About the author: Paul Misner has a doctoral degree from the University of Munich (1969) and has since taught at Boston College and the University of San Francisco. As a Senior Fulbright Fellow in Marburg in 1975-76, he is conducting researches in the history of ecumenism, especially in regard to the period between the World Wars.

PAPACY
AND DEVELOPMENT

STUDIES IN THE HISTORY
OF
CHRISTIAN THOUGHT

EDITED BY

HEIKO A. OBERMAN, Tübingen

IN COOPERATION WITH

HENRY CHADWICK, Oxford
EDWARD A. DOWEY, Princeton, N.J.
JAROSLAV PELIKAN, New Haven, Conn.
BRIAN TIERNEY, Ithaca, N.Y.
E. DAVID WILLIS, San Anselmo, California

VOLUME XV

PAUL MISNER

PAPACY AND DEVELOPMENT

LEIDEN
E. J. BRILL
1976

PAPACY
AND DEVELOPMENT

NEWMAN AND THE PRIMACY
OF THE POPE

BY

PAUL MISNER

LEIDEN
E. J. BRILL
1976

ISBN 90 04 04466 3

PRINTED IN THE NETHERLANDS

TO
MY PARENTS

TABLE OF CONTENTS

PART FOUR
COUNTERWEIGHTS TO ABSOLUTISM

ACKNOWLEDGMENTS

Thanks are due in the first place to Professor Heinrich Fries, Theology Faculty, University of Munich, who suggested this theme to me and helped me carry it through (in an earlier version) as a doctoral dissertation. The generosity and farsightedness of the Diocese of Pittsburgh and its bishop, the now Cardinal John J. Wright, made it possible for me to devote the greatest part of my time during the academic years 1965-1969 to researching this work, though of course no one beside myself is to be held accountable for the result. Like others before me, I have found the aid of the Rev. Charles Stephen Dessain, archivist of the Newman papers at the Birmingham Oratory, Edgbaston, to be invaluable. The encouragement of family, friends, and, in these last years, of my colleagues and deans at Boston College all deserve explicit appreciation, name by name, and I am sure that they will recognize that the lack of it does not imply any lack of gratitude for what they have contributed. My parents' contributions extend even to bearing part of the financial burden of publication, but that is not why this book is dedicated to them.

Everett, Massachusetts
June, 1975

ABBREVIATIONS

Apo   John Henry Newman. *Apologia Pro Vita Sua* (1864; 2nd. ed., 1865).
            Ed. Martin J. Svaglic. Oxford: Clarendon Press, 1967.
Dev   Newman. *An Essay on the Development of Christian Doctrine*. London:
            James Toovey, 1845.
Diff   Newman. *Certain Difficulties Felt by Anglicans in Catholic Teaching*.
            2 vols. New edition. London: Longmans, Green, and Co., 1897,
            1896.
DA   Newman. *Discussions and Arguments on Various Subjects*. New
            edition. London: Longmans, Green, and Co., 1897.
DS   *Enchiridion Symbolorum*. Ed. Heinrich Denzinger and Adolf Schön-
            metzer. 33rd ed. Freiburg: Herder, 1965.
LC   *Letters and Correspondence of John Henry Newman during his Life in
            the English Church*. Ed. Anne Mozley. 2 vols. London: Longmans,
            Green, and Co., 1897.
L&D   *The Letters and Diaries of John Henry Newman*. Ed. Charles Stephen
            Dessain and others. Vols. XI—. London: Nelson, 1962—.
LTK   *Lexikon für Theologie und Kirche*. 2nd ed. Ed. Josef Höfer and
            Karl Rahner. Freiburg: Herder, 1957-1967.
Migne, *PG* *Patrologia Graeca*. Ed. J. P. Migne. Paris, 1857-1866.
Migne, *PL* *Patrologia Latina*. Ed. J. P. Migne. Paris, 1878-1890.
NS   *Newman-Studien*. Ed. Heinrich Fries and Werner Becker. 9 vols. to
            date. Nuremberg: Glock und Lutz, 1948—.
Occ Serm Newman. *Sermons Preached on Various Occasions* (1867). New edition.
            London: Longmans, Green, and Co., 1894.
ODC   *The Oxford Dictionary of the Christian Church*. Ed. Frank Leslie
            Cross. 4th impression. London: Oxford University Press, 1963.
OS   *The Rediscovery of Newman: An Oxford Symposium*. Ed. John Coulson
            and A. M. Allchin. London: Sheed and Ward/SPCK, 1967.
PPS   Newman. *Parochial and Plain Sermons*. New edition. 8 vols. London:
            Longmans, Green, and Co., 1894-1896.
SD   Newman. *Sermons Bearing on Subjects of the Day*. New edition.
            London: Longmans, Green, and Co., 1891.
VM   Newman. *The Via Media of the Anglican Church*. 2 vols. New edition.
            London: Longmans, Green, and Co., 1895-1896.

INTRODUCTION

It was several months since John Henry Newman had laid down his pen upon completing the appeal to the reader at the end of his *Essay on the Development of Christian Doctrine* (1845). Having been preceded into the Roman Catholic Church by such younger Tractarians as William George Ward, Ambrose St. John, and finally John Dalgairns, he now was concerned that others with whom he had been close should not be long in following. Henry Wilberforce was one of his few confidantes, certainly the one of longest standing, now that Bowden and Froude were gone and Rogers declined to correspond with him. Henry was afraid to read Newman's book, and afraid to let him know that he hadn't read it. In early June, 1846, Henry wrote to Newman that the acceptance of the doctrine of the Pope's Supremacy was certainly the most formidable obstacle, it being so clearly a later development with no shadow of a consensus of the Fathers behind it. This elicited from Newman in the course of three letters [1] a clear and brief statement of his approach to the question of papal primacy at the end of his Anglican period and at the decisive point of his transition to Roman Catholicism.

Astonishingly, Newman brushes aside the difficulty of the late appearance of papal power as a problem in itself. The greater and more basic problem is that of the international unity (communion) of the church. This, however, is not a problem for one who would join the Roman Catholic communion, for its unity around the world is a palpable fact. Rather, it is the supreme difficulty for one who would remain out of communion with Rome (and the *orbis terrarum*) and in schism with Canterbury. That a particular bishop or a Pope should have peculiar status within the worldwide communion is a distinctly secondary issue, compared with the question as to which of the existing Christian bodies is the unified and ecumenical communion which alone can be God's church. In his third and last letter on this subject to Wilberforce, Newman clarifies:

---

[1] Of 10 June, 25 June and 4 July, 1846; text in *The Letters and Diaries of John Henry Newman*, ed. Charles Stephen Dessain (London: Thomas Nelson, 1961—), XI, 174-176, 181-184 and 190-192. This source will be referred to henceforth as *L&D*.

You do not seem to have apprehended, or rather I to have expressed, why I introduced what I said about 'the Church.' What I mean is this:—If we can get a tolerable notion *which* is the Church, and know (as we do) that it may be trusted because it is the Church, then comes the question *why* should not the Pope's Supremacy be one of the points on which it may be trusted?—For myself I have had so great experience of the correctness of the Roman view where once I thought otherwise, that I should be a beast if I were unwilling to take the rest on faith, from a confidence that what is still obscure to me is explainable. And it seems to me extravagant or unreasonable in you to demand proof of one certain particular tenet which it so naturally comes to the Church to decide. If the Roman Church be the Church, I take it whatever it is [2]—and if I find that Papal Supremacy is a point of faith in it, this point of faith is not to my imagination so strange, to my reason so incredible, to my historical knowledge so utterly without evidence, as to warrant me in saying, 'I *cannot* take it on faith.' [3]

This illustrates as well as any short passage can what a complicated, many-sided question was Papal Supremacy for Newman—the acute case of development of dogma, to paraphrase Karl Rahner [4]—and yet that the decisive question was for him the factual communion of the church. Were the unified and worldwide communion of believers in fact under the leadership of bishops in synod, then to that communion he would go; were it governed by an elected body, he would be willing, in theory at least, to swallow even that: but since the only communion to act like *the* church is the Roman Catholic one, it with its papal constitution commends itself to him.

There remain difficulties to be dealt with. Newman names three areas. His imagination had been cleansed of the stain which the perduring tradition of the papal Antichrist had afflicted it. [5] His

---

[2] "Whatever it is;" that is, as Newman explains in a gloss he added while copying this letter in 1876 (cf. *ibid.*, XI, 190 within double brackets), whether the Church is constituted as "monarchical, aristocratic or democratic."

[3] *Ibid.* The 1876 copy, also reproduced there, contains many interpolations and a comment of several sentences underscoring the importance of this passage in Newman's mind.

[4] Cf. art. "Papst," *Lexikon für Theologie und Kirche*, 2d ed. (hereinafter *LTK*), VIII, 46: "die verschärfte Frage der Dogmenentwicklung überhaupt."

[5] Cf. Newman, *Apologia pro Vita Sua*, ed. Martin J. Svaglic (Oxford: Clarendon Press, 1967), pp. 20, 50-59, 113-115 (references to *Apo* will always be to this edition). Newman speaks of a Tract of 1838 (*ibid.*, p. 114) in which he seems still influenced by the traditional Protestant interpretation of the prophecies concerning Antichrist, but in fact what he is referring to were Advent Sermons of 1835, not published until 1838. By 1838—indeed, already in 1835—he had repudiated the interpretation of Antichrist as having been realized in the papacy, cf. *The*

reason found little difficulty in the idea of an authoritative ruler representing the divine principle of authority in a religious body based on revelation, but as this was a point on which he would be challenged, we must examine his frame of mind as regards a strong central authority in the worldwide communion of the faith. Finally, he declares that even the greatest difficulty, which occurs in relation to historical knowledge, can be met. But to meet it he had to frame a whole new hypothesis, that of the development of doctrines (and structures) of the Christian life. On this hypothesis, the evidence which is available out of the first centuries for a developing papal power is such, in his opinion, that the counter-evidence presents no insuperable obstacle to accepting the Roman communion on its own terms.

From this account of the workings of Newman's mind in an essay which has been of unsurpassed importance for subsequent Roman Catholic theology, and upon a question which has seemed to many to be the *articulus stantis vel cadentis ecclesiae romanae*—the primacy of the papal power in the Church, defined as dogma by the First Vatican Council in 1870—certain questions arise, particularly from a historical point of view. Is Newman's reading of the development of the papacy a historically respectable interpretation? Is it more historically sensitive than were others available at the time? Theologically, as a confirmation of the Roman Catholic belief that papal power is ordained by God, why was his view of its development intelligible and persuasive to his not undemanding intellect? Moved by such questions, and mindful that Newman's *Essay on Development* has been appealed to by the most disparate theological spokesmen within and without the Roman Catholic fold, I have set out to investigate as objectively as possible just what were Newman's starting points, controversial aims, theological underpinnings, conclusions, and limitations as to the question of the Catholic doctrine of papal primacy in the context of his times which has already been so well interpreted by previous scholars.

If that is my aim, then the results also can be put briefly as follows, with a view to providing a sketchy orientation in reading the work. The question of the church's faithfulness to its origins (labeled "Antiquity" or "Apostolicity") versus its supranational, universal character ("Catholicity" and "Unity") was indeed decisive, as New-

Via Media of the Anglican Church (cited as *VM*; London: Longmans, Green, 1877), II, 208 and 219-222.

man himself repeatedly asserted, in his *Apologia* and elsewhere. In examining this first issue, then, I analyze an already well recognized factor in Newman's thought for its effect on his theology of the episcopate and the Roman primacy.

Secondly, however, a factor which is strange to most scholars and hence has been overlooked is shown to have been crucial for the argument of Newman's *Essay on Development*: the interpretation of prophecy as revealing God's design to set up an imperial church. I then found it necessary to investigate a complication to which too little attention has been paid in the research on Newman's idea of doctrinal development, namely the modifications which the theory underwent between his becoming a Catholic in 1845 and his revision of the *Essay* for republication in 1878. A tendency can be detected to downplay the element of novelty in his treatment of developments and to put the process more in terms of increasingly explicit knowledge than as historical change in the constitution of the church.

A third aspect of Newman's thought on the papacy comes to light in his late works. After actually living in an authoritarian church for decades, he was far from taking shelter in more and more rigid re- action against contemporary developments in society and learning, but instead mobilized the powers of his mind to counteract reaction and defensive narrowness within the Roman Catholic fold. Although his first biographer, Wilfrid Ward, appreciated this aspect of his work, it is only since the calling of the Second Vatican Council that it has begun to make itself felt in Catholic ecclesiology.

PART ONE

AN ITEM OF CONTROVERSY

CHAPTER ONE

UNTROUBLED ANTI-ROMANISM

Whatever else John Henry Newman may have been, he was an Englishman among Englishmen. Of the young Newman of the 1820's at Oxford it can be confidently said that by background and inclination he harbored more fervently anti-Roman sentiments than some others among his set. In this, however, he was more in harmony than were they with the popular convictions of a self-consciously Protestant people.[1] In the year of his evangelical conversion (1816) he had imbibed deeply of the prevalent Protestant interpretation of prophecies regarding Antichrist, prophecies which were seen as fulfilled in the Popes of Rome since the sixth or the eighth or the eleventh century. In 1829 he was still defending the ingrained national sentiment of No Popery on the grounds that priceless religious truths cannot be confided to the uncertain ministrations of human reasoning alone. One must find more reliable ways to maintain and pass on hard-won truths than by simply entrusting them to rational discussion without further ado. In a remarkable letter of 13 March 1829 to his mother, Newman named two such vehicles of truth: faith and another factor, which, he thought, ought not to be despised in the straitened circumstances of the church: "prejudice". Even though prejudice, that is, attachment to the traditional just because it has been received by previous generations, tends to bigotry, it is to be preferred to indifference or deism.

---

[1] For the anti-Romanism of the nation, cf. Owen Chadwick, *The Victorian Church* (London: Adam & Charles Black, 1966), I, 7-8 and 294-304; G. F. A. Best, "The Protestant Constitution and its Supporters," *Transactions of the Royal Historical Society* (series 5), 8 (1958), 105-127; E. R. Norman, *Anti-Catholicism in Victorian England* (London: George Allen and Unwin Ltd., 1968), pp. 13-22. For Newman's part in the agitation against Catholic Emancipation, cf. his own detailed and excited account in letters to his family of February and March, 1829 in Anne Mozley (ed.), *Letters and Correspondence of John Henry Newman* (London: Longmans, Green and Co., 1890), I, 175-181 (this work will be referred to henceforth as *LC*); Geoffrey Faber, *Oxford Apostles*, 2nd ed. (London: Faber & Faber, 1936), pp. 238-241; and Maisie Ward, *Young Mr. Newman* (New York: Sheed & Ward, 1948), pp. 154-158 with 224-236. The comparison of Newman with fellow Tractarians has been the object of a special study by Robert H. Greenfield, "The Attitude of the Tractarians to the Roman Catholic Church 1833-1850," unpub. diss., Oxford, 1956.

Was this then the substance of his objections to the papacy, unreasoning prejudice and national-religious pride? To write off his convictions on the Antichristian papacy so simply would be implausible. Nevertheless, the evidence does not permit a detailed refutation. His Christmas sermons of 1824,[2] in one of which he laid out his understanding of the fulfilment of the Antichrist prophecies in the Roman papal system, are no longer extant. As will be seen, Keble's example in 1827 showed him that one need not resort to the Antichrist theme in order to justify one's anti-Romanist stand. This does not mean that Newman already at this period dropped the identification of the Antichrist of scriptures with the Pope of Rome. But for a while the question was allowed to remain academic, despite the widespread discussion of the topic, in which Newman too participated.[3] The problem would again become urgent for him when he would begin to notice, at Froude's prodding, how much the Church of Rome still seemed to resemble the normative church of antiquity. But that time was not yet.

We do have some sermons from a period (1829-1830) after Newman had adopted "high" views of what the church is and should be, but before his anti-Romanism was exacerbated by the countervailing pull of the Roman Church with its majestic facticity. In them the themes of church unity and apostolicity are sounded, but without any of the tension between the two "notes" of the church such as will show up in 1833; in them also is a quiet presentation of the reason why one would not prefer the Roman communion to that of the Church of England. This is the way he takes up the doctrine of papal supremacy in his sermon of 29 June 1830:

> This passage [Mt 16:18-19], you may have heard, is made much of by the Papists or Romanists (as they are called)—the followers of the Pope—who assert that Peter by this text is proved to be the head of the Apostles, and that the Pope is the successor of St. Peter (though this of course is not proved by the text) and that therefore all Christians

---

[2] *Apo*, p. 57.

[3] Cf. Alfred William Benn, *The History of English Rationalism in the Nineteenth Century* (New York: Russell & Russell, 1962; first published in 1906), I, 333-336; Ernest R. Sandeen, *The Roots of Fundamentalism: British and American Millenarianism 1800-1930* (Chicago: University of Chicago Press, 1970), pp. 5-24. Newman's brother Francis adopted millenarian views for a few years starting around 1828, cf. Maisie Ward, *Young Mr. Newman*, p. 164 and Sandeen, *Roots*, pp. 29-38. See also Paul Misner, "Newman and the Tradition Concerning the Papal Antichrist," *Church History*, 42 (1973), 377-395.

should look upon the Pope as supreme visible head of the Church. Now I do not suppose that any of us are likely to fall away to Popery. It is not in the way for Churchmen to depart from their excellent forms and worship to the corruptions of the Romish Church. Men of unsettled minds, who wander from sect to sect, from Church to meeting, who despise all Church government and do what is good in their own eyes, these are the persons to fall into the opposite extreme (as they often do in fact) and, after an uncertain vagrant course, to settle at length in despair into an implicit superstitious belief of the Romish system. Such cases I say occur in fact. But sober Churchmen are in no danger from the Pope. Yet it may be useful to examine the text for our own satisfaction, even though our views of Scripture and truth are already too clear to feel perplexity by what is obscure.[4]

Newman then interprets, with ample patristic precedent,[5] Simon's name Peter as referring in the first instance to "the real foundation, Christ" and the profession, made first by Peter, that Jesus is the Christ. On this profession of faith Christ will build up his church. Since Peter and the other apostles are foundations in this sense, they should have the keys of the Kingdom of Heaven: "that is, should have the administration of the sacraments which convey the blessings of salvation, and should have authority to preach the gospel, to denounce vengeance on sinners, to excommunicate offenders, to restore the penitent, and to comfort the desponding, so that his words should be acknowledged as Christ's words at the last day. 'Whatsoever thou shalt bind on earth (put under condemnation) shall &c.' " [6] Peter then serves as a *type* of the ministerial office in general, in Newman's understanding of this famous scriptural passage.

Just as Newman saw in the figure of St. Peter a warning against dissent in the sermon just considered, so also he started from the same text in sermons of November, 1829 "against dissenters." [7] There is

---

[4] MS Sermon No. 246, "On St. Peter's authority—and thence on Church authority &c," pp. 3-4. This was one of the Saint's Days sermons initiated by Newman at St. Mary's, preached on weekday mornings, this one on 29 June 1830; preserved in the Newman Archives of the Birmingham Oratory and in the microfilm copy housed in the Beinecke Rare Book and Manuscript Library of the Yale University Library.

[5] Compare even e.g. Leo the Great, sermon 4, in Migne, *Patrologia Latina*, LIV, 150-151.

[6] MS Sermon No. 246, pp. 5-6.

[7] "The Unity of the Church," a conflation of three sermons given on November 8, 15, and 22, 1829, to be found in Newman, *Parochial and Plain Sermons* (London, 1868), VII, 230-242, with the text being Mt 16:18; the anti-dissent lesson was especially drawn out in "Submission to Church Authority," of 29 November 1829: *PPS*, III, 190-205.

no hint of an awareness that the lines of thought he is presenting could tell in favour of the Roman position in the future. After letting Matthew 16:18 ring out in his clear, high, memorable voice, Newman commenced: "In St. Peter, who is [in the text] made the rock on which the Church is founded, we see, as in a type, its unity, stability, and permanence."

Newman sees his ideal of the church united in visible organization everywhere confirmed in the New Testament. He cites the passages on the church as the body of Christ (I Corinthians, Ephesians), the church as "the pillar and ground of the truth" (I Timothy 3:15, a favorite verse which he of course attributes to St. Paul), the church as the bride of Christ and the "one new man" made out of the formerly hostile Jews and Gentiles (Ephesians), the church as spiritual building (I Peter 2:5). This implies an inexorable duty of maintaining unity with the official ministers of the new dispensation: "These are a few out of many passages which connect Gospel privileges with the circumstance or condition of unity in those who receive them; the image of Christ and token of their acceptance being stamped upon them *then*, at that moment, when they are considered as one." He points out in this connection that baptism itself, scripturally ordained as it is, is not conceivable outside the framework of a visible church. [8]

In all this the division of the Church of England from the church in other lands does not yet cause the slightest embarrassment. The Church of England is the church catholic in England, as is the Roman Church in some other parts of the world, the Greek Catholics still elsewhere, and so forth; [9] whereas sectarians everywhere live in flagrant opposition to the catholic church whose unity has been thus, though only imperfectly, maintained. That the Church should be one kingdom the world over, not just in each part of the world, was a consideration whose force would only later become apparent.

The reason for this, of course, is that division by countries and regions seemed to be a *fait accompli*, which was moreover mitigated by the common origins of the parts or branches of the church catholic, each of which could trace its descendance by way of ministerial succession to the undivided church of antiquity.

---

[8] *PPS*, VII, 231-236.
[9] *PPS*, III, 191.

I will mention one other guarantee, which is especially suggested by our Lord's words in the text, for the visible unity and permanence of His Church; and that is the appointment of rulers and ministers, entrusted with the gifts of grace, and these in succession. The ministerial orders are the ties which bind together the whole body of Christians in one; they are its organs, and they are moreover its moving principle.

Such an institution necessarily implies a succession, unless the appointment was always to be miraculous.

After confirming the necessity of a succession with an appeal first to the Pastoral Epistles and then to the experience of nations which fear instability when a dynasty is not maintained, he reiterates his position that the ministerial body forms the bond of union necessary to the continuance of the church, and that its orderly succession by ordination into the body is equally necessary. Fortunately, it is "a fact, that to this day the ministers of the Church universal are descended from the very Apostles. Amid all the changes of this world, the Church built upon St. Peter and the rest has continued until now in the unbroken line of the ministry." [10]

Multum in parvo! Such a concise summation of Newman's ecclesiology no doubt owes much to his editorial hand in 1842, when he reduced the three sermons of November 1829 into one short one for publication. It is not necessary to examine in detail the sources which influenced Newman's thought at this point.[11] I merely note that Newman apparently added an introductory allusion to the church as a fulfilment of kingdom prophecies only in the final rewriting.[12] It is

---

[10] *PPS*, VII, 237-240.

[11] Cf. the introduction and select bibliography by Eugene R. Fairweather (ed.), *The Oxford Movement* (New York: Oxford University Press, 1964), pp. 3-15 and 385-392; to that bibliography I would add only a special reference to *Apo*, pp. 54-57 and three recent works: Alf Härdelin, *The Tractarian Understanding of the Eucharist* (Uppsala: Almqvist & Wiksells, 1965), especially pp. 27-33, 41-44, and 65-69; A. M. Allchin, "The Theological Vision of the Oxford Movement," in *The Rediscovery of Newman: An Oxford Symposium*, ed. by John Coulson and A. M. Allchin (London: Sheed and Ward/SPCK, 1967), pp. 50-75 (this collection of essays will be referred to as *OS*); and Coulson, *Newman and the Common Tradition* (Oxford: Clarendon, 1970).

[12] Most MSS of Newman's published sermons disappeared after being sent to the printer. C. Stephen Dessain, of the Birmingham Archives, has informed me, however, that there does exist a MS of the sermon of 15 November 1829. The prophetical allusion, "Too many persons forget, or deny, or do not know, that Christ has set up a kingdom in the world," *PPS*, VII, 230, was written for the last time Newman preached the sermon on 24 August 1841.

clear enough that for the period in question the doctrine of the church contained in these sermons was directed against separatists and dissenters. It made confident use of Mt 16:18 and the figure of Peter as a type of Christian ministers wielding official authority.[13] Romanism was not a live option.

---

[13] Cf. also the sermon dated 14 December 1834, "The Christian Ministry," *PPS* II, 315: Peter is "the representative and type of" all legitimate Christian ministers; *ibid.*, p. 6: "the typical foundation of [the] Church."

CHAPTER TWO

CATHOLICIZING ANTI-ROMANISM

When Newman's family read the sermon on the unity of the church
and the succession of the ministerial order (November 1829) which
we have just presented, his sister Harriett wrote him, "We have long
since read your two sermons; they are very High Church. I do
not think I am near so High, and do not quite understand them
yet."[1]

Well might they be taken aback, for this was not the style of his
earlier religiosity which had led him into the church in the first place.[2]
Where had he come by these notions? Without covering all the ground
which has been gone over again and again since Newman himself
wrote of it in the *Apologia,* one must at least recall that Richard
Hurrell Froude enforced a radical anti-Erastianism, pounding away
relentlessly at those whose devotion to the established Church of
England was based principally upon appreciation of it as a branch of
the national government or a prop for the proper social order. This
kind of ecclesiastical Toryism was "humbug" to him; he contrasted
the "apostolicals" with the "peculiars" and the "conservatives,"
making the latter irreverently a term of opprobrium. Newman thus
was confirmed in the novel "idea of the Christian Church, as a divine
appointment, and as a substantive visible body, independent of the
State, and endowed with rights, prerogatives and powers of its own,"
which had been picked up from Whateley.[3]

---

[1] *LC*, I, 188-189.

[2] On Newman's "Evangelicalism," Maisie Ward's *Mr. Newman*, pp. 54-67
and 78-92, is still good. More recently David Newsome has contributed a short
study, "The Evangelical Sources of Newman's Power," *OS*, pp. 11-30, and a
long one on some contemporaries who were formed in Evangelicalism, *The
Wilberforces and Henry Manning: The Parting of Friends* (Cambridge, Mass.: Harvard
University Press, 1966). See also Thomas L. Sheridan, *Newman on Justification*:
A Theological Biography (Staten Island, N.Y.: Alba House, 1967).

[3] On Hurrell Froude, cf. Marvin R. O'Connell, *The Oxford Conspirators*:
A History of the Oxford Movement 1833-1845 (New York: Macmillan, 1969),
pp. 100-103; R. W. Church, *The Oxford Movement: Twelve Years, 1833-1845,*
ed. Geoffrey Best (1891; Chicago: University of Chicago Press, 1970), ch. 3;
Remains of the late Reverend Richard Hurrell Froude, ed. John Keble and John
Henry Newman (London, 1838), I, 307, 429 f. On Whateley's anti-Erastian
stand, cf. John Henry Newman, *Autobiographical Writings,* ed. Henry Tristram

Now Hurrell Froude—he remembered it as the most meritorious deed of his life—was instrumental in bringing Newman and the somewhat older John Keble together.[4] Keble in turn was responsible for setting up the terms of the Anglican-Roman controversy that was to shape Newman's thought from 1833 on. Keble's reverence for the ancient church, the church of the Fathers, the church as yet undivided and hence with its saving doctrine and usages still intact, was contagious. Not that Keble felt that the divisions that had cut across the Christian world since the end of the patristic age had nullified the church's authority or turned it into a mere outward sham of the true, invisible church. Not at all—the apostolic succession of bishops, guaranteeing as it did the transmission of Christ's grace through the orthodox preaching and apostolic ordinances, was the foremost sign that the visible church continued to embody Christ. Despite all its shortcomings, its unbroken link to the purer ages of the church of antiquity was assurance that the church even today, at least where episcopal succession was maintained and honored as in England, was the focus of God's work among men. In *The Christian Year* he went so far as to call the church (in one of his verse prayers directed to Christ) "Thy spouse, Thy very Self below." [5]

A corollary to this high view of the visible church, which Keble drew, much to the surprise first of Froude and then of Newman, was that the Roman Church could not be the fulfilment of Antichrist prophecies.[6] It too had episcopal government, however overshadowed by the pretensions of the bishop of Rome; it too honored the councils of antiquity, with whatever admixture of fraud; it was the successor to the old church catholic in other parts of the world, though it had been unfaithful to its patristic forebears "in adding many things to the Scriptures, and enforcing them as necessary conditions of Christian Communion." Deep as its fall may have been, the Roman Church was still a (misguided) sister of the Anglican and Greek communions and should not be denigrated as Antichrist: "Speak gently of our

---

(New York: Sheed & Ward, 1957), p. 69, and *The Oxford Dictionary of the Christian Church* (1963; hereinafter *ODC*), s.v. "Whateley, Richard" and "Erastianism."

[4] Cf. *Apo*, p. 29; *ibid.* on *The Christian Year*.

[5] John Keble, *The Christian Year* (London: Parker, 1876), p. 284: "St. Matthias' Day."

[6] Keble had come to this conclusion as early as 1824, cf. Kenneth Ingram, *John Keble* (London: P. Allan, 1933), p. 66; Froude's surprise: W. J. Baker, "Hurrell Froude and the Reformers," *Journal of Ecclesiastical History*, 21 (1970), 246; Newman's reaction, *Apo*, p. 57.

sister's fall." [7] This corollary was shared by a few Irish High Church-men such as William Palmer and Arthur Philip Perceval (so long as it was understood that Ireland fell to the English and not the Roman Communion) and was adopted by Froude and eventually by Newman, but it was not typical of early Tractarianism as such. As for Establishment churchmen and Evangelicals, not to mention dissenting Christians, the theme of the papal Antichrist was simply in possession. [8]

On the eve of the Oxford Movement's commencement, Newman undertook two noteworthy projects: he wrote his first major work, *The Arians of the Fourth Century*, and then went on a Mediterranean voyage with Hurrell Froude and his father, the Archdeacon (they departed in early December, 1832; Newman remained abroad until July, 1833). The Sicilian adventure was a major crisis in his life, associated, as previous ones had been, with illness. [9] When he got back, he oversaw the publication of *The Arians* and plunged into the work of creating the Movement. Up until his trip to Rome, Newman would sometimes use language strongly savoring of Antichrist when he spoke of the Roman Church: "the notorious insincerity and frauds of the Church of Rome"; "a corruption of Christianity"; "the Papal Apostasy." [10] In the verses he writes from there, it is clear that a certain fascination began to vie with the prejudices he had come with: the Mother Church of Rome is a cruel church, for her treatment of Christian England. Yet: "O that thy creed were sound! For thou dost soothe the heart, Thou Church of Rome." [11] The doom pronounced in Daniel's scroll upon the fourth kingdom rests on the city of Rome rather than the church situated there.[12] Even while he was writing *The Arians*, the Roman Church was to him no longer the only manifestation of Antichrist. The episcopacy of Paul of Samosata in

---

[7] Cf. R. H. Greenfield, *The Attitude of the Tractarians to the Roman Catholic Church*, pp. 42, 139; Keble, *Christian Year*, p. 365.

[8] Cf. Owain Jones, *Isaac Williams and His Circle* (London: SPCK, 1971), pp. 24, 57; David Newsome, *The Wilberforces and Henry Manning*, p. 177; R. W. Church, *The Oxford Movement*, ed. Best, p. 42.

[9] Cf. *LC*, I, 248-378, esp. pp. 363-78, and *Autobiographical Writings*, ed. Henry Tristram, pp. 109-38.

[10] Cf. Newman, "The Miracles of Scripture" (1826), in *Essays on Miracles* (London, 1870), p. 77; *The Arians of the Fourth Century*, 3d ed. (London, 1871), p. 474.

[11] Newman, "The Cruel Church" and "The Good Samaritan," in *Lyra Apostolica*, 1st American ed. (New York, 1844), pp. 249-50; cf. Gordon Huntington Harper, *Cardinal Newman and William Froude, F.R.S.: A Correspondence* (Baltimore: Johns Hopkins, 1933), p. 39.

[12] *Ibid.*, "Rome," p. 248.

Antioch, for instance, he portrayed as "so open a manifestation of the spirit of Antichrist as to fulfill almost literally the prophecy of the Apostle in his second Epistle to the Thessalonians." Arius, because he subordinated his religious teaching to his private ends, merely usurped the name of religion; this made him and his supporters "essentially antichristian." [13]

On the closing page of his book, Newman even allows himself to refer to the Arminian (in this context meaning, roughly, "rationalist") and Erastian elements in the Church of England in terms of "an Heretical Power enthralling" the church, of "the present tyranny ...the hand of Satan...the bonds of the Oppressor." He expresses his hope for a new Athanasius, one who rose up when most of the bishops of the church were Arian sympathizers and at length restored orthodoxy to its rightful pride of place. He believes that history supplies him with good reason for that hope: heresy has never taken over the church definitively; "it ever hastens to an end, and that end is the triumph of the Truth." [14] "Even the Papal Apostasy, which seems at first sight an exception to this rule, has lasted but the same proportion of the whole duration of Christianity, which Arianism occupied in its day; that is, if we date it, as in fairness we ought, from the fatal Council of Trent." [15] To call the post-Tridentine Roman Church "apostate" is equivalent to affirming that it is Antichristian, but in a no more precisely defined or concrete sense than that according to which the Arian churches were Antichristian; or even the liberal and rationalistic schools of thought in the Anglican communion (in the measure in which they would gain ascendancy and impose their views). Influenced by Froude, Newman now exempted the medieval papal church from the imputation of being Antichrist. What was Antichristian about the accursed Tridentine church was its elevation of late medieval corruptions to the status of required terms of communion, thus rendering England's breach of communion unhealable. [16]

---

[13] Newman, *Arians*, p. 3 (compare 2 Thessalonians 2:3-4 and Eusebius' *Church History*, VII, xxx, 9-10) and p. 259. Further evidence that Antichrist was not associated exclusively with Popery in his mind at this time is contained in two sermons of 1830 and 1832, cf. *PPS*, VII, 250 and *Fifteen Sermons Preached before the University of Oxford*, 3d ed. (London, 1871; referred to as *Oxford University Sermons*), pp. 120, 126, 135. Here "Liberalism," the "new school of error" is Antichristian.

[14] Newman, *Arians*, pp. 393-94.

[15] *Ibid.*, p. 474.

[16] Cf. *LC*, I, 338 and Froude's *Remains*, I, 307-08.

But now, viewing the Roman system at first hand, and with time to muse, Newman speaks of it gently, as compared with Bishop Newton,[17] but harshly, as compared with Keble. "There are great appearances of piety in the churches, still, as a system, the corrupt religion—and it is very corrupt—must receive severe inflictions; and I fear I must look upon Rome, as a city, still under a curse. . . ." One may suppose that the beginning of the apostasy occurred when the Pope assumed temporal sovereignty of this city under the prophetical curse, he admits. "But, granting this, it does not follow that the Church is the woman of the Revelation any more than a man possessed with a devil is the devil. That the spirit of old Rome has possessed the Christian Church there is certain as a matter of fact . . . . The revivification of ancient Rome in modern has often been noticed; but it has been supposed that the Christian Church is that new form of the old evil, whereas it is really a sort of *genius loci*, which enthralls the Church which happens to be there . . . ." [18] This represents a certain softening of Newman's position against the Roman Church, as he tells us in his *Apologia*: he never again thought of her as Antichrist pure and simple. But it still enabled him to use hard words in plenty against her when he felt he had to for the defense of the Church of England. [19]

The opportunity, or rather the necessity, to explore many sides of the three-cornered controversy (Protestantism—[English] Catholicism—Romanism) that was to characterize Tractarianism was not long in coming.[20] Forty-seven *Tracts for the Times* were available when they were gathered up, in November, 1834, for their first volume. The Preface to this volume and six of the Tracts may fairly be said to be concerned to repel any suspicion of Romanism, indeed, to be

[17] For Bishop Thomas Newton's *Dissertations on the Prophecies* (London, 1754-1758 with numerous editions through the first part of the nineteenth century), cf. *Apo*, p. 20 and Paul Misner, "Newman and . . . Antichrist," *Church History*, 42 (1973), 382-385.

[18] Cf. *LC*, I, 331 and 342 (letters from Italy of March and April 1833). Compare *DA* (i.e., John Henry Newman, *Discussions and Arguments on Various Subjects*, London, 1872), p. 3; *Historical Sketches* (London, 1872), II, 127; *PPS*, II, 318; *University Sermons*, p. 120. Froude writes Newman in 1834, cf. his *Remains*, I, 389: "I have a theory about the beast and woman too, which conflicts with yours; but which I will not inflict on you now."

[19] *Apo*, pp. 57-59, 113-15. Newman's most violent anti-Romanist utterances of this period (roughly 1833-1837) can be found in his "Retractation of Anti-Catholic Statements" (1843), *VM*, II, 428-33.

[20] Cf. R. W. Church, *The Oxford Movement*, ed. G. Best, pp. 28-29 and 68-90.

strengthening the Church of England against any attacks or defections
which might be expected from that quarter.[21] In Tract 38 (July 1834),
after some exceptionally vigorous denunciation of various corrupt
Roman practices and doctrines, Newman stated explicitly that "the
claim of the Pope to be Universal Bishop cannot be maintained." [22]

The most interesting document for our purposes, however, is
"Home Thoughts Abroad," composed about the same time (1833 or
1834), though only published in 1836 (in the *British Magazine*).[23]
Here the shape of Newman's as yet future struggle over the rival
claims of the Roman and the English communions is uncannily fore-
shadowed. Three Englishmen sojourning in Rome speak of the
prospects facing their church and discuss what tack should be taken
to cope with the evident untrustworthiness of the State to look after
the true interests of Christianity as it ought, according to Establishment principles. The three are Newman's rendering of Froude, Keble,
and himself, under the cover names of Ambrose, Basil and Cyril
respectively. Throughout the piece the papacy is present in the minds
of the speakers as a concrete model for a church independent of the
State, and on the desirability of this autonomy on the part of the
church there is no disagreement among them, now that the State
was declining to support the church as it had in the past, at least in
theory. Even Keble's mouthpiece says forthrightly, "I give up high-
churchmanship." [24] Froude leaps from this anti-Erastian starting
point to the question, "Why should we not unite with this imposing
communion? " He adduces, perhaps with more than a little coaching
from the author who is putting words into his mouth, the patristic
idea of the true church as being a far-flung communion, characterized
by catholicity (that is, unity and universality). Here occurs already, for
the first time in Newman's writing, the appeal to Augustine's handling
of the Donatist controversy (but on his friend's lips). What is especially significant for our understanding of Newman's subsequent

---

[21] See especially Tracts 20 (by Newman), 36 (by A. P. Perceval), 38, and 41
(both by Newman, entitled *Via Media*).
[22] The original Tract 38, called "Via Media, No. 1," as published in *Tracts
for the Times*, I (Oxford, 1834), has unnumbered pages. This sentence occurs on
the last page, where four dots appear in the later edition, *VM*, II, 34.
[23] Reprinted in Newman, *DA*, pp. 1-43, under the title "How to accomplish
it." Cf. Gary Lease, *Witness to the Faith*: *Cardinal Newman on the Teaching Authority
of the Church* (Pittsburgh: Duquesne University Press, 1972), p. 29 to supplement
Newman's account in *Apo*, pp. 104-06.
[24] *DA*, p. 23.

development is that a letter of Augustine's, which he cites here, twice appeals to the spread and catholicity of the true church as the self-evident fulfilment of prophecy.

> Seeing that at this day we have before our eyes the Church of God, called Catholic, diffused throughout the world, we think we ought not to doubt that herein is a most plain accomplishment of holy prophecy. . . . Please to tell me, then, how the Church of Christ has vanished from the world, and is found only among you [Donatists, confined to Africa]; whereas our side of the controversy is upheld, without our saying a word, by the plain fact, that we see in it a ful-filment of Scripture prophecy.[25]

To be sure, the prophecies referred to by Augustine are promises of the New Testament, Matthew 28:19 and the like. But to Newman the transition from these back to Isaiah will not prove insuperable.

When Froude is forced to concede that the universality of communion, which was such an undeniable fact in Augustine's day, has been disrupted for centuries, he falls back on the argument that the Roman Church is the most considerable communion left after the break-up, and the direct heir of the former united church as well. But here Newman interposes to warn him that he has shifted his ground from catholicity to apostolicity, where facts do not speak for the Romanists of the present day. "Foundation we have as apostolical as theirs," Newman maintains, "and doctrine much more apostolical. Please to keep to the plain tangible *fact*, as you expressed it when you began, of the universal or catholic character of the Roman communion."[26] The issue is joined, then, in 1833 as in 1840, on the question of England's episcopal apostolicity and Rome's papal catholicity.

As the three go on talking, it appears that many of the reforms urged as valid on account of their precedent in antiquity, and feasible on account of their continuity with the English church, are more Catholic than Protestant. Froude again challenges the assumption that union with Rome is out of the question, thus bringing Newman (and Keble) down to the essential hindrance which prevents it.

> "Pardon me," I said, in answer, "Basil [Keble] thinks the Roman Church corrupt in doctrine. We cannot join a Church, did we wish it

---

[25] *Ibid.*, p. 7, Newman's translation of part of Augustine's Epistola 49, to the Donatist Honoratus; cf. Migne, *PL*, XXXIII, 190.

[26] *DA*, p. 10.

ever so much, which does not acknowledge our Orders, refuses us the Cup, demands our acquiescence in image worship, and excommunicates us, if we do not receive it and all other decisions of the Tridentine Council. While she insists on this, there must be an impassable line between her and us; and while she claims infallibility, she must insist on what she has once decreed; and when she abandons that claim she breaks the principle of her own vitality. Thus, we can never unite with Rome." [27]

Keble, accepting this, adds that reform in the separated bodies must take precedence over dreams of reunion, for which neither communion is even remotely prepared. Why profess papal prerogatives, he asks, when there may be no Pope in Rome by the time the communions proceed to the point of reunion?

To Froude's skepticism that the Church of England is ready for religious orders or the principles of apostolic Christianity, such as the apostolic succession, the power of the keys, the sacredness of church ordinances,[28] Newman replies, "Our generation has not yet learned the distinction between Popery and Catholicism. But, be of good heart; it will learn many things in time." [29]

---

[27] *Ibid.*, pp. 28-29.
[28] *Ibid.*, p. 36.
[29] *Ibid.*, p. 43.

CHAPTER THREE

THE VIA MEDIA

Newman's major effort to work out the distinction between Popery and Catholicism and to construct a realizable Via Media between Protestantism and Romanism issued in his *Lectures on the Prophetical Office of the Church Viewed Relatively to Romanism and Popular Protestantism* (1837).[1] In these lectures he traces all the corruptions of the Roman Church back to the doctrine of infallibility "viewed...as a practical system."[2] The Roman Church had nowhere solemnly defined its infallibility, but it operated on the basis of it, as when Trent insisted on transsubstantiation for anyone who wished to maintain communion with the church and anathematized those who would not accept the doctrine. Neither had Trent defined the nature of the papal sovereignty, but it was clearly a *sine qua non* of Romanism. In one rather marginal passage which concedes quite a bit to the proponents of the Pope's supremacy under cover of a strong anti-Romanist tone, Newman attacks what he calls "the doctrine of the Pope's universal Bishoprick."

> That St. Peter was the head of the Apostles and the centre of unity, and that his successors are the honorary Primates of Christendom, in the same general sense in which London (for instance) is the first city in the British Empire, I neither affirm nor deny, for to make a clear statement and then to defend it, would carry us away too far from our main subject. But for argument's sake I will here grant that the Fathers assert it. But what there is not the shadow of a reason for saying that they held, what has not the faintest pretensions of being a Catholic truth, is this, that St. Peter or his successors were and are universal Bishops, that they have the whole of Christendom for their own diocese in a way in which other Apostles and Bishops had and have not, that they are Bishops of Bishops in such a sense as belongs to no other Bishop; in a word, that the difference between St. Peter and the Popes after him, and other Bishops, is not one of mere superiority and degree, but of kind, not of rank, but of class.[3]

The venerable Anglican theme of usurpation (of episcopal and civil prerogatives on the part of the Pope) is here touched upon.

---

[1] Referred to as *Prophetical Office*, 1st ed., London, 1837, reprinted in a 3rd ed. in *VM*, I, pp. 1-355; cf. *Apo*, p. 67.

[2] *VM*, I, 84.

[3] *VM*, I, 180-181; cf. Tract 71 in *VM*, II, 103.

Antiquity recognized that the bishop of Rome enjoyed a "primacy in honour and authority," though not one that amounted to "sovereignty" or "universal jurisdiction." [4]

Though Newman does not go into the distinction between "authority" and "universal jurisdiction" here, he had discussed Royal Supremacy in the pages of the *British Magazine*, and it is clear that what he means is determined by Article 37 of the Thirty-Nine Articles ("The Bishop of Rome hath no jurisdiction in the realm of England") and by the Oath of Supremacy ("No foreign prince, person, prelate, state, or potentate, hath, or ought to have, any jurisdiction, power, superiority, preeminence, or authority, ecclesiastical or spiritual, within this realm").[5] In his articles on "The Convocation of the Province of Canterbury" in the *British Magazine* (1834-1835) he had already confronted the problem of reconciling his anti-Erastian principles with the Royal Supremacy. The jurisdiction or authority in question here must be considered as that which concerns the civil authority in the arrangement of matters external to the apostolic foundation of the church. What the Oath of Supremacy calls "spiritual" or "ecclesiastical" is so called from the point of view of the civil magistrate; from the point of view of the churchman, such areas are more properly called "semi-civil," as entailing the cooperation of the State in the ordering of church affairs.[6] After all, is not Article 37 headed, "De *civilibus* Magistratibus"?

In any case, the Pope's primacy had long been in abeyance and would continue to be "as long as he upholds a corrupt system." [7] The system was corrupt by reason of late and adventitious doctrines from which the popes could not retreat, having put their authority at stake on them. Thus the system of infallibility formed a vicious circle in which the Roman communion had imprisoned itself without hope of escape. Newman sees the Pope chiefly as the figurehead and instrument of this system, which replaces reliance on antiquity (apostolicity) with its claimed gift of standing infallibility. "And thus

---

[4] *VM*, II, 103.

[5] Quoted by Newman in 1841 in Tract 90, *VM*, II, 340 (Article 38 in the numbering followed by Newman).

[6] Cf. *Historical Sketches* (London: Longmans, Green, 1872), III, 413-416, 420. In support of Newman's distinction between papal primacy rightly understood and the Roman primacy of jurisdiction, cf. Derick W. Allen and A. Macdonald Allchin, "Primacy and Collegiality: An Anglican View," *Journal of Ecumenical Studies*, 2 (1965), pp. 71-75, citing Elizabeth, James I and Bramhall.

[7] *VM*, II, 103, cf. *ibid.*, I, 195, 199.

their boasted reliance on the Fathers comes at length to this,—to identify Catholicity with the decrees of Councils, and to admit those Councils only which the Pope has confirmed." [8] This high and mighty way of manipulating scripture and the testimony of the Fathers to its own purposes leads to the basic corruptions of Roman teaching: to filling in and perfecting the system beyond what is written, then insisting upon such human developments as *de necessitate salutis*, and finally leveling out religious doctrine to conform to the semi-rationalistic mentality of Roman scholasticism. [9]

Did the idea of a *Pope* exercising this infallibility constitute a special difficulty, over and above the general difficulty of a standing infallible authority differently institutionalized? It did, insofar as this office of the Pope was made a mandatory object of faith and was considered to be of divine institution; for this doctrine is itself not part of the teaching of antiquity. Or, if certain hints and precedents can there be found, it is an opinion "of a nature such as not to demand enforcement"—it is not one of those essential truths which one must insist upon as necessary to salvation or as terms of communion. [10] The infallibility claimed by the Roman Church, unlike the indefectibility which Newman vindicates for the universal church, sought to make up for its lack of authority in all the Christian churches by a particularly unyielding consistency. This stance was perhaps further accentuated by a centralizing institution such as the papacy. But even if the papacy were not a factor, a council of bishops from a branch of the church, which called itself ecumenical, and invoked the Roman idea of infallibility, would be just as pernicious. For Newman the infallibility of the pope was a natural consequence of any doctrine of the continuing infallibility of the church of which he was *de facto* head. The question that preoccupied him, however, was not whether the pope, by divine appointment, was or was not an infallible teacher in the church, but whether the communion of which he was the head still enjoyed the attribute of infallibility in any meaningful sense. [11]

A center of unity, around which the various branch communions of the church could group themselves, was thus very far from being

---

[8] *VM*, I, 57.

[9] *VM*, I, 89-105.

[10] *VM*, I, 248. It is attested to at most in the "Prophetical Tradition," not in the official "Episcopal Tradition."

[11] *VM*, I, 203 and 110; cf. "The Fall of La Mennais," *Essays Critical and Historical* (London, 1871), I, 169. The passage from *Apo*, p. 106 about the divine institution of the papacy is to be interpreted in the light of the above.

anathema to Newman, if only it did not have to be achieved at the cost of purity of doctrine. A primacy of the bishop of Rome was of itself a desirable thing, provided it did not place itself in the service of doctrinal corruptions. That the claim to be divinely protected in its affirmations of doctrine did not draw Newman's fire more often and more directly is curious. It is never mentioned in his published letters of this period. Perhaps this can be explained by a sort of bad conscience about the authority which the State was allowed to exercise over the Church of England. Newman justified the latter to himself and his readers in the *British Magazine*, with safeguards and reservations, to be sure. But Froude's influence was in the background, constantly wearing away at Newman's subtleties. Was it not the lesser of two evils, he asked, if a foreign church usurped the power of nominating bishops from the local ecclesiastical authority, rather than delivering it into the hands of the civil power? [12] Given the strength of this anti-Erastian factor in Newman's mind, the surer course seemed to him to hold up those errors solemnly insisted upon by Rome at Trent: the veneration of images, the honor paid to the Virgin Mary and the saints, the doctrine of purgatory and prayers for the dead. These were evident departures from the teaching of the earlier, still united church and certified the Roman Church's disrespect for apostolic truth most plainly. The infallibility of the Pope and his primacy were not yet formally dogmatized by the Church of Rome —this would happen only after Newman had long been a member of that communion, in 1870. Still, the ultimate root of Rome's corruption lay in treating the later decisions of one branch of the church as superceding the witness of the undivided church of the Fathers. Infallibility, thus practised, made a mockery of the vaunted apostolicity of the Roman Church.

Newman was not unhappy with the defense he fashioned against Popery while extolling "Catholicism." But even then a note of apprehension sounded softly, yet ominously.[13]

---

[12]   Cf. Froude's *Remains*, III, 220-225.
[13]   *LC*, II, 197, 206; *VM*, I, 16.

CHAPTER FOUR

THE SEARCH FOR NEW FOUNDATIONS

In later years Newman returned many times to the summer of 1839
and the combination of readings concerning the patristic church that
turned out to be of decisive importance in the "history of his religious
opinions." [1] It was the Monophysite controversy that he had immersed
himself in, only to be confronted from another quarter with St.
Augustine and the Donatists again. Even before these two remote
episodes reacted in his imagination in September of 1839, he had
been impressed with the timeliness, so to speak, of certain aspects of
the Council of Chalcedon—"the great power of the Pope (as great as
he claims now almost), and the marvellous interference of the civil
power, as great almost as in our kings." [2] Later on in the summer it
struck him how the Pope had been on the right side as always at
Chalcedon, and how the Anglicans were in the position of the schismatic churches (great parts of Christendom they were, more considerable than England) that refused to accept the Chalcedonian decrees. [3]

But though a Pope, Leo the Great, figured in this first unsettling
of Newman's mind about the Via Media of the Church of England,
it would not do to give the impression that the Pope's authority
immediately became the cardinal point in his reconstruction of the
controversy with Rome. The primary question was still that of
catholicity. Now, however, he had become intellectually unnerved in
a new way by Augustine's insistence on the not to be questioned
validity of the testimony given by the whole church, the church
spread over the face of the earth and united against all local schisms
or heretical sects. To meet this challenge he again went back to the

---

[1] The parts of Newman's *Apologia* that deal with this blow to his Anglicanism
are in substantial agreement with his earlier public and private descriptions, but
do not convey the full force of the parallels. Cf. *Apologia pro Vita Sua*, ed. Svaglic,
pp. 108-111, 130; *Certain Difficulties Felt by Anglicans in Catholic Teaching* (London,
1850), I, 378-387, 392-393; *Correspondence of John Henry Newman with John Keble
and Others ... 1839-1845* (London: Macmillan, 1917), pp. 16-19, 24-25, 219;
Cardinal Newman and William Froude, F.R.S.: A Correspondence, ed. Gordon
Huntington Harper, pp. 36-59; and *LC*, II, 254-258 and 261-62.

[2] Letter to Frederic Rogers of 12 July 1839, *LC*, II, 254.

[3] Cf. *Correspondence ... 1839-1845*, p. 24; Harper (ed.), *Cardinal Newman*,
p. 44; Maisie Ward, *Young Mr. Newman*, p. 462.

Anglican theologians of the previous centuries and came up with a
defense in the *British Critic* of January, 1840, in an article named
"The Catholicity of the Anglican Church." [4]

The question gnawing at Newman's mind during these years of
transition may be put thus: is not the Church of England in schism?
Do not Augustine's strictures against the Donatists apply to it? Or
had he, Newman, been the victim of a temporary loss of perspective
when he let the words, "*Securus judicat orbis terrarum,*" so affect him? [5]
He looked into the matter more closely, and found that Augustine
indeed held that the visible catholicity of the church was one of her
essential notes. Anglicans relied on Ignatius of Antioch and Cyprian
for their theory of the essentially diocesan set-up of the church, but
Augustine even reinterpreted Cyprian, making what he had said
about the unity of the church apply unambiguously only to the universal church, *ecclesia universa toto terrarum orbe diffusa.*[6] However,
Newman's Anglican convictions rallied, and he was able to give
reasons why this un-Anglican attitude of "St. Austin especially, as
the spokesman of other Fathers," [7] need not be taken as an absolute
principle of churchmanship always and everywhere. In "Home
Thoughts Abroad" he had argued that present circumstances (long-
standing divisions in church communion, for instance) had rendered
the principle unworkable. Now, however, he takes a different tack
and brands it a development subsequent to the first three centuries
and hence not essential (a typically "Protestant" argument which
goes against the grain for Newman). Augustine did view communion
with the church around the world as an essential condition for
membership in the true church, he concedes, but earlier Fathers had
not.

Indeed, he says, Roman Catholic controversialists "will grant
perhaps that the papacy is a development," [8] and the phenomenon
seems almost to be postulated by other cases in the history of the
church's teaching. But development creates as many problems as it
solves. Neither Romans nor Anglicans can put forth a consistent
theory of development—it would go to unwelcome lengths in either

---

[4] Reprinted in *Essays Critical and Historical*, II, 1-73.

[5] Cf. *LC*, II, 257.

[6] *Essays Critical and Historical*, II, 35.

[7] *Ibid.*, p. 38.

[8] *Ibid.*, p. 44; this remark could apply to Wiseman, who was Rome's spokesman
in this controversy; cf. Hugo M. de Achával, "An Unpublished Paper by Cardinal
Newman on the Development of Doctrine," *Gregorianum*, 39 (1958), 585.

case, "against individual branches and against the Pope." [9] The theory of development forgets that there also occur aberrations and deteriorations in the life of the church.

Of course, it had not been merely the attitude of St. Augustine towards his fellow Africans, the Donatists, that had impressed Newman so thoroughly in 1839. Rather, it was the comment that this supplied to the story of Chalcedon and its aftermath. With his articles in the *British Critic* of January 1840 and July 1841 [10] he felt he had said all that could be said for the catholicity of the Anglican communion in its estrangement from the rest of the catholic world. He brought up several cases from the fourth century, known to him from his preparatory work for his book on *The Arians*, which purported to show that schism was sometimes tolerated in the ancient church. For instance, Lucifer of Cagliari seems to have decided at one point that, to paraphrase Jerome, the whole world really *had* become Arian, definitively. He withdrew from communion with all other bishops, thinking himself the only orthodox one left. And yet he was never anathematized nor was his cult discouraged by the Roman Church in later years.[11] Another Catholic saint, Meletius of Antioch, "lived and died out of the communion of Rome and Alexandria." Some other bishops who, unlike Lucifer or Meletius, actively consorted with the semi-Arian camp were also treated indulgently by the orthodox. It thus seemed that the ancient church acted, in some cases at least, according to the Anglican and Cyprianic theory of the strictly episcopal constitution of the churches.

On this theory, what was to be said of the Pope as center of unity? Unity, Newman insisted, was not achieved by communion with the Pope; serious a duty as intercommunion of the churches might be in itself, it is quite secondary where the unity of the church is concerned. The essential unity of the church stems from its one origin and its faithfulness to that origin.[12] It was, therefore, a unity of doctrine and to some extent of practice ("apostolic usages"), but it did not contain within itself an unconditional demand for intercommunion at any price, still less for communion with the Pope. The origin bespoke

---

[9] *Essays Critical and Historical*, II, 45.

[10] "The Catholicity of the Anglican Church" and "Private Judgment," the latter reprinted in *Essays Critical and Historical*, II, 336-374.

[11] *Ibid.*, II, 65-68 (cf. *Arians*, p. 364) and 373. Cf. Jean Stern, "Traditions apostoliques et Magistère selon J. H. Newman," *Revue des sciences philosophiques et théologiques*, 47 (1963), 55.

[12] *Essays Critical and Historical*, II, 18, repeated in Tract 90 (1841), *VM*, II, 341.

church unity around the local bishop (Ignatius). Each diocese was essentially independent. Schism then was separation from one's bishop. The only schismatic activity in which a duly inducted bishop could be involved would be meddling in the affairs of another diocese, or "erecting altar against altar," as the Romanists were doing in England.[13] But mere separation of bishops, mere lack of communion between them, could not be schism, much as it was to be deplored.

Newman's considered application of this line of thought to the papacy is well brought out in the following passage.

> Bishop is superior to bishop only in rank, not in real power; and the Bishop of Rome, the head of the Catholic world, is not the centre of unity, except as having a primacy of order. Accordingly, even granting for argument's sake that the English Church violated a duty in the sixteenth century, in releasing itself from the Roman Supremacy, still it did not thereby commit that special sin which cuts off from it the fountains of grace, and is called schism. It was essentially complete without Rome, and now, whether by rebellion or not, it is free from it; and as it did not enter into the Church Invisible by joining Rome, so it was not cast out of it by breaking from Rome. These were accidents in its history, involving, indeed, sin in individuals, but not affecting the Church as a Church.[14]

Thus the papal primacy was like royal supremacy, the patriarchal system, or any number of ecclesiastical arrangements which can be made and unmade, since they are not a matter of *ius divinum*.

Among Newman's collaborators in the Tractarian Movement, which included many younger men by 1840-1841, the mood had changed. William George Ward and his ilk always seemed to give the benefit of the doubt to Roman Catholicism in any question that came up as to whether Rome or Canterbury were more genuinely "catholic." Newman found it difficult to maintain his claim that the Anglican communion's catholicity was sufficient. In this frame of mind he wrote Tract 90, "Remarks on Certain Passages in the Thirty-Nine Articles," and published it in early 1841. Whereas in earlier years he was glad to be able to point to certain doctrinal corruptions which had been irrevocably proclaimed by the Council of Trent, now he wanted to reconcile as much as possible the official teaching of the Roman Church with the official norms of the Church of England, the Thirty-

---

[13] *Essays Critical and Historical*, II, 23 and 30.
[14] *Ibid.*, pp. 24-25, repeated in Tract 90, *VM*, II, 342-343.

Nine Articles. He made much of the distinction between the official teaching of both communions on the one hand and popular beliefs on the other. By showing that the differences were not radical or numerous on the official level, he felt he could lend much-needed support to his view about the unity of the church; for if the church were one and universal, despite its division into branches, then a certain unity of doctrine must be at hand. Tract 90 was therefore a continuation of the work started in "The Catholicity of the Anglican Church" of the previous year.[15] It repeats the latter's notion of schism, and outlines the place which may be granted the Pope in such a view of the church.

These efforts of Newman's reached quite a different audience than the one which occupied him as he wrote it. The Anglican Church at large was scandalized: a furore ensued.[16]

> When the affair of No. 90 happened, Manning said "Shut up your controversy, and go to the Fathers, which is your *line*." Well *they* had been the beginning of my doubts, but I did so. I began to translate St. Athanasius. The truth kept pouring in upon me. I saw in the Semi-arians the Via-medians, I saw in the Catholic Church of the day the identical self of the Catholic Church now;—as you know a friend by his words and deeds, or see an author in his works.[17]

So now, in the autumn of 1841, under the impact of a third object lesson from the church of the Fathers, this one involving his hero, Athanasius, in the fourth century, the strength of the Roman position again loomed up and threatened to engulf him.

His former objections to Rome did not disappear totally, however. Rather, the most obstinate of them remained for a long time as "difficulties." Foremost among them was the Tridentine Council's decree on the (permissibility of the) veneration of images.[18] In the

---

[15] Cf. the comment of the Oratorian editors, *Correspondence* ... *1839-1845*, p. 74.

[16] See Church, *Oxford Movement*, ch. xiv; Chadwick, *The Victorian Church*, pp. 181-189; O'Connell, *The Oxford Conspirators*, ch. xvi.

[17] *L & D*, XII, 357 (to Henry Wilberforce on 30 November 1848).

[18] Council of Trent, Session 25, 3 December 1563 (DS, no. 1823). This is included in all lists of hindrances to union drawn up by Newman: *DA*, pp. 17-18; *Tracts for the Times*, I (Tract 33); *VM*, II, 34 (Tract 38); *VM*, II, 105-113 (Tract 71); *VM*, I, 265 (*Prophetical Office*); letter of 17 November 1834 given in M. Ward, *Young Mr. Newman*, p. 461. Other Tractarians also include it in their lists: A. P. Perceval in Tract 36, and William Palmer of Worcester College in his *Narrative of Events Connected with the Publication of the Tracts for the Times*, new ed. (London, 1883), pp. 144-148.

lists of unacceptable Romanist doctrines which Newman composed
from time to time, Trent's defense of indulgences, the Catholic
practice of praying to the Virgin Mary and to the saints, and the custom
(sanctioned by Trent) of praying for the dead, together with the
doctrine of purgatory are regularly pilloried. In about half of these
lists papal usurpations or the Pope's claim to be universal bishop are
mentioned. After Tract 90, Newman assured a professor from Maynooth who had written to him that, quite apart from possible differences over transsubstantiation, he objected firmly to "the extreme
honours paid to St. Mary and the Saints"[19] as well as to the doctrines a-
bout indulgences and sacred images. Moreover, Catholics in England
compromised religion by joining forces with a liberal political party.[20]
But if the papacy was a difficulty on its own, he did not mention it.
During all this time (1840-1841), however, he did not think well of
individual conversions to the unity of the Roman Catholic Church
(even granting that one's objections could be overcome), but felt
that one should work for a union of the churches on mutually agreed
upon terms, which would effectively shut out recognition of papal
claims.[21] Though the difficulty presented by the papal primacy as
received in the Roman Church did not yet seem acute, it would become more and more urgent for Newman as the other objections
yielded to explanation one by one over the next two years.

---

[19] *Correspondence ... 1839-1845*, p. 123, letter to Dr. Charles William Russell
of 13 May 1841. Cf. "Private Judgment" (July, 1841), however, *Essays Critical and
Historical*, II, 367.

[20] Newman's aversion to Daniel O'Connell, *Apo*, p. 117, was so great that he
lapsed into Antichrist talk about his policies as late as 1841, cf. *Apo*, p. 174.

[21] Cf. *Apo*, pp. 171, 174.

CHAPTER FIVE

ON THE DEATHBED

The years 1841 to 1845, which Newman characterizes as deathbed
years in respect of his membership in the Anglican Church,[1] are also
the ones during which Newman's opinions on the question of papal
power had to be clarified and indeed reversed, as far as the critical
question of fact was concerned. There is no better way to take stock
of his positions on many questions connected with the papacy as he
stood uncertainly at the threshold of far-reaching developments in
his own thinking, than to reconstruct as far as possible how he viewed
the history of the papacy at the beginning of the 1840's. In history
he found the concrete facts which weighed more with him than ever
so many speculative difficulties.

The letters of Ignatius of Antioch had an influence on Newman's
interpretation of the church's life from the beginning which can hardly
be exaggerated. It was in his framework of monepiscopacy that
Newman looked at every description of the church in action that he
came across. Ignatius' prescription for church order seemed to supply
what was missing elsewhere and correct the details of other pictures
which did not agree with that one. Ignatius extolled the ideal of unity
in submission to the local bishop in terms which have hardly ever
been exceeded in the letters which he wrote to various communities
(to the Ephesians, the Magnesians, the Philadelphians, etc.) on his
way to be martyred in Rome around the year 110. The "monarchical
episcopate," to which Ignatius is the first to attest, is the guarantee of
sound doctrine. The other two ranks of the ministry, presbyters and
deacons, assist the bishop and may be trusted implicitly as long as
they hold to him loyally. Outside the communion of those who are
gathered around the bishop there is no union with God, who is one
and whom the one bishop represents. Naturally this doctrine was
well-known to episcopal-minded churchmen, since it was such an
early and clear statement of the necessity of the episcopal system.
Newman himself started to make notes on the original text of Ignatius' letters in 1828; [2] he speaks of the influence Ignatius' view of the

---

[1] Cf. *Apo*, p. 137.
[2] Cf. *Apo*, p. 35.

episcopacy had on his Tractarian ecclesiology; [3] and in 1870 he put out a study "On the Text of the Epistles of St. Ignatius," [4] which he tells us was begun in those notes of 1828.

Since Ignatius' time (and even before, as he thought), the church had always been organized around bishops. Bishops consecrated other bishops, when sees fell vacant, and strove to keep up a communication with the other local churches, just as Ignatius had done with his surviving letters. The most prominent early historian of Christianity, Eusebius of Caesarea, whom Newman read carefully and often cited, confirmed this view of the monarchical episcopate as the trustee [5] of the divine *depositum* of revelation. Irenaeus of Lyons (*c.* 130-200) had especially developed the idea of a public succession from the bishops of the present back to the apostles. For Newman as for Eusebius his testimony was so early as to speak for the very first generations of the church. The monarchical episcopate in unbroken succession from the apostles, therefore, was one of the few church institutions that must always and everywhere be maintained, being *de jure divino*.[6] Irenaeus praised the Roman See for doing in a conspicuous manner what every apostolically founded bishopric did. This was surely one of the reasons that Newman and his fellows hankered after union with Rome, even when they declared it impossible, more than they did after Constantinople, say, or Alexandria or Moscow.

Cyprian of Carthage, in the middle of the third century, was another authority of the first magnitude for Newman's view of church history and its lessons. Indeed, one may see Newman's great struggle, now commencing, as a process of reconciling Cyprian's episcopalism with Augustine's universalism, or even as a process of emancipating himself from Cyprian's influence, though such a phrase would have seemed irreverent to him. Cyprian thought of the church as the one body of Christ its head, teaching the same doctrine everywhere under the care of its bishops. The duty of maintaining communion and concord in the church at large devolved in a special way upon the bishops, whereas it was each Christian's task to preserve the *sacramentum unitatis* [7] with their respective bishops and through them with the

---

[3] Cf. *Apo*, pp. 55-56.

[4] Cf. *Tracts Theological and Ecclesiastical*, new ed. (London, 1895), p. 93.

[5] Cf. *PPS*, III, 199.

[6] "From the first it has been believed that the Catholic system is Apostolic;" cf. "Primitive Christianity," *Historical Sketches*, I, 402 (originally in the series "Church of the Fathers," published in the *British Magazine*, 1833-1836).

[7] Cyprian uses this expression in his treatise *De ecclesiae unitate*, 4 and 6, cf.

catholic church. Cyprian's ideal of church unity, with its appealing reliance on the brotherly love and harmony which the Holy Spirit was to bring about among the bishops, had of course not been able to stem the tide of divisions that had washed over the church after his time. So despite his insistence upon unity "throughout the whole world,... over the universal earth," for the seamless garment of Christ which was the church,[8] one must conclude that local unity around one's own bishop is more basic and essential than the ecumenical communion of episcopal churches.

Though not essential, it was natural, desirable, and yes, providential that webs of communion grew up around prominent and ancient sees. An orderly arrangement patterned after that of the imperial "dioceses" was a need of the time, and was met by the formation of "metropolitan, patriarchal, and papal systems," [9] which derived their authority from their evident usefulness or from the decrees of councils. Rome, from the interplay of these and like factors, came to enjoy an influence surpassing that of any other see. But Gregory the Great turned away the flattery of Easterners and would not allow himself to be styled the "ecumenical bishop"—and this as late as the year 598.[10] True as this account of the rise of ecclesiastical structures beyond the episcopate was, Newman learned, still under Cyprian's influence, that there were greater depths which had to be plumbed. Was the church really left to the ministrations of thousands of bishops, each one monarch in his bailiwick? Where did that leave the promise made to St. Peter by Christ, made so much of by Cyprian, that there would be *one* church in which he would be responsible for the power of the keys?

In theory, as Newman saw it at this point,[11] each bishop was

---

C. Thornton's translation in *The Treatises of S. Caecilius Cyprian* (Oxford, 1840, *Library of the Fathers*, vol. III, part 1), pp. 134 and 136, for which Newman supplied the preface. Cf. *LC*, II, 7, 189, 248, and 251. Cf. also Norbert Schiffers, *Die Einheit der Kirche nach John Henry Newman* (Düsseldorf: Patmos, 1956), pp. 79-90.

[8] Cf. the Oxford ed., *Treatises of Cyprian*, pp. 135-36; also G. S. M. Walker, *The Churchmanship of St. Cyprian* (Richmond, Va.: John Knox Press, 1968), p. 49.

[9] Newman, "The Catholicity of the Anglican Church," *Essays Critical and Historical*, II, 24.

[10] Cf. letters of Gregory I to John the Faster, Patriarch of Constantinople, and to Eulogius, Patriarch of Alexandria, in Carl Mirbt, ed., *Quellen zur Geschichte des Papsttums und des römischen Katholizismus*, 6th rev. ed. by Kurt Aland (Tübingen: J. C. B. Mohr, 1967), pp. 244-45 (nos. 488 and 490); used by Newman in *Prophetical Office, VM*, I, 183-84; cf. *Essays Critical and Historical*, II, 127.

[11] Cf. Newman's note, *Treatises of Cyprian* (Oxford, 1840), pp. 150-52, and

"sovereign and supreme over the whole flock of Christ," just as each apostle had been. This was the divine-right foundation of which the Petrine passage in Matthew 16 speaks. Now to this foundation had to be added in the course of time "certain ecclesiastical regulations," in order to accommodate the abstract theory to the actual state of human nature, as he puts it; in order, that is, to bring a certain minimal order out of the chaos which would result if several bishops' authority were called into play on different sides of one and the same local issue. From the "bishops at large" which every bishop would be if matters were left in their original God-given form, mutual agreement created "bishops by restraint."

> First, Bishops have been restrained, as regards Christ's flock, into local districts called Dioceses; next as regards each other, by the institution of Synodal meetings or Councils, the united decisions of which bind each Bishop as if it was his own individual decision; and moreover, still for the sake of order, by prescribed rules of precedence.

These restraints on the ecumenical power of individual bishops are not of divine institution and a necessary condition of grace, but "are part of the mere ecclesiastical system," which is binding for the sake of order, but which once destroyed need not be built up again on exactly the same lines.

The church then maintained these institutions, all based on the divine-right episcopacy, for many centuries. Bishops such as Athanasius, Basil, Cyril of Jerusalem, and Chrysostom in the East, such as Ambrose of Milan and several Popes in the West (Julius, Damasus, Leo, Gregory),[12] were further signs of God's graciousness in bestowing "the Catholic system" upon his church at its origins. What God did not do was to extricate his church altogether from the effects of men's weakness and malice. The unity of the whole church, that highly prized mark of the early centuries which made it possible to recognize apostolic truth in the voice of ecumenical councils, suffered shipwreck, first by the dissension of East and West, irreparably then in the sixteenth century. For this reason one had only antiquity to judge by.[13]

In the Dark Ages, it became convenient for petitioners, whether

---

his letter of May, 1844 to Mrs. William Froude in Harper, *Cardinal Newman*, pp. 52-54.

[12] Cf. Newman, "The Church of the Fathers," *Historical Sketches*, II, 41-45; "Primitive Christianity," *ibid.*, I, 342-474.

[13] Cf. Tract 71 (1836), reprinted in *VM*, II, 134.

princes, religious clergy, or the lower secular clergy, to appeal to Rome against the policies of bishops or rulers. Taking advantage of the general ignorance, some such parties forged decretals, passing them off as the work of earlier and more enlightened centuries which testified to the supreme authority of the Roman Pontiff. These later were accepted as genuine in all good faith. The "reformation of the eleventh century," [14] though initiated with the aid of the emperor, turned out to be a case study of successful anti-Erastianism on the part of Hildebrand, who covered himself and the papacy with glory by his selfless and tireless efforts *pro ecclesiae libertate*. The papacy worked its own aggrandizement, however, at the expense of the episcopate. The fact that kings and commoners were constantly dealing with Rome over the bishops' heads led to a reduction of their status in fact; and theory followed. Of course, it could also be a source of strength for hard-pressed bishops to be able to appeal to the international and sacralized prestige of the Pope against the importunities of a king, as the case of Becket showed. [15]

Newman's historical view of the papacy seems to have stopped, for all practical purposes, on this high plateau of the Gregorian reform and its consolidation under Innocent III. Perhaps through lack of time or interest he refrained from commenting on the decline of the papacy in the late middle ages. Writing on royal supremacy in "The Convocation of the Province of Canterbury," he had ample opportunity to call a pox down upon both tax-grabbing Popes and expropriating kings. However, the former are mentioned without any animus whatsoever, whereas his contempt for Henry VIII and for William of Orange is barely kept within bounds. [16] Froude, it is true, worked out an interpretation according to which the Popes' excessively centralizing bureaucracy set off a reaction (dated from the statute of *Praemunire* in 1353) on the part of the English crown against the papacy's encroachments on its rights; [17] but there is no evidence

[14] Thus Newman renamed his review of John William Bowden's *Life of Gregory VII* (*British Critic*, April 1841), when he republished it in *Essays Critical and Historical*, II, 249-317. Bowden was a close friend of Newman's from undergraduate days until his death in 1844. Note also Newman's earlier remarks (after Gibbon) on Gregory VII and Innocent III in "Fall of De la Mennais," *British Critic* (October 1837), reprinted in *Essays Critical and Historical*, I, 153.

[15] Cf. *ibid.*, 273-74 and 173; *VM*, I, 184; cf. also *Historical Sketches*, II, 28; and Froude's *Remains*, III, 221 and IV, 449.

[16] *Historical Sketches*, III, 343, cf. 397-400.

[17] Froude's *Remains*, III, 225-27 (from 1833?).

that Newman accepted it. Even Newman's awareness of the manifold conciliarist movement of the late middle ages [18] is so scanty as to be non-existent, despite the many points of theoretical and historical contact which would seem to make it a congenial ally in any controversy between the Church of England and the Church of Rome.[19] Boniface VIII, to mention another medieval figure embarrassing to whomever would defend the infallibility or even the sagacity of the Roman See in the middle ages, likewise seems to be a discovery Newman would make only decades later.

As for the time of the Reformers, Newman certainly held them to be more injurious to the church than the popes had been. They caused the break-up of Christendom and infected a large part of what was left with heresies and with an anti-ecclesiastical spirit. The English Reformation was only better than the continental one, because it took place without a revolution against the essential (episcopal) structure of the church. The English had the happiness to be committed neither to Protestant principles (though they usually gloried in them, to be sure) nor to the Council of Trent, which went beyond what Antiquity had attested. The Reformers were responsible for that unhappy Council, too, by provoking the old church into reaction.

Though Trent had taught little or nothing strictly false, it had had the presumption to set itself up as the arbiter of the universal church, whereas it only represented one branch. It tolerated popular corruptions of doctrine, dogmatized peculiar Roman practices, and anathematized other branches for not accepting new doctrines. This made it impossible for other, more orthodox episcopal churches to keep communion with Rome, which should have remained the center of church unity; and Pope Paul IV had ratified and aggravated this impossibility by insisting on a new creed, based on Trent's decisions, as terms of communion. Arrogance had crowded out love.

The papacy of Newman's own day, he thought, agreeing in this with Lamennais, was embroiled in the obligations of a temporal prince, making it impossible for the Pope to act with the independent spirit of a Gregory or an Innocent. The papacy could not aspire to a

---

[18] Recent research on conciliarism has been admirably drawn together and presented by Francis Oakley, *Council Over Pope? Towards a Provisional Ecclesiology* (New York: Herder & Herder, 1969).

[19] The only mention of conciliarism I have been able to find in Newman occurs in *Prophetical Office*, *VM*, I, 184-85 and 188; it appears more as a thrust in controversy than as a serious objection.

truly leading position in the church as long as it was held down by "worldly alliances and engagements." [20] At least it could be said for the papacy that its "engagements" were on the side of order and stability, as part of the restoration effected by the Congress of Vienna in 1815. And yet Rome threw away the credit for this too; for it seemed as if the Pope blessed the efforts of English and Irish Catholics to achieve a better civil standing by attacking politically the privileged position which religion, represented by the Church of England, had hitherto enjoyed in Britain. Everything the *Times* printed about the conspiracy of Popery, Whiggery, and Liberalism seemed to be verified. [21]

The path from this view of the papal church in 1840-1841 to October, 1845 was trod at an exceedingly slow pace. Still, the differences between the account just given of Newman's reading of history and that which will appear in his *Essay on the Development of Christian Doctrine* are, some of them, not minor at all. At what points do Newman's views change? Which changes are most significant in allowing him to come to the decision to embrace the Roman communion and be embraced by it? One can mark but few.

First there is the recurring doubt that perhaps the whole theory expounded in "The Catholicity of the Anglican Church" and for the next two years was a chimera. Second, the Arian controversy itself, upon reexamination, exhibited the same dire parallels of a restricted communion trying to forge a Via Media (and ending condemned for heresy) that had so unnerved him in 1839 in the cases of Donatism and Monophysitism. Third, the Church of England took or submitted to actions which Newman could only interpret as showing that its first principle was not antiquity and purity of doctrine but Erastian deference to the interests of the national State. A few words on each point are in order.

The Cyprianic theory of communion and schism which Newman had put forth in "The Catholicity of the Anglican Church" seemed paradoxical to some of his readers, who felt Wiseman had the better of him in the latter's article on "The Anglican Claim of Apostolical Succession." [22] One interested reader, a lawyer, wrote to him about it, and Newman was forced to concede that Wiseman had indeed "fixed

---

[20] *Essays Critical and Historical*, I, 156.
[21] Letter to Ambrose Lisle Phillips of 12 September 1841, in *Apo*, p. 174.
[22] Cf. *Apo*, p. 109.

on our weak point," as his *Prophetical Office* and other Tractarian writings had fixed on his: [23] the constantly recurring question of catholicity versus apostolicity. The case seems to have been somewhat more serious than just this, however. In May, 1844, while explaining his change of mind to Mrs. William Froude, he states that the correspondence with the lawyer, with whom he was only slightly acquainted, "had the effect of convincing me that it was absurd to call the Roman Catholics schismatics in England." He recalls his theory, "that since there is but one Bishop and Church in each place, and our succession, not the Roman, has possession in England, therefore the Roman succession and Church are intruders here" (just as, *mutatis mutandis*, Ignatius or Cyprian would have thought). The lawyer argued, however, that the real bone of contention was not on what side of the English Channel one found oneself, but consisted of matters of doctrine and practice, or, to put it differently, not a question of schism but of heresy: "His plain argument was, how preposterous that a man who across the Channel believes in purgatory, the Mass, the Pope's Supremacy etc. must all of a sudden, if he comes to England, change his creed and worship, and become a member of a local community which denies all he has hitherto believed?"

This palpable absurdity led him to abandon "the Anglican theory of local Episcopacy itself," [24] that is, the conception that every bishop *per se* is a bishop at large, a duplicate of every other bishop, all joint tenants of the one episcopate held *in solidum* by all; and that only pragmatic necessity has led to "bishops by restraint." In the short term it led him to emphasize the qualities of churchliness that he could still recognize in the Church of England; in the long, to the acknowledgment of papal supremacy by divine right, that is, of the superiority in "real power," not only in organizational rank, of one bishop over the others.

In the sketch of Newman's view of the history of the episcopate and the papacy between 1839 and 1841 which began this chapter, no notice was taken of the Arian controversy, a special interest of Newman's since 1832. Its relevance to his question about catholicity was not apparent until he began work on Athanasius again in the summer of 1841. But now he saw the same dynamics at work in the prolonged battle for Nicean orthodoxy which also characterized the Protestant-Tridentine-Anglican struggle since the sixteenth century:

[23] Letter to John W. Bowden of 5 January 1840, *LC*, II, 263.
[24] Cf. Harper, *Cardinal Newman*, pp. 52-53.

as was the case in the later controversies regarding Donatism and Chalcedonian orthodoxy, which had already made him fear for the Anglican Via Media, so now too in this earliest and most basic controversy which had been fought out on the grand scale of a truly ecumenical church he found the same pattern. There was a strong and unmitigated challenge from one extreme (Arius/Luther); there was an opposite extreme, which the Roman church and its Pope made its own (Nicea-Athanasius-Pope Julius/Trent-Bellarmine-Pope Paul IV); and there was a middle party, convinced that peace could be achieved if only one did not insist on sharp doctrinal formulations which went beyond scripture (many bishops, among them Eusebius of Nicomedia and Eusebius of Caesarea, enjoying the confidence and support of the court/the bishops and other Erastian supporters of the Anglican establishment). Just as the main body of the church at length settled for Nicean orthodoxy, rejecting all the tergiversations of a Via Media, as the judgment of posterity went against the isolated communion of the Donatists, as Chalcedonian orthodoxy in time became the undisputed foundation of orthodox Christology, so it was to be feared that the Anglican experiment, far from being a promising new departure, would turn out to be just the last of a series of newly discovered attempts at impermissible compromise. "I had hitherto read ecclesiastical history with the eyes of our Divines, and taken what they said on faith, but now I had got *a key*, which interpreted large passages of history which had been locked up from me. I found everywhere one and the same picture, prophetic of our present state, the Church in communion with Rome decreeing, and heretics resisting. Especially as regards the Arian controversy, how could I be so blind before! except that I looked at things bit by bit, instead of putting them together." [25]

Lastly, just as Newman was seeing the English communion's fate prefigured in that of the semi-Arians, his bishops began to act more and more like them. Thinking that he had purchased their neutrality as between his Tract 90 and its Protestant attackers by his silence, he was chagrined to find the bishops taking the Protestant stand in their charges, and condemning the Tract.[26] Not only that, but in October, 1841, Parliament passed a bill to set up an Anglo-Prussian bishopric in

---

[25] Cf. Harper, *Cardinal Newman*, p. 45 (letter to Mrs. William Froude of 5 April 1844); Newman, *Certain Difficulties Felt by Anglicans in Catholic Teaching*, I, 378-87; *Apo*, p. 130.

[26] Chadwick, *The Victorian Church*, I, 188.

Jerusalem, with the concurrence of Archbishop Howley and Bishop Blomfield. To Newman this seemed a portent that could not be overlooked. As he wrote to Robert Wilberforce at the end of 1841:

> One special test of the heretical party is absence of *stay* or *consistence*, ever shifting, ever new forming—ever consumed by internal strife. Our present state ... is a most miserable and continual fulfilment of this Note of error. ...
>
> Another is a constant effort to make alliances with other heresies and schisms, though different itself from them. Thus the semi-arians attempted the Donatists, and the Arians, the Meletians. ... Now, I confess, miserable as this Prussian business is to my mind in itself, it is rendered still more stumbling and unsettling by its apparent fulfilment of this Note of error. ... [27]

The other setbacks that followed for the Tractarians did not seem to affect the scales for Newman; [28] having elevated the episcopal authority in the church, he had no recourse when it disavowed him. Or rather, unlike Lamennais, he could still go one higher, and remain in the church.

But for the immediate future, a period which Newman himself estimated would last "many years," his intention was to withdraw from controversy and see if the passage of time would not show him after all that he had been the victim of a delusion, that only excitement made the Roman Church temporarily appear as the truly Catholic communion.

In the letter to Robert Wilberforce, just quoted, Newman alludes to the considerations which still induce him to remain in the English communion, no matter what his doubts about its quality *qua* church. The mark of schism and error which he perceives upon the Church of England "has led me to look out for *grounds* of remaining where Providence has placed me.... It has also forced me back upon the *internal or personal Notes of the Church*: and with thankfulness I say that I have received great comfort there...." [29] These grounds are laid out in great detail in the four sermons he had just preached at St. Mary's, sermons in which he stresses the grace so evidently passed

---

[27] Quoted in Newsome, *The Wilberforces and Henry Manning*, p. 290, along with other valuable new material showing that Newman's later judgment on the Church of England was already present in late 1841. On the Jerusalem bishopric see *Apo*, pp. 130-36 and Chadwick, *The Victorian Church*, I, 192.

[28] Cf. Church, *The Oxford Movement*, ch. xvi: "The Three Defeats: Isaac Williams, Macmullen, Pusey."

[29] Newsome, *The Wilberforces and Henry Manning*, p. 290.

on to communicants in the Church of England.[30] From the standard outward signs or "notes" of Christ's presence in the Church: the bond of catholic unity, the public succession of sacramental ministers from the apostles, "which have well nigh deserted us," he turns to those which only the eye of faith can perceive, especially the "note of sanctity." These must suffice, as they did even for such a one as the prophet Elijah, born in schism from Jerusalem as he was. Though the Church of England is only Samaria, it is enough, until and unless God issue "some clear indisputable command... to leave it." [31]

Thus Newman, by the beginning of 1842, had prepared himself for an indefinitely long wait, though in a psychological posture that called for a resolution. At what point did he shift from defending Anglicanism and the duty of remaining within its fold to defending the contemporary shape of Roman Catholicism and making a plea for joining its communion? He tells us that it was at the end of 1844,[32] although his mind had been working on the defense of developments for some time previous.[33] Writing to Mrs. William Froude on June 1, 1845, in the midst of his work on the *Essay on Development*, he reveals that he had counted on six months rest after finishing the translation and notes of St. Athanasius at the end of the previous year. "And then I found all of a sudden this new work come before me, and I could not deny its claim on me. I have been thinking about some work or other since last March year, and turning the subject in my mind at odd times." [34] In fact, the archives at the Birmingham Oratory contain a packet of papers on the subject of doctrinal developments which were begun on March 7, 1844.[35] Newman was working on an edition of Athanasius through the rest of 1844, but we may safely assume that his deprecatory reference to "odd times" connotes no lack of interest. Indeed, the sermon on "The Theory of Development in Religious Doctrine" of February, 1843, had been in his mind in connection with the general topic of his University Sermons for years, even

---

[30] Sermons xxi through xxiv of *Sermons Bearing on Subjects of the Day* (referred to as *SD*; new ed. by W. J. Copeland, London, 1869); cf. *Apo*, pp. 138-45 and M. Ward, *Young Mr. Newman*, pp. 382-86. Cf. also Newman, "Private Judgment," *Essays Critical and Historical*, II, p. 362, and his later reflections in *DA*, I, 70-88.

[31] Cf. *SD*, pp. 318, 328-35, 355-61; Greenfield, *Attitude*, p. 361.

[32] Cf. *Apo*, p. 205.

[33] *Ibid.*, p. 142: "the end of 1842."

[34] Harper, *Cardinal Newman*, p. 66. Cf. *Correspondence ... 1839-1845*, p. 278.

[35] Cf. Owen Chadwick, *From Bossuet to Newman: The Idea of Doctrinal Development* (Cambridge: University Press, 1957), pp. 230-31.

before the summer of 1839.[36] By July 14, 1844 he had got so far as to declare candidly, if only in confidence, that the principle of developments had reconciled him "to the (apparently) modern portions of the Roman system." Moreover, this declaration is accompanied by no expressions of fear lest he be suffering under a delusion.[37]

For our present purposes, it is of the greatest interest to note that the question of the development of papal supremacy is dealt with in detail and as the natural test case of the approach which Newman hopes will lead him out of his dilemma. The Froudes would read in the letters of May 19 and July 14, 1844 that the primacy of the Pope had indeed been formed, to all outward appearances, by the "restraint" laid upon other bishops' ecumenical powers over the first few centuries; but that this process was the gradual fulfillment of the prophecy made to Peter in Matthew 16. Therefore, the papacy could very well be an institution *de iure divino*, even though it did not make its appearance until long after the apostolic age. A seemingly subtle change in comparison with Newman's views of 1840—the introduction of the notion of propecy in conjunction with developments not only in the old, but also in the new Gospel covenant—has led to a diametrically opposed judgement on the papacy. Papal supremacy, a difficulty mentioned at once by his Anglican friends as an insuperable obstacle to joining Rome,[38] presented Newman for the time being with no problem other than of defending it as a primitive doctrine on the hypothesis of development.

---

[36] Sermon xv of *Oxford University Sermons*; cf. Günter Biemer, *Newman on Tradition* (New York: Herder and Herder, 1967), pp. 51-54; James J. Byrne, "The Notion of Doctrinal Development in the Anglican Writings of J. H. Newman," *Ephemerides Theologicae Lovanienses*, 14 (1937), 230-286; also the letters to the Froudes of 14 July 1844; Harper, *Cardinal Newman*, p. 58, and of 9 June 1844: Jean Stern, *Bible et Tradition chez Newman* (Paris: Aubier, 1967), p. 97.

[37] Harper, *Cardinal Newman*, pp. 58-59; compare *Apo*, p. 179.

[38] Cf. Newsome, *The Wilberforces and Henry Manning*, p. 291.

PART TWO

PROPHECIES OF KINGDOM AND CHURCH

CHAPTER SIX

THE PATRISTIC IDEA OF ANTICHRIST

The battle for Newman's soul was fought out on the terrain of apostolicity and catholicity of the Church. So much Newman assures us—and the supporting evidence is there, as we have seen. But it is also well known that for him, at least, the Antichristian taint that the Protestant interpretation of prophecies attached to the church of Rome was an essential component of the Via Media.[1] In the *Apologia* he tells us that the anti-Roman interpretations of Antichrist prophecies stained his imagination until 1843, although they lost their grip on his intellect earlier.[2] The decisive blow was not any interpretation of prophecy, but the realization of his possible schismatic situation. Later, in a note on Dean Church's account of the Oxford Movement, he insisted that the alternative between Christian and Antichristian church character did not come into his "great question." [3] He acknowledged, however, that he may have been obliged in controversy to deal with the matter, though it did not affect his personal stance or decision any more.

All this is quite correct, but it has had the unfortunate effect of putting students off the scent of a development in Newman's thought, which, if secondary, is by no means unimportant. I mean the further use of the argument from prophecy in Newman's ecclesiology. This argument plays a subdued, but crucial, role in his *Essay on the Development of Christian Doctrine*. Without it his construction of the development of the papal institution and doctrine does not stand up. To show how this is so, therefore, we must first give an account of the changing role played in Newman's thought by the Antichrist theme and its relationship to the Roman church. This can be briefly summed up in this chapter, since I have treated it in detail elsewhere.[4] The next

---

[1] *Apo*, pp. 57-60.

[2] *Ibid.*, p. 20.

[3] Quoted in R. W. Hunt, "Newman's Notes on Dean Church's *Oxford Movement*," *Bodleian Library Record*, 8 (1969), 135.

[4] Paul Misner, "Newman and the Tradition concerning the Papal Antichrist," *Church History*, 42 (1973), 377-395; cf. also Maurice Nédoncelle, "Newman, théologien des abus de l'Eglise," in *Oecumenica*, 2 (1967), 116-132, esp. pp. 116-122, of which I was unaware when composing my article.

chapter will then present the alternative ecclesiological interpretation of Old Testament prophecies, which culminates in an affirmation that an outwardly splendid, imperial church is in harmony with God's will.

Newman was introduced to the tradition concerning the Antichrist by the *Dissertations on the Prophecies* of Bishop Thomas Newton (1704-1782), who did more than any other churchman of the eighteenth century to restore credit to the whole enterprise of interpreting prophecies. As Christopher Hill has shown, the excesses of radical Puritans in the tumultuous years 1640-1660 were such as to make churchmen put aside the appeal to prophecy as a much too dangerous instrument. The sophisticated intellect of Enlightenment critics, on the other hand, found interpretations of prophecy to be apt targets of their ridicule. Newton, however, rescued the anti-papal interpretations of Antichrist prophecies from the sectarian underground where they had taken refuge and furnished them with a scholarly foundation which even skeptical men of learning could not easily pick apart. Newman, at fifteen, was impressed.

We have seen how under the influence of Froude and Keble, Newman pulled back from any direct identification of the papal church as Antichrist. In 1835 he was far enough removed from Bishop Newton's way of thinking to state that the Antichrist prophecies had not yet been fulfilled, so that the question of identifying him was as yet premature (*Advent Sermons on Antichrist*, Tract 83).[5] This did not prevent him from assailing Antichristian elements, as he saw them, in the Roman system (especially in *Prophetical Office* of 1837).[6] Nevertheless, the view which the Fathers held of the nature of Antichrist ruled out any papal application, as he saw it. He used 2 Thessalonians 2:6-7 to demonstrate this: "that which withholdeth," that which was restraining the mystery of lawlessness in the time of the Fathers, was still restraining it, was not yet "out of the way." This restraining factor is none other than the "present framework of society," which he views as the heir of the Roman Empire and thus as partaking of the nature and destiny of Daniel's fourth beast. Its dissolution will usher in the time of the Antichrist proper. In the meantime "the mystery of iniquity doth already work" (2 Thess. 2:7) and "even now

---

[5] Reprinted as "The Patristical Idea of Antichrist," *DA*, pp. 44-106.
[6] See above, Ch. III, and *VM*, II, 428-433.

already is it in the world" (1 John 4:3).[7] "The whole world lieth in wickedness" (1 John 5:19).[8] But this is not yet the time of Antichrist.

The years 1835-1840 were years of increasing suspicion against the Tractarians because of their softness on Romanism. How serious the situation was becoming should have been apparent to all at the latest in 1838 when Keble and Newman published Froude's *Remains*.[9] In the ensuing uproar Newman was forced to take a clear stand on whether or not the Pope was Antichrist. To the dismay of many Tractarians, he said no, the Pope was not Antichrist.[10] Never again would he make the allusions to Rome with Antichrist rhetoric which he had made just the previous year in his *Prophetical Office*. Though he alienated many supporters with this stand, he himself regarded the step as a liberating one, which helped focus attention on the real issues of apostolicity and catholicity of the two communions.

In respect to this turning-point of 1838 it may be said that the *Apologia* gives the internal or psychological history of Newman's religious opinions and hence highlights the crisis of 1839 at the expence of this very public crisis of 1838. The *Apologia* contains no mention of Newman's "Letter to Faussett" (*VM*, II, 195-257, a reply to Godfrey Faussett, *The Revival of Popery*, Oxford, 1838), which marks the first occasion on which he wrote that the Church of England was just as liable to the Antichrist charge as was the Church of Rome: in either case the charge could only come from a radical Protestant position which rejected the testimony of Antiquity. The *Apologia* also dates the *Advent Sermons on Antichrist* to 1838 instead of 1835 and most commentators have followed this dating. Though both the *Advent Sermons* and the "Letter to Faussett" appeared in June, 1838, they are distinct steps along the way of the Antichrist tradition. Already in 1835, but most definitely in 1838, Newman was further along this path than he gives himself credit for in the *Apologia*.[11]

The change announced briefly in the "Letter to Faussett" in 1838 and to be developed more in the following years consisted simply in this, that the last remnants of the Antichrist polemic, even in the attenuated form in which Newman had used it, was swept away, and

---

[7] *DA*, p. 51.

[8] *PPS*, VII, 27.

[9] Maisie Ward, *Young Mr. Newman*, pp. 332-333; Misner, "Newman and ... Antichrist," p. 379.

[10] *VM*, II, 208.

[11] *Apo*, p. 114.

the argument from history and from purity of doctrine was left to stand on its own merits. Newman did not think his position was any the weaker for this change.[12] By it however he broke with an imposing Church of England tradition and denied himself henceforth the opportunity of "revil(ing) Popery in order to say strong Catholic things."[13]

Two years later, on the rebound from his shock of recognition as holding a despicable compromise position with dogmatic truth (see above, Chapter IV), Newman made one last and very effective effort to undermine what he considered a false and dangerous argument from the controversy between Anglicanism and Romanism, the argument from Antichrist prophecies. In a long article in the *British Critic* of October 1840, called "Todd's Discourses on the Prophecies relating to Antichrist," [14] he developed the point he had made so briefly in the "Letter to Faussett," that Antichrist prophecies tell as surely against an episcopal church as they do against Rome. While doing so, he made clear what he now considered the offence of the papal system in general to be,[15] and also what the Roman Catholics in England in particular were doing wrong.[16] But his first concern was to scotch the use of Antichrist talk against Rome *within* the High Church wing in England.

The target of the Protestant interpretation of Antichrist prophecies was, he maintained, the doctrine that the church represents Christ and continues his work, not merely the reputed excesses of the papacy. For if Christ has in fact left a representative behind him, then it may issue authoritative commands in religious affairs, it may convey the power of the Spirit by its visible acts. But if the doctrine of the church as representative of Christ is spurious, then its acts of "authority"

---

[12] See "State of Religious Parties" of April 1839 in *Essays Critical and Historical*, I, 305-307.

[13] Letter to Keble of 22 August 1838 in *LC*, II, 235.

[14] "Todd's . . . Antichrist" is reprinted under the title, "The Protestant Idea of Antichrist," in *Essays Critical and Historical*, II, 112-185.

[15] *Ibid.*, p. 173: "And what is the Pope but a bishop? his peculiarity lying not in his assuming to be *omnibus numeris* a bishop, but in his disfranchising all bishops but himself; not in his titles nor in his professed gifts, which are episcopal, but in his denying these to other bishops, and absorbing the episcopate into himself."

[16] *Ibid.*, p. 180: "What is the real place of the Church of the middle ages in the divine scheme need not be discussed here. If we have been defending it, this has been from no love, let our readers be assured, of the Roman party among us at this day. That party, as exhibited by its acts, is a low-minded, double-dealing, worldly-minded set, and the less we have to do with it the better . . ." and more in that vein.

and of "grace" are usurpations, are acts of Antichrist.[17] One "cannot consistently hold that the Pope is Antichrist, without holding the principle of establishments, the Christian ministry, and the most sacred Catholic doctrines, are fruits of Antichrist." [18] Therefore, those who believe in the church as a society Christ founded to represent him on earth should not use the Antichrist epithet against any Christian communion or hierarchical figure.

Newman notes that in fact various sectarian authors apply the Antichrist label also to the episcopal Church of England. Indeed, being so labelled is tantamount to a mark of the true church.[19] That it is applied frequently to the pope only shows how close the pope is to being a true type of the Christian hierarchy.[20] Protestant talk about the Antichrist prophecies as having already been fulfilled in a branch of the Christian Church is based on the principle that no one and no institution can represent Christ on earth, and hence turns against the Anglicans as surely as against Rome.

Newman might well have been satisfied with thus setting to rights the terms of the controversy. Tract Ninety and its consequences, however, were just down the road, as we know. What is less well known is the role an alternative set of prophecies bearing on the church would continue to play in his thinking.

---

[17] *Ibid.*, pp. 170-72. Alf Härdelin gives a clear presentation of this point in his *Tractarian Understanding of the Eucharist*, p. 105.

[18] *Essays Critical and Historical*, II, 115.

[19] *Ibid.*, p. 166.

[20] *Ibid.*, p. 173, cf. *DA*, p. 19.

CHAPTER SEVEN

THE IMPERIAL IMAGE OF THE CHURCH

In the same autumn of 1816 when he read Bishop Newton's *Dissertations* on the Antichrist prophecies, Newman also fell under what he came to consider a contrary influence, that of the Church Fathers. "I read Joseph Milner's Church History, and was nothing short of enamoured of the long extracts from St. Augustine, St. Ambrose, and other Fathers which I found there." It was a dozen years before he came back to the Fathers again in a serious way, but since he was destined to do so, Newman later saw in the combination of the two books, Newton and Milner, "the seeds of an intellectual inconsistency." [1] On the one hand, the Fathers led him to a high view of the church realizing the "sacramental system," according to which God condescended to communicate invisible grace through visible agencies; on the other hand, as he was to say in his *Essay on the Development of Christian Doctrine*, "The school of Hurd and Newton consider that Christianity slept for centuries upon centuries, except among those whom historians call heretics." [2] The issue was joined on a matter of theological and historical judgment: had the church of the Fathers been that divine instrument to which they themselves bore testimony, or had it been the Antichristian power that Protestants saw in it?

That the Christian church was in some sense a fulfilment of Old Testament prophecies bearing on the vindication of Israel has always been a common notion. To speak of "the kingdom of God" or the "kingdom of Christ" in this connection has *prima facie* biblical and traditional warrant. So it is nothing specially indicative of a trend in Newman's thinking when we find him speaking of the "mediatorial kingdom of Christ" as "the object of prophecy from the first ages of the Jewish church" in 1827. At this time, after all, he was in his "Noetic" period, his mind had not yet been aroused to subtle dangers of Christian rationalism, and his reference to this theme simply indicates what a commonplace it was. [3] There is as yet no stress on the

---

[1] *Apo*, p. 20.
[2] *Dev* (1845), p. 129; compare Ch. II, Sec. II, no. 14 of revised editions.
[3] MS Sermon No. 160, pp. 1-5, followed by notes on the criticism it received

aspect of domination or of authority in church officers, which will soon characterize his image of the church *qua* imperial power.

The imperial image comes flooding out in some writings of 1833-1836, a series of descriptions of "The Church of the Fathers" which Newman published in the *British Magazine*. The more he read the Fathers, the more he saw the ruling hand of providence behind the champions of the church: Athanasius against the Arians and the semi-Arian emperors, Ambrose against Justin and Valentinian,[4] Basil and Gregory also, although the Cappadocians "did not live to see the Churches, for which [they] laboured, in a more Catholic condition." [5] Nor did he neglect to point out the prelates who carried on the struggle in their own remarkable way in the middle ages, Hildebrand especially, and Thomas Becket.[6]

With this historical fulfilment now vividly before his mind's eye, Newman was in a position to reenact and appropriate the post-Constantinian application of Old Testament types and prophecies to the present age of the church.[7] The vehicle for this striking development is a two-part sermon dating from early 1835, called "The Kingdom of the Saints." [8] There he presented a picture of the church as an aggressive political force on the world scene.

> Christ preached that "the kingdom of God was at hand." He founded it and made Peter and the other Apostles His Vice regents in it after His departure, and He announced its indefinite extension, and its unlimited duration. And, in matter of fact, it exists to this day, with its government vested in the very dynasty which His Apostles began, and its territory spread over more than the world then known to the Jews; with varying success indeed in times and places, and varying consistency and unanimity within; yet, after making every allowance for such partial failures, strictly a visible power, with a political influence founded on invisible pretensions.[9]

Being a "kingdom" with a governing "dynasty" and "territory" and

---

(not apropos of our investigation, cf. *Apo*, p. 25). See also John Coulson, *Newman and the Common Tradition*, pp. 64 f.

[4] *Historical Sketches*, I, 342-374.
[5] *Ibid.*, II, 49.
[6] *Ibid.*, II, 20; I, 344-345.
[7] See Heinrich Fries, "Wandel des Kirchenbildes," in *Mysterium Salutis*, IV/1 (Einsiedeln: Benziger, 1972), pp. 235-249 for the historical importance of the imperial church theme; Rudolf Hernegger, *Macht ohne Auftrag* (Olten: Walter, 1963), pp. 242-252 (Eusebius of Caesarea's theology of history).
[8] *PPS*, II, 232-254, note especially pp. 244-245 and 236-239 for material which follows.
[9] *Ibid.*, p. 245.

"political influence," the church naturally comes into conflict with the Roman Empire into which it is born, only avoiding strife for longer or shorter periods because it disclaims "the use of force." [10]

At first, it seemed as if "ten thousand orderly societies," each resembling the others but neverthless local and "without any sufficient system of correspondence or centre of influence," were springing up everywhere. They constituted a series of rival states or kingdoms, rivals, that is, not among themselves, but to the civil power. They traced their origins back "through a continous line of their Bishops to certain twelve or fourteen Jews, who professed to have received it from Heaven" ; and despite appearances, "they were bound one to another by the closest ties of friendship; the society of each place to its ruler, and their rulers one with another by an intimate alliance all over the earth. At length, they took the place of the Empire under which they had had such modest beginnings, and "ruled as supreme" :

> ruled, united under one head, in the very scenes of their former suffering, in the territory of the Empire, with Rome itself, the seat of the Imperial government, as a centre.[11]

Newman is thus forced to look to Rome for fulfilments of prophecies about the kingdom of God! The papacy itself was quite a legitimate form of Christ's foundation considered as kingdom, apart from the question of whether it had defiled itself with false doctrine. The sentence just quoted applies in the first place to the Roman church of the fourth, fifth, and sixth centuries, when Popes such as Leo and Gregory held sway. But he applies the prophecies of the Messianic kingdom expressly to the middle ages as well,[12] and we know that names like Hildebrand and Innocent III represented the imperial church, the "Theocratic Church" [13] to Hurrell Froude.

How then did this stand to his Anglicanism? Could a preacher in the Church of England hold such a view? Could anyone but a Romanist regard the pretensions of medieval popes as "parts of the Divine Dispensation" ? Newman counters this objection with a repetition of his standpoint, that the medieval church government did in some sort actually fulfill certain prophecies; but this need not mean that the fulfilment took place exactly as "intended" by God. After all, the

---

[10] *PPS*, II, 244; cf. also 238.

[11] *Ibid.*, pp. 236-39; cf. *Essays Critical and Historical*, I, 151.

[12] *PPS*, II, 248-49; also p. 239: "Five centuries compass the rise and fall of other kingdoms; but ten were not enough for the full aggrandizement of this."

[13] *Apo*, p. 35; cf. Froude's *Remains*, III, 224.

Israelites were rebuked for setting up a monarchy, yet this was to a certain extent blessed and the fulfilment of prophecy.[14] In the age of the Gospel, too, human weakness and sin and inattention to God's word will have diminished the fulfilments which otherwise might have come to pass.

> The Latin ecclesiastical system of the Middle Ages may anyhow be the fulfilment of that gracious design, which would have been even more exactly accomplished, had Christians possessed faith enough to keep closely to God's revealed will. For what we know, it was intended that all the kingdoms of the earth should have been made subject to the spiritual rule of the Church. The infirmity of man defeated this purpose; but it could not so far defeat it, but some sort of fulfilment took place.[15]

No Evangelical or fundamentalist of later years could surpass the earnestness and ingenuity of Newman's prophetical interpretations as we find them in these sermons on "The Kingdom of the Saints." They are indications of his continued efforts to develop a consistently ecclesiological interpretation of prophecies. This makes them a counter-part to his *Advent Sermons on Antichrist* of the same year. The juxtaposition and contrast of the two incompatible sets of prophecies, however, did not take place until 1841, in the article to which we have already referred, "Todd's Discourses on the Prophecies relating to Antichrist," although Newman had had it in mind at least since 1838.[16] At the close of this essay he sketched an argument for his doctrine of the church as an authoritative representative of Christ, an argument which is also based on scriptural prophecies. The question he posed was typical. Which of the two sets of prophecies, the Antichrist ones or the imperial ones, were fulfilled in the church of the Fathers and of the middle ages?

In fact, Newman formulated the question even more pointedly: "If the history of Christian Rome corresponds to the denouncements of the Apocalypse, does it not more closely and literally correspond to the promises of Isaiah?" [17] Can anyone doubt that what Isaiah sang of the glory of Jerusalem was fulfilled in the church triumphant of the fourth and ensuing centuries? "You shall be called the priests of the Lord, the ministers of our God shall you be named; you shall

---

[14] *PPS*, II, 251, with reference to Dt 17:14-20.

[15] *Ibid.*, pp. 252-53.

[16] *LC*, II, 251; cf. R. W. Hunt, "Newman's Notes on Dean Church's *Oxford Movement*," *Bodleian Library Record*, 8 (1969), 135.

[17] *Essays Critical and Historical*, II, 182.

enjoy the wealth of the nations, and in their glory shall you revel"
(Isaiah 61:6; Newman also cites here Isaiah 2:2, 54:17, 59:21,
60:17-18).

The importance of such prophecies for Newman emerges from the
careful treatment he devotes to them a year later (27 November 1842)
in a sermon with the precise and uncompromising title, "The Christian
Church an Imperial Power." [18] It is a clear sign not only that inhibi-
tions arising from Antichrist prophecies were behind him, but also
that the prophecies of the imperial church which had supplanted
them were weighing heavily against the equilibrium between apostolicity and catholicity which he had painstakingly reinstated after the
blow of 1839. In his article on "Catholicity" [19] he had mentioned the
patristic idea of the church, in one of its aspects, as a unified political
entity, but mainly as a difficulty to be dealt with. Now, after a period
of despairing of the external marks of the church,[20] he returned to
the subject with a vengeance. Newman's "kingdom-ecclesiology,"
as I may call it, emerged stronger than ever from the crisis in which it
had been plunged.

As before, the Isaianic texts receive the lion's share of Newman's
attention in "The Christian Church an Imperial Power," though he
also cites verses from several messianic psalms and from Daniel,
Micah, Zechariah and Ezekiel, as well as his favorite (because he
considered it the oldest and most primitive), Genesis 49:10, "The
sceptre shall not depart from Judah until Shiloh come, to whom is the
gathering of the people." He had learned his exegetical methods from
the Alexandrians Clement, Cyril, and Athanasius; [21] when applied to
the prophecies of Kingdom, they led him to the imperial picture of
the church.

Newman laid great stress on the public, authoritative and aggressive
steps by which the church came to rival and eventually supplant the
Roman Empire.[22] He insisted that beside the mission to teach and
show mercy, the church has a mission, entrusted to its officers, of
ruling, and he insisted further "that the nations are subject to them." [23]

---

[18] *SD*, pp. 218-236.
[19] *Essays Critical and Historical*, II, 9 (see above, Ch. IV).
[20] See above, Ch. V.
[21] Cf. *Arians*, pp. 56-63.
[22] *SD*, pp. 228 and 234; cf. *Essays Critical and Historical*, II, 176-179.
[23] *SD*, p. 227. See Norbert Schiffers, *Die Einheit der Kirche nach John Henry
Newman*, pp. 281 and 230-235: J. Richard Quinn, *The Recognition of the True*

Only in one respect did Newman point out a difference between the church and civil regimes: the church was not founded by violence and should not use violence to maintain itself.[24] The sermon which deals with this thought, "Sanctity the Token of the Christian Empire," breathes a different spirit than the rather bellicose or should we say "triumphalistic" sermons preceding it.

Here the thought of service instead of domination comes to the forefront, but it is also insisted upon that it is proper for the church to have "power, and influence, and credit, and authority, and wealth," though she should not seek these things. In a like vein, touching upon the matter of the papacy, Newman wrote that "universal dominion, or Catholicity" comes to the church because she has not been ambitious for it. "They shrink and flee from the episcopate of the world, and they are crowned with an ecumenical dominion: they write themselves servants of servants [Gregory the Great], and they become vicars of Christ." [25]

Otherwise he refrained from any definition or delimitation of the "imperial power" which he attributed to the apostles. That might lead him into a discussion of the state's competence, which was not his concern. In the sermon on "The Christian Church an Imperial Power" he wished above all to make it clear that he was not speaking merely of a metaphorical or invisible empire. If the church is a kingdom, it is "a body politic, bound together by common laws, ruled by one hand, holding intercourse part with part, acting together." [26] If the church is more than a kingdom, if it is an empire, then it extends its power beyond its own boundaries.[27]

> What is wanting ... to the picture of a great empire, comprising all that a great empire ordinarily exhibits? Extended dominion, and that not only over its immediate subjects, but over the kings of other kingdoms; aggression and advance; a warfare against enemies, acts of judgment upon the proud; acts of triumph over the defeated; high imperial majesty towards the suppliant; clemency towards the repentant; parental care of the dutiful. Again, these passages imply, in the subjects of the kingdom, a multitude of various conditions and dispositions; some of them loyal, some restrained by fear, some by interest, some partly subjected, some indirectly influenced. [The

---

Church according to John Henry Newman (Washington: Catholic University Press, 1954), pp. 56-65, 71-98.

[24] *SD*, p. 237.
[25] *Ibid.*, pp. 246 and 248.
[26] *Ibid.*, p. 220.
[27] *Ibid.*, p. 228.

passages quoted from Isiaah] involve, in consequence, though they do not mention, a complex organization, and a combination of movements, and a variety and opposition of interests, and other similar results of extended sway. Of course, too, they involve vicissitudes of fortune, and all those other characteristics of the history of a temporal power which ever will attend it, while men are men, whether, as in the case of the Jews, they are under a supernatural Providence or no.[28]

The sacralization of ecclesiastical authority, which had been such a prominent feature of Christian history since Constantine, could hardly have a more eloquent defense than these sermons and the parts of the *Essay on Development* which build on them.

It is obvious that such a line of thought has little appeal to Christians of a forward-looking, liberal disposition. Perhaps that helps to account for the oblivion into which this aspect of Newman's thought has fallen. One would hardly suspect its weight from reading John Coulson's excellent studies, for example.[29] Even Harold Weatherby, who maintains the strange position that Newman should have defended the Christian polity of former ages consistently to the end, instead of letting himself and those who relied on him into a compromise with modern ideas, does not capitalize on these texts as he might.[30] It must be said to Christopher Dawson's credit, however, that he saw clearly how the prophetical images presented themselves to Newman.[31] The atmosphere of cultural despair which was so strong in Catholic circles between the World Wars may have been favorable to discerning this profoundly anti-libertarian element in Newman's world view at mid-century. But Dawson developed the perspective to see Newman's other side, too, calling him "almost the only Christian thinker who realized the anti-Christian character of the trend to secularism without indulging in wishful thinking or identifying the cause of the Church with that of the political reactionaries. . . . He never accepted the fundamental historical pessimism which is so common today." [32] But

---

[28] *Ibid.*, p. 234.

[29] See especially Coulson, *Newman and the Common Tradition. A Study in the Language of Church and Society* (Oxford: Clarendon Press, 1970).

[30] Harold L. Weatherby, *Cardinal Newman in His Age. His Place in English Theology and Literature* (Nashville: Vanderbilt University Press, 1973), esp. pp. 246-259.

[31] Christopher Dawson, *The Spirit of the Oxford Movement* (New York: Sheed & Ward, 1933), 108-109.

[32] *Idem*, "Newman and the Modern World," *The Tablet*, 226 (5 August 1972), 733-734 (an essay dated May 1945).

this is a global judgment that presupposes familiarity with the Roman Catholic part of Newman's life. Though the imperial image of the church yields pride of place to other aspects in Newman's later Catholic writings, it remains a factor in his ecclesiology, the more disconcerting because it is presupposed rather than defended.

PART THREE

THE THEORY OF DEVELOPMENT
AND THE PAPACY

CHAPTER EIGHT

THE *ESSAY ON DEVELOPMENT* AND ITS ARGUMENT

Newman's *Essay on the Development of Christian Doctrine* is one of those works of genius in which a man's whole store of learning is mobilized under great existential pressure. Insofar as the question of papal powers in the church was a burning issue in the Tractarian Movement and in Newman's life at this juncture, we should expect to find it treated in detail in this work. Some of Newman's first critics felt that acceptance or rejection of the papal claims was the central issue of the whole *Essay*; they tended to regard the space devoted to other topics and to broad historical descriptions as so much window-dressing. Many later commentators have followed in their footsteps, apparently feeling that in the circumstances it could not have been otherwise. I find, however, that to describe the role of the papal controversy in this work is not so simple. This issue is not truly central—apostolicity and catholicity are—but it *is* dealt with at length directly and indirectly.

Our purchase on the *Essay* will have to be gained at several levels, one after the other or when necessary simultaneously. I will first note some leading lines of the *Essay*, which are basic to its understanding. Then the special "antecedent probabilities" which in Newman's argumentation prepare the way for accepting the development of the papacy on its own terms are examined (Chapter IX). The revealed character of the papal church as an object of divine prophecy is an element of his case for it as a legitimate development which deserves special attention (Chapter X). Having clarified all these presuppositions, we can then turn to the actual historical process by which the papal primacy came to self-realization, as Newman presented it (Chapters XI-XIII). Finally, the reception which his hypothesis received in Roman Catholic theology, the appeals made to it in 1870 when the papal primacy was defined as dogma by the First Vatican Council, and the revisions which Newman made in the Essay for its third edition of 1878 will round out the account of his thinking in respect to the historical development of papal primacy (Chapter XIV).

A critical edition of the *Essay on Development* is much to be desired. The first two editions (1845 and 1846, virtually identical) are rare books, though now there is a paperback edition of the first edition, slightly altered in the notes.[1] It will not do, however, to consult only the revised (third) edition of 1878, since Newman subjected it to a complex revision and rearrangement of material. Owen Chadwick made a first attempt to determine what subtle differences in theory or method may be detected through these changes; his brief analysis remains a boon to researchers, along with his thorough study of the background and tendencies of the first edition.[2] The most valuable aid to date for students of the *Essay* is a German edition, which Johannes Artz has provided with a wealth of highly reliable notes. Besides tracking down allusions and supplying documentation to fill out Newman's sparse references, Artz draws attention to many of the textual variations between the first and third editions.[3] There was no point in attempting a truly critical edition in German translation, of course; nevertheless, it is the nearest thing to doing for the *Essay on Development* what Martin Svaglic did for the *Apologia*.

Newman entitled his work very deliberately an Essay, and he was not always confident that it would stand the test of time.[4] It is well to remember that the first edition, at least, was emphatically "an hypothesis to account for a difficulty." [5] Although he refers to "the Theory

---

[1] *An Essay on the Development of Christian Doctrine* by John Henry Newman, the Edition of 1845, ed. with an introduction by J. M. Cameron (Baltimore: Penguin, 1974), hereinafter referred to as *Dev*, ed. Cameron. Cf. Ottis Ivan Schreiber, "Newman's Revisions in the Essay on the Development of Christian Doctrine," in Charles Frederick Harrold's edition of the *Essay* (New York: Longmans, Green and Co., 1949), pp. 417-435.

[2] Owen Chadwick, *From Bossuet to Newman. The Idea of Doctrinal Development*, pp. 187-191 and 245-249.

[3] John Henry Newman, *Über die Entwicklung der Glaubenslehre*, durchgesehene Neuausgabe der Übersetzung von Theodor Haecker, besorgt, kommentiert und mit ergänzenden Dokumenten versehen von Johannes Artz (Mainz: M. Grünewald, 1969), hereinafter referred to as *Dev*, ed. Artz. The monograph on the *Essay* with which Artz introduces this edition was first published as "Entstehung und Auswirkung von Newmans Theorie der Dogmenentwicklung," *Theologische Quartalschrift*, 148 (1968), 63-104 and 167-198. Charles Stephen Dessain offers a selective but valuable bibliographical introduction in *Victorian Prose: A Guide to Research*, ed. David J. Delaura (New York: Modern Language Association, 1973), pp. 177 f.

[4] Chadwick, *From Bossuet to Newman*, p. 186.

[5] *Dev*, p. 27; ed. Cameron, p. 90 (Introduction). My citations of Newman's *Essay on the Development of Christian Doctrine* will observe this form: *Dev*, followed by the page number in the first (1845) and second (1846) editions, which are practically identical, and then by the page number in Cameron's 1974 re-issue of the first edition. Following this in parentheses will be the place in the revised edition of 1878 according to chapter, section, and number. This will enable the reader to consult any edition.

of Developments," he operates with the elements of many potential theories of development and does not try to systematize them, since he is feeling his way quite empirically from one communion of Christians to another.[6] It is only at times and as though carried away by his argument that he shows enthusiasm for change in itself, as when he says, "Here below to live is to change, and to be perfect is to have changed often." [7] The basic theme remains the permanence and identity of faith through all transformations. Change is a difficulty, not normally a positive recommendation for him. He seeks the Christian communion which has changed the least and remained most profoundly the same since the days of the Fathers.

All the same, it had become historically evident that great transformations of one kind or another had in fact taken place in the course of Christian tradition. Newman had emancipated himself from the prevailing viewpoint that such changes were all undesirable. In his sermon on "The Theory of Developments in Religious Doctrine" (1843), he had recognized that faith is in part at least an "Idea" and that this idea could not remain inert in the minds of those who received it. The analogy of an influential idea, one which impresses itself on many minds in a social setting over a period of years and thus makes its mark on history, is drawn out to great effect in the *Essay* (Chapter I). What was at issue for Newman was whether this analogy could serve as a hypothesis to explain both the constancy and the change in a tradition founded by divine revelation.

If that were so, it would not do simply to accept the prevailing view that the "rule" of Vincent of Lerins provided a sure guide for distinguishing what is essential Christian doctrine, namely that "Christianity is what has been held always, everywhere, and by all." [8] Newman therefore found it necessary to mount an attack in the Introduction of his *Essay* against this commonly accepted dictum. But this was a

---

[6] Nicholas Lash, "Faith and History: Some Reflections on Newman's 'Essay on the Development of Christian Doctrine,'" *Irish Theological Quarterly*, 38 (1971), 229.

[7] *Dev*, p. 39; ed. Cameron, p. 100 (I, 1, 7).

[8] Newman's paraphrase in *Dev*, p. 8; ed. Cameron, p. 74 (Introduction). The so-called rule of Vincent of Lerins, from his *Commonitorium*, II, 3, deserves to be quoted once in full: "*In ipsa item catholica ecclesia magnopere curandum est, ut id teneamus, quod ubique, quod semper, quod ab omnibus creditum est; hoc est etenim vere proprieque catholicum.*" It was constantly cited in controversies between the confessions since the Reformation, usually with transposed word order, "Quod semper etc." Cf. Jaroslav Pelikan, *Historical Theology: Continuity and Change in Christian Tradition* (Philadelphia: Westminster, 1971), p. 5.

delicate undertaking, since he was not prepared to declare himself against its presupposition, that Christian faith, where and insofar as it exists, preserves its identity intact. What he wished to do was rather to suggest that the identity of an idea is compatible with considerable modifications in its expressions over a sufficiently long time.

The novelty of this contention and its difficulties are well known, as is clear from Chadwick and Pelikan. If there is one clear-cut case which would seem to vindicate the application of this rule, it is that of the Catholic teaching about the place of the Pope in the church. Because Newman comes to this very issue while discussing Vincent's rule, it will repay us to look at this section of his Introduction to the *Essay*.

The Anglican application of this rule had of course insisted that, the papacy being a development which had not attained recognition in many parts of the church during the period of Antiquity, it could therefore not be regarded as a binding doctrine of Christian faith. This was the use that Newman himself had made of it in *Prophetical Office*.[9] Still, he had recognized that the application of such a general rule called for a great deal of sensitivity to other considerations, to the testimony of Scripture, the extant sources and so forth, in other words that it was rarely a decisive procedure all by itself. In this he was following in the footsteps of his great Anglican forebears, who had developed a theological method of reliance upon the Scriptures in conjunction with tradition and reason. In their appeal to tradition, the rule of Vincent confirmed them in their preference for the first five centuries (Antiquity).[10] However, in the patristic studies of George Bull (1634-1710), the model of Antiquity tended to become absolutized. This had the double effect of playing down the role of Scripture and theological reason on the one hand and of inviting theological prejudices to invade historical studies on the other; it was after all desperately important that the historical record support orthodoxy, once it had become the dominant guide to faith.

Since Newman had accepted Bull's *Defensio Fidei Nicaenae* whole-

---

[9] *VM*, I, 55, cited in *Dev*, p. 9; ed. Cameron, p. 76. (Introduction), cf. *VM*, I, 180-185.

[10] Cf. Henry R. McAdoo, *The Spirit of Anglicanism: A Survey of Anglican Theological Method in the Seventeenth Century* (New York: Scribner, 1965), pp. 316-414; Gareth Vaughan Bennett, "Patristic Tradition in Anglican Thought, 1660-1900," in *Oecumenica 1971-72: Tradition in Lutheranism and Anglicanism*, ed. by Günther Gassmann and Vilmos Vajta (Minneapolis: Augsburg, 1972), pp. 63-85; and Thomas M. Parker, "The Rediscovery of the Fathers in the Seventeenth-century Anglican Tradition," *OS*, pp. 31-49.

heartedly when he was writing his *Arians*, he now felt he had been taken in by a pseudo-critical scholarship with untenable stress on the identity of convictions among both pre-Nicene and post-Nicene Fathers. It was *this* understanding of the patristic period and its authority according to the dictum of Vincent of Lerins that he had to refute. However, he included in his criticism any and all attempts to retain the rule as a serviceable, practical guide. (He had no problem therefore in following Father Perrone's Roman interpretation of Vincent, to the effect that some doctrines could be shown positively to fulfill the requirements and thus to be authentic, but the rule could not stand as a negative criterion against all other teachings which did not enjoy such testimony.) [11] The basic reason was that only a complete skeptic could use the rule consistently, discarding every doctrine that did not measure up.

Anglican controversialists in particular found themselves being inconsistent, according to Newman. They all accepted orthodox trinitarian dogma, of course, but even Bull could not demonstrate that the earlier Fathers had expressed themselves correctly here.[12] The doctrines of purgatory and original sin display a similar history, yet Anglicans accept the one and reject the other.[13] Belief in the real presence in the Eucharist is well enough attested in Antiquity that Tractarians accept it. Newman, for his part, can only consider it a genuine affirmation of faith. The thought then occurs to him:

"And do not the same ancient Fathers bear witness to another doctrine, which you disown? Are you not as a hypocrite, listening to them when you will, and deaf when you will not? How are you casting your lot with the saints, when you go but half-way with them? For of whether of the two do they speak the more frequently, of the Real Presence in the Eucharist, or of the Pope's Supremacy? You accept the lesser evidence, you reject the greater."

In truth, scanty as the Ante-Nicene notices may be of the Papal Supremacy, they are both more numerous and more definite than the adducible testimonies in favour of the Real Presence.[14]

---

[11] Cf. "The Newman-Perrone Paper on Development," ed. by T. Lynch, *Gregorianum*, 16 (1935), 423.

[12] *Dev*, pp. 11-17; ed. Cameron, pp. 77-82 (Introduction).

[13] *Dev*, pp. 17-19; ed. Cameron, pp. 82-84 (Introduction).

[14] *Dev*, p. 20; ed. Cameron, pp. 84-85 (Introduction); anticipated in his letter to William Froude in Harper, *Cardinal Newman*, pp. 58-59, also excerpted by Newman in *Apo*, p. 179. This letter shows how Newman's thought proceeded from Tract 85 to *Dev*.

Newman thus linked together the history and destinies of the tradition of papal power with the tradition of trinitarian belief, arguing that if we have grounds for believing the one from a benevolent interpretation of Antiquity, we have analogous grounds for accepting the other as well. This parallel would draw down upon him the ire of Anglican critics for overlooking the differences between the two kinds of developments and attempting a fallacious *reductio ad absurdum*.[15] It is an example, by no means the most strained, of Newman's habitual approach to questions controverted among Anglicans: you must either take the Catholic position whole or resign yourself to utter rationalism and disbelief (an approach that characterized Tract 85, which we shall have occasion to mention again). In this case, however, the argument is made with a high degree of sensitivity to historical nuance, something which Mozley failed to give Newman credit for. We have seen that Newman, after sounding the motif of papal supremacy at the beginning of his discussion of the Vincentian canon, returned to it only by a series of steps and comparisons, so that the direct comparison is that between primacy and Real Presence, not primacy and trinity. [16]

Nevertheless, the common predicate of all these doctrines is that they lack that full, clear, primitive consensus which Bull had led him, as an Anglican, to invoke. Not that the earlier Fathers lacked a *belief* or *inward* knowledge [17] in a Son and a Holy Spirit who were just as divine as the Father was. "But nothing in the mere letter of those documents leads to that belief. To give a deeper meaning to their letter, we must interpret them by the times which came after." [18] If trinitarian orthodoxy emerges somewhat more plainly from the controversies of Antiquity than does papal primacy, that can be explained by the nature of the case and by the circumstances. One need

---

[15] Cf. especially J. B. Mozley, *The Theory of Development* (London, 1878), pp. 149, 202. See David Nicholls, "Newman's Anglican Critics," *Anglican Theological Review*, 47 (1965), 377-395 and Maurice Nédoncelle, "Le développement de la doctrine chrétienne: J. B. Mozley, critique anglican de Newman," in *Oecumenica 1971-1972*, pp. 166-169.

[16] The comparison was not only historically well taken, but of great topicality to Tractarians wondering what guides of faith they could trust. Pusey's sermon setting forth this "Anglican doctrine" in 1843 had been condemned by the vice chancellor of the university and six doctors of divinity. Cf. Alf Härdelin, *The Tractarian Understanding of the Eucharist*, p. 140, and G. H. Harper, *Cardinal Newman*, p. 43.

[17] Compare *Oxford University Sermons*, p. 323.

[18] *Dev*, p. 13; ed. Cameron, p. 79 (Introduction).

only reflect that theology and christology are much more central to faith than ecclesiology; moreover, the doctrine concerning bishops and apostolic succession had to be established as a preliminary to doctrine about papal authority, since the pope was (in the normal Anglican view of the matter) an episcopal successor of an apostle. But not even this basic Anglo-Catholic teaching could be upheld against a strict application of the Vincentian canon.[19]

All this insistence of Newman's on the formation in the course of time of Catholic teachings would seem naturally to lead to what has been called a transformistic theory of developments, according to which the centuries bring forth new variations which cannot be said to be identical in substance with what went before. Yet all commentators are clear that Newman refused to resolve the tension between historical change and permanent identity; his whole effort was towards reconciling them hypothetically if he could, but never at the price of giving up permanence and continuity of doctrine. He sometimes gives the impression that he wants to have it both ways: a given Catholic doctrine was always held, and yet it found expression at a more or less late date. This gives rise to certain equivocations, which Owen Chadwick has underscored.[20] In our present connection, it is remarkable that Newman appealed repeatedly to Vincent of Lerins' notion of organic growth in the body of received doctrines, although he rejected the same author's rule for determining what doctrine is to be received.[21] This may be regarded as more Vincent's inconsistency than Newman's, because Newman accepted development by growth as being but one modality among several by which dogmatic development has taken place, whereas Vincent evidently thought that it was the only analogy which sufficiently preserved the

---

[19] *Dev*, p. 10; ed. Cameron, p. 77 (Introduction).

[20] Chadwick, *From Bossuet to Newman*, esp. p. 160. Cf. Nédoncelle, *Oecumenica 1971-1972*, p. 171, and my own somewhat less favorable interpretation of these oscillations, "Newman's Concept of Revelation and the Development of Doctrine," *Heythrop Journal*, 11 (1970), 32-47, with literature, and Nicholas Lash, *ibid.*, 48-54. On "transformistic" (liberal) theories of the history of dogma, see Jan H. Walgrave, *Unfolding Revelation: The Nature of Doctrinal Development* (Philadelphia: Westminster, 1972), pp. 179-277 or more briefly in his preface to Newman, *Essai sur le développement de la doctrine chrétienne*, tr. Luce Gérard (Paris: Centurion, 1964), pp. 31-37.

[21] Cf. *Dev*, ed. Artz, note 113, for references, *Dev*, p. 58, ed. Cameron, p. 117 (V, I, 1). On the question of "growth" and "progress" in the history of dogma, see Oskar Köhler in *Mysterium Salutis*, IV/2, 537-540.

identity of permanent teaching.[22] Catholic teaching remains the same through all its changes, just as a human being is the same person through all the stages of his life.

That this analogy from the growth of a living organism (acorn-oak, grub-butterfly, embryo-adult) lies behind a good many passages of the *Essay* is clear. It has caused many commentators to fasten upon it as the chief operative model of Newman's insights, precipitately, I think. Without going into a full discussion of this point, I may state that (1) the analogy of the individual human mind and the development of an idea in it is very much in the foreground. Perhaps the closest analogy Newman used was (2) that of a cultural development, the way, that is, of an idea or complex of ideas in a society. He knew (3) how to give logic its due as well as (4) the finer perceptions of the human spirit which precede rigorous and systematic discourse. He certainly acknowledged (5) the motions of the Holy Spirit in the life of the church, which cannot be reduced to anything resembling biological laws. The peculiar sort of providence which consists of (6) prophecy and fulfilment will concern us later. Despite his general insistence on the harmony and continuity of developments in doctrine, he had a well-tuned historical sense which allowed him to see the irony and (7) accidental character of many an important development. The place of (8) conflict (dialectic) in the development of doctrine was large, given the history of controversies. Given his opposition to liberal philosophies of development, however, he tended to see every development which was once received by the Church to be a definitive and irreversible acquisition which could not be abandoned without peril. The organismic analogy (9) certainly played its part here.

From this we can appreciate how consistently Catholic (and Anglican) he felt his view to be. Despite his insistence that developments cannot be limited to a given period near the origins of Christianity (Antiquity), he was sure that what Antiquity had brought forth would never have to be repudiated. It is in this context that he takes up his argument for papal primacy as a Catholic given. Already in Tract 85 Newman had stressed the criteriological superiority of the fifth century over those that preceded it (a thesis unprecedented in Anglican divinity, so far as I can tell). Still enjoying the unimpaired vigor of catholic unity and the infallibility that went with this unity,

---

[22] Cf. Jaroslav Pelikan, *The Christian Tradition: A History of the Development of Doctrine* (Chicago: University of Chicago Press, 1971—), I, 333-339.

the church of the fifth century had had enough time to put forth all its parts, as it were, and to settle down to the full consciousness of its faith. Christianity could now recognize itself as a fully-fledged organic system and give an account of itself in which the proportion of one part to another could be set forth in the perspective afforded by long experience and many trials of growth. The records of the fifth century are full enough, in contrast to the earlier ages, to provide later generations of Christians with adequate guidance on questions for which the Bible had no clear answer. "The fifth century acts as a comment on the obscure text of the centuries before it, and brings out a meaning which, with the help of that comment, any candid person sees really to belong to them." [23]

When writing Tract 85 (1838), Newman was of the opinion that one could find fundamental truths of Christianity such as the Trinity or the inspiration of the four Gospels in the records of the earlier centuries, but the canonicity of certain other books and of the Bible as a whole were still not determined clearly enough. He maintained, that is, the classicist notion of church history. Now, in the *Essay*, he was vindicating for the church of all times the indefectibility Christ promised her, even in certain cases where development continued past antiquity. So his hermeneutical principle of interpreting the earlier evidence in the light of the later underwent a corresponding expansion. Now he called it a "general probability... that doctrine cannot but develop as time proceeds and need arises, and that its developments are parts of the Divine system, and that therefore it is lawful, or rather necessary, to interpret the words and deeds of the earlier Church by the determinate teaching of the later." [24] Realizing that this would seem to erect uncritical and anachronistic interpretations of history into a principle, Newman defended its application to such cases as the obscure beginnings of the papal primacy in a lengthy

---

[23] *DA*, p. 237-238; cf. Chadwick, *From Bossuet to Newman*, pp. 127-129. Newman quoted this passage himself in *Dev*, p. 143; ed. Cameron, p. 189, but omitted it from the revised edition, III, II, 8.

[24] *Dev* (1878), IV, III, 8. The corresponding passage in the first edition, p. 171 (ed. Cameron, p. 213), reads: "To this [i.e., the particular antecedent probabilities making for a papal primacy,] must be added the general probability, which has been shown in the foregoing Chapter [Chapter II in all editions], that all true developments of doctrine and usage which have been permitted, and this in the number, have been divinely approved; and, again, the probability in particular in favour of the existence, in some quarter, of an infallible authority in matters of faith."

discussion of similar procedures by such historians as Niebuhr, Gibbons, Thirlwall, Heeren, and Mosheim.[25]

Newman's mode of argumentation thus begins to take shape. Far from aiming at presuppositionless historiography, his approach gives an explicit account of how much weight he attached to the antecedent probability of any disputed development (Chapter II of all editions). The other side of his argumentation in each case will then consist of a rehearsal of the historical evidence that can be adduced relative to the expectation. The bits of evidence, considered one by one, need not be compelling. Especially if they are examined apart from the antecedent probabilities which can be reasonably elaborated, the historical testimonies will not suffice in disputed cases to convince the observer with prejudices to overcome. But the convergence of probabilities, antecedent and posterior, should be of such a texture as to win over those who in other important matters realize that practical certitude arises from an accumulation of probabilities.[26]

The seven famous tests of true developments, or of fidelity in development, which Newman discussed in the first chapter of his *Essay* (postponed to Chapter V in the revised edition), are not particularly successful.[27] Newman quite properly downgraded them in rearranging his book for the 1878 edition. The fact that they do not include any distinctively theological criteria, but only general notions, is due to their original place at the head of the *Essay* and to their rather extrinsic role of providing a way to divide the too ample material. Newman's real criteria are of course scripture and tradition, with tradition now being seen in the guise of continuing church life and calling for the protection of a strong church authority (Chapter II, Section II). The catholicity of the tradition now counted more than its antiquity. If one asks what the underlying organizational principle of Newman's *Essay* is, Wilfrid Ward has long since supplied the answer: the center of gravity around which the rest revolves are those three vast tableaus of the church in the first centuries, in the Arian troubles of the fourth century, and in the eminently Catholic fifth and sixth centuries. Each culminates with Newman drawing the historical parallel to the Roman communion of the nineteenth century,

---

[25] *Dev*, pp. 179-202; ed. Cameron, pp. 219-239 (mostly omitted in rev. ed., III, II, 4).

[26] On Newman's argumentation from probabilities, see the references in *Dev*, ed. Artz, note 41a.

[27] Chadwick, *From Bossuet to Newman*, p. 155.

showing that the changes wrought by the Tridentine consolidation were insubstantial compared with the overwhelming sameness between the earlier Christians, *humani generis hostes* as they were considered, and the modern Roman Catholics.[28]

When Newman imagines Athanasius and Ambrose coming to Oxford and turning away "from many a high aisle and solemn cloister which they found there" and asking "the way to some small chapel where mass was said," can we doubt that he was appealing to something very like the Vincentian canon? "It cannot be doubted what communion they would mistake for their own," [29] he wrote with a touch of irony which he removed from the 1878 edition. And yet it was a Vincentian canon transmuted by a new sense of history. This, to Newman, did not demand a theory of free and unchecked developments as the liberals presumed. But the rule of Vincent would have to be complemented by another view: *quod et sensim, quod denique, quod a communicantibus.*[30]

---

[28] Wilfrid Ward, *The Life of John Henry Cardinal Newman* (London: Longmans, Green, and Co., 1912), I, 88-91. This material is contained in Chs. IV and V in the 1st ed., Ch. VI in the rev. ed. See *Dev*, ed. Artz, notes 411, 426, 427, and 486, and Chadwick, *From Bossuet to Newman*, pp. 142-144.

[29] *Dev*, p. 139; ed. Cameron, p. 185 (II, III, 5).

[30] Cf. *Apo*, p. 110 on Augustine's *Securus judicat orbis terrarum*: these words "decided ecclesiastical questions on a simpler rule than that of Antiquity; nay, St. Augustine was one of the prime oracles of Antiquity; here then Antiquity was deciding against itself. . . . the deliberate judgment, in which the whole Church at length rests and acquiesces, is an infallible prescription and a final sentence against such portions of it as protest and secede." The force of "prescription" is that of Tertullian's usage as in *De praescriptione haereticorum*.

On the whole question of Newman and Tradition, see the literature cited in *Dev*, ed. Artz, note 76. I am especially indebted to Heinrich Fries' studies, "Newmans Beitrag zum Verständnis der Tradition," in *Die mündliche Überlieferung*, ed. Michael Schmaus (Munich: Hueber, 1957), pp. 63-122, also in *Vitae et Veritati*, Festgabe für Karl Adam (Düsseldorf: Patmos, 1956), pp. 103-143, and "Die Dogmengeschichte des fünften Jahrhunderts im theologischen Werdegang von John Henry Newman," in *Das Konzil von Chalkedon* (Würzburg: Echter, 1951-1954), III, 421-454.

CHAPTER NINE

ANTECEDENT PROBABILITIES OF A PAPAL PRIMACY

Newman's contention that developments are legitimate and inevitable in the church as elsewhere needs no defense today. That some developments are somehow covered and especially sanctioned by the Christian revelation, however, remains as controversial an issue as ever. To Newman it seemed a necessary corollary. The Apostles may well have received revelation so fully that it satisfied all their questions. "Still the time at length came, when [revelation's] recipients ceased to be inspired; and on these recipients the revealed truths would fall, as in other cases, at first vaguely and generally, and would afterwards be completed by developments." [1]

It is not enough at that time to have recourse to scripture. There are no firm answers there for such pressing questions as: whether scripture is inspired and what books it contains; whether infants should be baptized; whether there is forgiveness of post-baptismal sins; what the state of the departed before the general resurrection is. If God had left us without provision for finding the answers, we would of course have to tolerate our lot; but in fact the scriptures, with their obscure prophecies gradually becoming clearer in the light of events, seem to suggest the means of revelation's "own growth or development." [2] The summation is Newman's:

> Thus developments of Christianity are proved to have been in the contemplation of its Divine Author, by an argument parallel to that by which we infer intelligence in the system of the physical world. In whatever sense the need and its supply are a proof of design in the visible creation, in the same do gaps, if the word may be used, which occur in the structure of the original creed of the Church, make it probable that those developments, which grow out of the truths which lie around them, were intended to complete it. [3]

After discussing the indicators ("tests") by which developments reveal their authenticity or lack of it, Newman returned to the theme of developments grounded in revelation. Here (Chapter II, Section II)

---

[1] *Dev*, p. 95; ed. Cameron, p. 149 (II, 1, 2).
[2] *Dev*, pp. 97-113; ed. Cameron, pp. 151-164 (II, 1, 4-16).
[3] *Dev*, pp. 101-102; ed. Cameron, p. 154 (II, 1, 8).

he showed, always in the realm of probability, that (1) some developments must receive a seal of approval analogous to the credentials
with which the original revelation was furnished, and (2) that this
requires an infallible authority of or in the church, which can designate
developments as true or false, genuine or spurious.

As to the first point, he constructed a foil by positing the existence
of all kinds of divine revelations which are not authenticated as such:
private illuminations, for example, and the treasure of godly wisdom
set at large even in the pagan world without sufficient sign of its
divine origin. Against these he contrasted Christianity, "which comes
to us as a revelation, as a whole, objectively, and with a profession
of infallibility." [4] On this he based a very short and simple argument,
or, as some would have it, assertion.

> If then there are certain great truths, or proprieties, or observances,
> naturally and legitimately resulting from the doctrines originally
> professed, it is but reasonable to include these true results in the
> idea of the revelation, to consider them parts of it, and if the revelation
> be not only true, but guaranteed as true, to anticipate that they will be
> guaranteed inclusively. Christianity, unlike other revelations of
> God's will, except the Jewish, of which it is a continuation, is an
> objective religion, or a revelation with credentials; it is natural then
> to view it wholly as such, and not partly *sui generis*, partly like others.
> Such as it begins, such let it be considered to continue: if certain
> large developments of it are true, they must surely be accredited
> as true.[5]

To establish the second point, the infallible authority which can
judge and distinguish between true developments and false, Newman
worked from two angles, from the angle of Christianity considered as
a *revealed* religion, and from the angle of it considered as a religious
society. As a revealed religion, it constitutes an external authority
giving voice to the revelation, and its authority corresponds to the
authority that conscience exercises in a natural religion without an
authenticated revelation. As a religious society with a creed to be
maintained, Christianity must have within it a recognized organ (to
take the final step in the argument from antecedent probability) by
the authority of which the different members of the social body may
be kept in a unity of faith.

> If Christianity be a social religion, as it certainly is, and if it be based
> on certain ideas acknowledged as divine, . . . and if these ideas have

---

[4] *Dev*, p. 118; ed. Cameron, p. 168 (II, ii, 5).
[5] *Dev*, pp. 118-119; ed. Cameron, p. 169.

various aspects, and make distinct impressions on different minds, and issue in consequence in a multiplicity of developments, true, or false, or mixed, as has been shown, what influence will suffice to meet and to do justice to these conflicting conditions, but a supreme authority ruling and reconciling individual judgments by a divine right and a recognized wisdom? ... If Christianity is both social and dogmatic, and intended for all ages, it must, humanly speaking, have an infallible expounder.[6]

Newman named three candidates which could be considered for this post of guide in matters of faith: "the voice of Scripture, or of the Church, or of the Holy See." [7] As far as scripture was concerned, however, Newman had already as an Anglican insisted that the Bible needs an interpreter, and that the church, with her gift of "indefectibility," performed that function.[8] Thus he did not feel called upon to labor the point in *Development*: he simply states that the purpose of scripture is not to provide by herself a living and present guidance, any more than the scroll of Isaiah by itself sufficed for the Ethiopian eunuch. With him, the common sense of mankind cries out, "How can I understand, unless some man guide me?" [9]

With scripture out of contention for the office of living guide, Newman was not at pains to distinguish between the voice of the church and that of the pope, since the latter would only be conceivable to him as the voice of the former. Nevertheless, he was ready enough to accept Bellarmine's papal position, which he had occasion to cite in this section. One feels he refrained from endorsing papal infallibility explicitly only because it was not yet a dogma of the Catholic Church: it did not yet need to be justified as an accomplished development. Newman managed to reveal his mind on the point rather unambiguously, although the position of the pope in the church belonged to a later stage of his argumentation. For, in drawing out an analogy between the order of creation and the order of the church to the effect that, as the Creator follows up the hexaemeron with continual conservation, so we can expect him to follow up a revelation with continual teaching, Newman wound up with the quotable flourish, "As creation argues continual governance, so are Apostles harbingers of Popes." [10]

---

[6] *Dev*, pp. 127-128; ed. Cameron, pp. 176-177 (II, ii, 13).
[7] *Dev*, p. 124; ed. Cameron, p. 174 (II, ii, 11).
[8] *Prophetical Office*, eighth lecture; see above, Chapter III.
[9] *Dev*, p. 126; ed. Cameron, p. 175 (II, ii, 12).
[10] *Dev*, p. 124; ed. Cameron, p. 173 (II, ii, 10).

One would nevertheless be mistaken to think that Newman attributed probative value (in the sense of antecedent probability) to these remarks about the pope. Here in Chapter II, Section 11, his whole marshalling of probabilities must be seen as tending to the proof of the necessity of an infallible doctrinal authority of the *church* as a whole. Whether the pope is a bearer of this authority is a subordinate question, to be settled on another level, as we shall shortly see. Newman himself thought that this was an important point, because it meant that he had an argument for the infallibility of the church that was entirely independent of the complicated and difficult questions connected with the papacy. Before one got into the question of papal infallibility, one already had ground for accepting the one communion on the face of the earth which claimed to exercise this so necessary teaching authority.[11] Accordingly, (1) Newman in the *Essay* did not even treat in set terms of *papal* infallibility. As far as he was concerned, the infallibility of the church might find its ultimate criterion in the actual reception of a doctrine solemnly proclaimed by pope or ecumenical council in (morally speaking) all the churches that hold communion with Rome. He made no dogmatic statements, in other words, about the *seat* of infallibility. (2) Papal *primacy* (or, in his terminology in the *Essay*, "supremacy") does not occupy the key position in his argumentation which the infallibility of the church does. It is treated on a second plane, as one of the things to be accepted on the authority of the infallibly teaching church; or, to put it under another, but just as germane, aspect: papal primacy is one of the alleged corruptions or arbitrary additions of the Roman Catholic Church to the Gospel truth, and Newman had to show that, on the contrary, it was a legitimage development.

The passages in the *Essay on Development* which treat directly of the papal supremacy are oddly hidden away in the first edition. There is the listing of the evidences from the first three centuries in the Introduction, then fifteen pages, unheralded in the table of contents, in Chapter III, Section iv, "Instances in Illustration," and finally various scattered allusions, of which the most powerful is the evocation of Pope Leo the Great's influence at Chalcedon, underlined by the concluding parallel between the Christianity of the fifth and sixth centuries and the contemporary Church of Rome (Chapter V, Section iii). One

---

[11] *Dev*, pp. 126-127; ed. Cameron, pp. 175-176 (II, 11, 12); ed. Artz, note 226.

of Newman's major changes for the edition of 1878 was to bring the papal material from the Introduction into the main treatment and give it a heading of its own (revised edition, Chapter IV, Section III, "Papal Supremacy"). The emphatic placement of the papal passages in the revised edition has led unwary critics to see them as the center of gravity of the whole *Essay*.[12] Even critics of the first edition tended to see the papal question as decisive, understandably enough.[13] This, however, was at least in part a misunderstanding.

In and under all Newman's assertions about the development of the papacy is the matter we discussed in Chapter VII above, i.e. his use of the analogy of a kingdom (or empire) to the status of the Christian church. Prophecy had predetermined that the last age was to see "a power visible in the world and sovereign over it," and these are characteristics "which are accurately fulfilled in that historical Christianity to which we commonly give the name." [14] The seed parables of the Kingdom anticipate "the development of Christianity, both as a polity and as a doctrine." [15] It was against this background of eschatological prophecies in scripture being applied to church history that Newman posited, in the principal passage on papal supremacy in his *Essay*, an "antecedent probability of a monarchical principle in the Divine Scheme."

> It is the absolute need of a monarchical power in the Church which is our ground for anticipating it. Blackstone has expressed the principle in a sentence, quoted in an earlier page, as it relates to kingly power. A political body cannot exist without government, and the larger is the body the more concentrated must the government be. If the whole of Christendom is to form one Kingdom, one head is essential; at least this is the experience of eighteen hundred years. As the Church grew into form, so did the power of Pope develope; and wherever the Pope has been renounced, decay and division have been the consequence. We know of no other way of preserving the *Sacramentum Unitatis*, but a centre of unity.[16]

---

[12] For instance, William Robbins, *The Newman Brothers: An Essay in Comparative Intellectual Biography* (Cambridge, Mass.: Harvard University Press, 1966), pp. 102-107.

[13] For instance, James B. Mozley, in an article in *The Christian Remembrancer* of January 1847 went so far as to see "the doctrine of Papal Infallibility" as "the keystone of Mr. Newman's whole argument," *The Theory of Development*, p. 83. Frederick Denison Maurice, *The Epistle to the Hebrews* (London: Parker, 1846), Preface, pp. xli, xlvi, sees the matter much more in perspective.

[14] *Dev*, p. 3; ed. Cameron, p. 70 (Introduction).

[15] *Dev*, p. 112; ed. Cameron, p. 163 (II, I, 16).

[16] *Dev*, p. 170; ed. Cameron, p. 212 (IV, III, 8); in the rev. ed. the sentence

Stated so baldly and with such questionable generalizations from history, the argument seems less than overpowering. But as one probes all the seemingly soft places in Newman's conception of the necessity and growth of the papal primacy, one finds that he could defend it at every point with considerations which, in the last analysis, all had the same basis, namely, that the church is a unitary realm.

In the phrase *sacramentum unitatis* one might at first suspect an allusion to the Eucharist, especially since Newman first brought it up in connection with Ignatius of Antioch,[17] who, as is well known, wrote of the importance for unity of the eucharistic assembly around the bishop.[18] Augustine also, and Thomas of Aquinas called the Eucharist the *sacramentum unitatis*.[19] However, the phrase is in reality a clue that Newman was carrying on a running battle with one very particular theology of church unity, that of St. Cyprian and of his Anglican upholders.[20] For it was Cyprian who came closest to the episcopal theory of church unity, he who pleaded passionately for unity while at the same time rejecting the pretensions of the pope to be its special protector, and it was he who used the phrase *sacramentum unitatis*.[21] There is no particular eucharistic reference in Cyprian's use of the term; it may be translated almost as "the sacred duty and privilege of" Christians to hold to their bishops in "unity." It is an expression which could well be suggested by the Epistle to the Ephesians (Eph 1:9-10; the *mystery* of his will... to *unite* all things in Christ), from which Cyprian quotes (Eph 4:4) in the same breath with *sacramentum unitatis*.[22]

To those who accepted the *sacramentum unitatis* in the Cyprianic sense, Newman now had to make clear that this notion or fact of ecclesiastical life was capable of, required, and had in fact undergone,

---

about Blackstone no longer appears, *Dev*, pp. 154-155, the citation in question having been shifted to a later page, namely Ch. V, Sec. vi, 5.

[17] *Dev*, p. 165; ed. Cameron, p. 208 (IV, iii, 2).

[18] Cf. Ignatius' Letter to the Ephesians, 20, 2; to the Philadelphians, 4.

[19] Cf. *Summa Theologiae*, IIIª, qu. 82, a.2 ad 3, citing Augustine *super Ioan.*, Tract. 26, no. 13 (Migne, *PL*, 35, 1613).

[20] See above Ch. V; cf. ed. Artz, note 439.

[21] Cf. the translations of *The Treatises of S. Caecilius Cyprian* (Oxford 1840, in the *Library of the Fathers*, vol. III), 134, 136. Newman was one of the Editors of this series and supplied the preface for this volume, dated 25 April 1839. Cf. letters in *LC*, II, 189, 248, 251.

[22] The expression occurs in what Bévenot considers the earlier text in ch. 7, and in the *textus receptus*, here discussed, also in ch. 4 (end). Bévenot translates "the mystery of Oneness," Cyprian, *De Lapsis and De Ecclesiae Catholicae Unitate*, ed. and tr. Maurice Bévenot (Oxford: Clarendon Press, 1971), p. 65.

a further development. Augustine was the principal witness of the factual development, which he helped to carry out. Newman had relived it in his own intellectual history,[23] and a great aim of his *Essay* was to make it intelligible and imitable on the part of his former comrades-in-arms. As attractive as Cyprian's theory of church unity was, in its reliance on the brotherly love and harmony which the Holy Spirit was to bring about among the bishops, it did not hold up "in the harsh realities of ecclesiastical life." [24] Anglicans, including Newman, had recognized this, and had concluded that church unity on the international level must not be essential. Cyprian would not have taken this step, judging from his emphasis on unity "through the whole world,... over the universal earth." [25] So now Newman too takes up the theme of unity, not on the diocesan level, but among the churches, internationally.[26] Implicitly he was making his characteristic challenge to the Tractarians: do not retreat from Cyprian's position, once you have gained it, but go on to appropriate the consequent development as well. It was nothing to the purpose that St. Cyprian had explicitly withstood the pope's power, "for when a doctrine or ordinance has to be developed, collision or disturbances seem previous conditions of its final adjustment." [27]

If all this seems to be devoting a great deal of attention to a factor that is just mentioned briefly in the section of the *Essay* on the papal supremacy, I must admit that that is quite so. The theme, however, of the international unity of the kingdom-church is basic to the whole section, and is presupposed there. This we know from several letters which Newman wrote in 1846 to Henry Wilberforce, whose main obstacle to accepting Roman Catholicism seemed to be the papacy.[28] Newman was miffed, as well he might have been, when it turned out that Wilberforce was proposing difficulties to him about the pope's

---

[23] See above Ch. IV, note 4, and Ch. V, notes 22-24.

[24] Berthold Altaner, *Patrologie*, (Freiburg: Herder, 1958), p. 160; similarly in Newman's 1855 novel, *Callista* (London, 1895), p. 322.

[25] *De ecclesiae unitate*, 5; cf. *Treatises of Cyprian*, Oxford ed., 135; *ibid.* 136 for Cyprian's concern for Christ's "seamless garment." Cf. also *Dev*, p. 351; ed. Cameron, p. 362 (VIII, I, 8) and *VM*, II, 134.

[26] Thus "bond of communion," "*Sacramentum Unitatis*," "international bond," all in *Dev*, pp. 165-175; ed. Cameron, pp. 208-216 (IV, III, 2-13).

[27] Letter of 29 April 1844 to William Froude in Harper, *Cardinal Newman*, p. 56, and in *Letters of John Henry Newman*, eds. Derek Stanford and Muriel Spark (Westminster, Md.: Newman Press, 1957), p. 112.

[28] Cf. letter of 8 June 1846 in *L & D*, XI, 174-75; also in Ward, *Life*, I, 618-21. See above, Introduction.

supremacy without having read his *Essay*.[29] But the annoyance was beneficial for us in later generations, since we may observe, most clearly in the letter of June 25,[30] how Newman refers immediately to the thought of "one Catholic organized church or kingdom" in all the world as the basic consideration in the question of the papacy. The thought and even the wording is the same as that of the *Essay on Development* in the central passage devoted to "the Church of the Fourth Century" (Chapter IV, Section 11; Chapter VI in the revised edition). Here he utilized the literature stemming from the Donatist controversy to refute all varieties of the branch theory of Christian unity or disunity, especially such as he had lent his name to. The way Newman now viewed church unity is summed up by saying, "The Church is a kingdom," and not, as heretical churches always turn out to be, merely a "family" which "continually divides and sends out branches... each of them as independent as its original head." [31]

This was a change with far-reaching implications. The following citation about the church of the fourth century, though lengthy, is indispensable for establishing the context in which Newman thought of the papal role.

> It may be possibly suggested that this universality which the Fathers ascribe to the Catholic Church lay in its Apostolical descent, or again in its Episcopacy; and that it was one, not as being one kingdom or Augustinian *civitas* "at unity with itself," with one and the same intelligence in every part, one sympathy, one ruling principle, one organization, one communion, but because, though consisting of a number of independent communities, at variance (if so be) with each other even to a breach of communion, nevertheless all these were possessed of a legitimate succession of clergy, or all governed by Bishops, Priests, and Deacons. But who will in seriousness maintain that relationship, or that sameness of structure, makes two bodies one? England and Prussia are both of them monarchies; are they therefore one kingdom? England and the United States are from one stock; can they therefore be called one state? England and Ireland are peopled by different races; yet are they not one kingdom still? If unity lies in the Apostolical succession, an act of schism is from the nature of the case impossible; for as no one can reverse his parentage, so no Church can undo the fact that its clergy have come by lineal descent from the Apostles. Either there is no such sin as schism, or unity does not lie in the Episcopal form or in the Epis-

---

[29] *L & D*, XI, 215.

[30] *Ibid.*, pp. 181-184, also printed in part in Ward, I, 129-30.

[31] *Dev*, p. 246; ed. Cameron, p. 275 (VI, 11, 4); compare Barrow's "universal empire," cited *Dev*, p. 169; ed. Cameron, p. 211 (IV, 111, 6).

copal ordination. And this is felt by the controversialists of this day;
who in consequence are obliged to invent a sin, and consider, not
division of Church from Church, but the interference of Church with
Church to be the sin of schism, as if local dioceses and bishops with
restraint were more than ecclesiastical arrangements and by-laws
of the Church, however sacred, while schism is a sin against her
essence. Thus they strain out a gnat, and swallow a camel. Division is
the schism, if schism there be, not interference. If interference is a
sin, division which is the cause of it is a greater; but where division is
a duty, there can be no sin in interference.

Far different from such a theory is the picture which the ancient
Church presents to us; true, it was governed by Bishops, and those
Bishops came from the Apostles, *but it was a kingdom besides*; and as a
kingdom admits of the possibility of rebels, so does such a Church
admit of sectaries and schismatics, but not of independent portions. . . .

It was a vast organized association, coextensive with the Roman
Empire, or rather overflowing it. Its Bishops were not mere local
officers, but possessed a power essentially ecumenical, extending
wherever a Christian was to be found. . . . [The evidence points to]
a unity throughout Christendom, not of mere origin or of Apostolical
succession, but of government.[32]

In the aforementioned letters to Wilberforce Newman brings this
thought directly and explicitly to bear on the question of the papal
supremacy. The connecting link was the recognition that the historical
continuation and contemporary realization of Augustine's "Teaching,
Sacramental, organized Body called the Church" could be none other
than the Roman communion. The conclusion was simple:

since that communion received the Successor of St. Peter as the
Vicar of Christ and the Visible Head of the Church, such he was.[33]

On this view no violence was done to the positive content of episcopal
ecclesiology after the manner of Cyprian and the Tractarians. Rather,
the doctrine of apostolic succession and the theory of church unity
based on it were taken up into a higher unity, both in the theoretical
and the political sense. This higher unity was the Catholic *communio*.
International *communion* characterizes Newman's Catholic view of

---

[32] *Dev*, pp. 258-264; ed. Cameron, pp. 285-290, emphasis mine. The revised
edition, Ch. VI, Sec. II, 13-14, omits copious extracts from Gibbon's *Decline
and Fall*. All of this Section II should be read to fill out the notion of *sacramentum
unitatis*. A recent parallel is Ludwig Hertling, *Communio: Church and Papacy in
Early Christianity*, tr. and introd. by Jared Wicks (Chicago: Loyola University
Press, 1972, originally 1943).
[33] Note of 17 February 1876 on copy which Newman made of his letter of
4 July 1846 in *L & D*, XI, 191; cf. *ibid*. XIII, 283-84.

church unity, as union with one's bishop had characterized his Anglican view.

The episcopal constitution of the church, considered in her socio-political aspect as requiring a ruling authority, was God-given, and so was the "monarchical" (papal) element, according to Newman.[34] How did he reconcile these two forms of government in his own mind while writing *Development*? It would appear from the section on the papal supremacy that he simply considered the episcopacy a divine ordinance intended for local government, whereas the papacy was destined to care for the unity of the whole ecumenical communion. But in the long passage about the church of the fourth century, from which we have just quoted, there are hints of a more developed view, building on and presupposing the notion of "bishops by restraint." [35] It was an approach which Ultramontanes would probably not comprehend, for it enabled Newman to establish the priority of universal rule in the church over diocesan, metropolitan, and patriarchal set-ups, while at the same time extolling the episcopal office as the basis of the papal development.

Newman spoke of bishops endowed with "a power essentially ecumenical, extending wherever a Christian was to be found." [36] A "restraint," however, was normally laid on the exercise of this power by the device (*juris ecclesiastici, non divini*) of diocesan boundaries and locally confined jurisdiction, accepted by the bishops for the sake of good order. Anglicans had of course developed this idea in a way that put papal claims in a bad light, as a purely human development. Newman saw rather a confirmation for the authenticity of the teaching concerning the ecumenical unity of the church, the *sacramentum unitatis*, which he then utilized in conjunction with other evidence in his argument for the papal supremacy. If he had been asked in 1845, "What then is the place of the Pope, if all bishops have an ecumenical power, only bound by church law?" he certainly would not have answered with a discussion of collegiality, the synodal structure of the church, or the relative autonomy of local churches, as one would today.[37]

---

[34] *Dev*, p. 167; ed. Cameron, p. 210 (IV, III, 5).

[35] Newman wrote Mrs. Catherine Froude in May, 1844, that development lent an entirely new aspect to the meaning of "bishops by restraint," cf. above, Ch. V, notes 11 and 24.

[36] *Dev*, p. 263; ed. Cameron, p. 290; in the third edition, after Vatican I, this was changed to "a quasi-ecumenical power," p. 266 (VI, II, 14).

[37] Maurice Nédoncelle, "La suprématie papale d'après l'*Essai sur le développement* de Newman," in *Parole de Dieu et sacerdoce*, eds. E. Fisher and L. Bouyer (Paris:

Presumably he would have said something to the effect that the bishops' ecumenical responsibilities were a temporary provision for the international bond of unity until conditions permitted the Roman bishop to exercise his God-given monarchical office; when this became possible, it became mandatory for the bishops to subordinate their ecumenical concerns to the direction of the Pope.

The prophetically anchored unity of the kingdom is then the most basic of the antecedent probabilities in Newman's cumulative argument for the papacy. Taken for itself, however, it is by no means probative. Congenial as the monarchical solution to the problem of church government and unity is to Newman's kingdom-ecclesiology (and to his political stance), an *a priori* argument is here insufficient. Newman let slip a phrase which could mislead, "the absolute need of a monarchical power in the Church." [38] But of course Blackstone's authority for this principle would not settle the question. No, to arrive at the "presumptive interpretation" of the total evidence bearing on papal supremacy, one needed, beside the "antecedent probability of a monarchical principle on the Divine Scheme" (so Newman on the same page, but more accurately), its "actual exemplification" in history as well. The two sides of the argument only avail if taken together and as reinforcing one another.

Newman himself realized that the argument from the need of a monarch was not so "absolute." That, at least, was the interpretation he gave thirty years later to his letter to Henry Wilberforce of 4 July 1846. The jottings he added in 1876 are put in parentheses in the following extract:

> it seems to me extravagant or unreasonable in you to demand proof of one certain particular tenet which it so naturally comes to the Church to decide. If the Roman (Catholic) Church be the Church, I take it (and submit to it) whatever it is (monarchical, aristocratic or democratic)—and if I find that Papal Supremacy is a point of faith in it, this point of faith (though not capable of proof on its own merits) is not to my imagination so strange, to my reason so incredible, to my historical knowledge so utterly without evidence, as to warrant me in saying, "I *cannot* take it on faith." [39]

Desclée, 1962), 143-144. Some basic texts of Vatican II on collegiality etc. are the Constitution on the Liturgy, art. 41, and the Dogmatic Constitution on the Church, arts. 22-27, in *The Documents of Vatican II*, ed. Walter M. Abbott (New York: America Press, 1966).

[38] See note 16 above.

[39] *L & D*, XI, 190.

He contemplated the possibility, therefore, even in 1846, that God might have found other means than the papacy to safeguard his church's unity, admitting equivalently that the antecedent probability in favor of a monarchical constitution of the church was not *a priori* of itself conclusive. In the event of a democratic or other constitution, of course, he would have had to find other arguments than those based on the need for a head in a government, and he would have expected a different historical development. Whether Newman would ever have found his way into a democratic church may be doubted, humanly speaking. Luckily for him, the argument for "Popedom" fell together from elements which had long since been part and parcel of his outlook. His difficulty had not really been with the idea of papal monarchy, but with the fear that it had fallen victim to, and been made a thrall of, corruptions in doctrine.

There are certain expressions of Newman's which arouse the suspicion, as Acton was to charge, that Newman was constructing with his theory of development a way to disregard history, "emancipate" himself from history, and allow the voice of the present church to "supersede the study of the past." [40] The letter to Wilberforce is a case in point. In the reflections added in 1876 Newman said:

> There are men, as I suppose T. W. Allies, who have been converted to the Catholic Church by their belief in the divine Mission of St. Peter and his successors: I on the contrary, (though thinking that much might be said positively for that divine mission from Scripture, Tradition, History and reason, and that that doctrine was much more than "not strange," "not incredible," not "without evidence") mainly received it on the word of the Universal Church, that is, on faith.[41]

Acton's stricture is, however, exaggerated. Even here Newman sought to give history its due, and in fact he always concedes it at least a negative, controlling function, both as regards antecedent probabilities and the possibility of a dogmatic definition by the church.[42] That

---

[40] In unpublished notes quoted by Chadwick, *From Bossuet to Newman*, p. 129, who defends Newman ably, *ibid.*, pp. 138, 146. Cf. however Hugh A. MacDougall, *The Acton-Newman Relations* (New York: Fordham University Press, 1962), pp. 156-164.

[41] *L & D*, XI, 190. Cf. Thomas W. Allies, *The Church of England cleared from the Charge of Schism* (London, 1846—the charge was Newman's), then his change of heart in 1850, *The See of St. Peter*.

[42] *Dev*, (1878), Ch. III, Sec. II, 11-12, which seems to be new material.

is, no matter how probable a development may appear, if the church has solemnly declared against it in her history, or if other historical facts render it untenable, then it can be no legitimate development.[43]

---

[43] *Dev* (1878), III, ii, 12, apparently new material; compare *Dev*, p. 4; ed. Cameron, p. 71 (Introduction, 4: Chillingworth's taunt of "popes against popes"). Cf. James M. Cameron, "Newman and the Empiricist Tradition." *OS*, pp. 92-94.

CHAPTER TEN

PAPAL AUTHORITY: A PROMISE OF SCRIPTURE

Nowhere in his published work did Newman go into any detail about the scriptural basis of Peter's or the Pope's primacy. The *Essay on Development* is no exception, since here two short paragraphs are sufficient to indicate their place in his argument. The Petrine passages of Matthew 16, Luke 22, and John 21, it is clear, are liable to different interpretations, papal and non-papal. It is therefore necessary to put them into some wider context than the Gospels in which they stand to arrive at any certainty about their bearing. What that context should be is not in doubt for Newman. Church history has supplied the "comment" on the texts by witnessing the emergence of a development that fulfills them, and that in accord with the more general antecedent probabilities which have been noted. The Petrine passages are an inspired "counterpart to these anticipations." [1]

This approach entails an understanding of these passages as being in some broad fashion prophetic, which could arouse the suspicion of special pleading. If it is special pleading, however, it is not reserved for the papacy, but is based on a theme which pervades the *Essay*, the theme of development in biblical revelation as a whole. In Chapter II, Section 1, Newman had pointed out that, although revelation could conceivably have taken place in a solitary act once for all [2] or in a succession of "communications independent of each other," as a matter of fact it furnished instead an example of growth, the small beginnings expanding in stages where all that is new is found to have been present from the first. The whole of revelation was given globally, as it were, in the protoevangelium of Genesis 3:15. All that came afterwards formed parts of a process which could properly be called development, since "the earlier prophecies are pregnant texts out of which the succeeding announcements grow; they are types." Since this is the way of the scriptures, Newman argued, it is antecedently probable that an analogous process would take place in regard to *New* Testament texts. After all, "the *effata* of our Lord and His Apost-

---

[1] *Dev*, p. 171; ed. Cameron, p. 213 (IV, III, 9).
[2] "Milman's View of Christianity," in *Essays Critical and Historical*, II, 233; cf. *Dev*, VIII, 2, 12 and ed. Artz, note 560.

les are of a typical structure, parallel to the prophetic announcements above mentioned, and predictions as well as injunctions of doctrine." Among such fertile texts is "Thou art Peter, and upon this Rock I will build my Church." [3]

Newman had one more Old Testament analogy which, being concerned with sacred authority, fit the case of the papacy the best, and this he saved for the place in the *Essay* where he treated papal supremacy *ex professo* and spoke of the Petrine passages.

> It should be observed ... that a similar promise was made by the patriarch Jacob to Judah: "Thou art he whom thy brethren shall praise: the sceptre shall not depart from Judah till Shiloh come"; yet it was not fulfilled for perhaps eight hundred years, during which long period we hear little or nothing of the tribe descended from him. In like manner, "On this rock I will build My Church," "I give unto thee the Keys," "Feed My sheep," are, not precepts merely, but prophecies and promises, promises to be accomplished by Him who made them, prophecies to be interpreted by the event,—by the history, that is, of the fourth and fifth centuries, though they had a partial fulfilment even in the preceding period, and a still more noble development in the middle ages. [4]

This was surely an unusual way to deal with the Petrine texts, though it had its precedents in the exegesis of Bishop Newton and the deed of William Warburton, who founded the lecture series named after him to demonstrate the truth of revealed religion "from the completion of the prophecies in the Old and New Testaments." [5] In a way, of course, such an uncritical appeal to prophecies was already obsolescent when Newman wrote; in another way, however, Newman was exploiting a very modern approach to history, some of whose exponents were beginning to perceive the social structures of historical developments. The French Protestant liberal, François Guizot, whom Newman cited in the *Essay* several times, may stand as a case in point. Had he not suggested "that Christianity, though represented in prophecy as a kingdom, came into the world as an idea rather than

---

[3] *Dev*, pp. 102-104; ed. Cameron, pp. 155-157 (II, i, 9-10).

[4] *Dev*, p. 172; ed. Cameron, pp. 213-214 (IV, iii, 9). We have noticed Newman's use of Gen. 49:10 above, Ch. VII, cf. *SD*, p. 219. He came back to it in *Grammar of Assent* (London: Longmans, Green, 1870), p. 442.

[5] Cf. Misner, "Newman and ... Antichrist," *Church History*, 42 (1973), 384. Newman appealed to the Warburtonian Lectures of John Davison (1824) in a related connection: *Dev*, p. 157; ed. Cameron, p. 201 (III, i, 9). Cf. *Essays Critical and Historical*, II, 400-404, for other remarks of Newman on these lectures and *Dev*, ed. Artz, note 246.

an institution, and has had to wrap itself in clothing and fit itself with armour of its own providing, and to form the instruments and methods of its prosperity and warfare?'' [6]

If this old-new perspective enables one to account for aspects of Christianity which are otherwise overlooked, the hypothesis of development is strengthened. The perspective is different from that of his Via Media, but much of the content can be taken into it unchanged. As we saw in Chapter I, Newman had long held that Matthew 16 constituted Peter as a *type*, a scriptural image of church authority[7]. The fulfilment which corresponds to that type cannot be known with precision from scripture. It must be judged according to the meaning in which it was accepted by the church, as is the case for all scriptural passages which are neither complete nor self-explanatory. For the Anglican Newman this meant the undivided church of Antiquity; when this could no longer satisfy, the full organic growth of the fourth and fifth century and the catholic consent of later ages had to be consulted; and when Newman had identified the Catholic communion of the present, he accepted also the authority recognized in it as providing the sense of what remained obscure in scripture.

By viewing the matter in this light we are also able to cut through the confusions strewn by Newman about the different senses of scripture. The problem is this: in *Arians* as in the *Essay on Development* and elsewhere, Newman upheld the superiority of the "mystical" or "ecclesiastical" sense of scripture over its "literal" sense; [8] whereas in elaborating the Kingdom-ecclesiology from Old Testament prophecies, he stood by Hooker's rule in favor of an exclusively "literal" interpretation. [9] But there is one passage in the *Essay* where development of

---

[6] *Dev*, p. 116; ed. Cameron, p. 167 (II, ii, 3); ed. Artz, notes 177, 178. Cf. G. P. Gooch, *History and Historians in the Nineteenth Century* (Boston: Beacon Press, 1959, 1st ed. 1913), p. 181: "Guizot was the first to dissect a society as the anatomist dissects a body, the first to study the functions of the social organism as the physiologist those of the animal."

[7] See also *Lectures on the Doctrine of Justification* (1838; London: Longmans, Green, 1874), pp. 245-246; *VM*, I, 180-185.

[8] For the Tractarian context of this question, see Alf Härdelin, *The Tractarian Understanding of the Eucharist*, pp. 31-37; A. M. Allchin, "The Theological Vision of the Oxford Movement," *OS*, pp. 50-75, about Pusey's lectures on Types and Prophecies.

[9] See Jaak Seynaeve, "Newman (doctrine scripturaire du Cardinal)," *Dictionnaire de la Bible, Supplément*, VI, 460-467 for documentation. Hooker's rule, as stated by Newman in *SD*, p. 184, is: "Where a literal construction will stand, the farthest from the letter is commonly the worst." Compare *SD*, pp. 196, 235, and *PPS*, II, 245.

the papal church is specifically linked up with scripture "interpreted in a mystical sense" and not "confined to the letter." [10] Does this indicate a substantial shift in Newman's interpretation of prophecies? If so, it might be illegitimate to make the Kingdom ecclesiology of his Anglican period so decisive for his argument in the *Essay*. I think this is not the case, however, and that what we meet in his discussions of the "mystical" and "literal" senses of scripture is a wide-ranging terminological inconsistency and vagueness, rather than a more profound change in Newman's approach.

Newman never distinguishes more than two possible senses of scripture at any given time. The duality is always seen in the context of the history of doctrine in the patristic church, where he found orthodox Fathers appealing to an extended or even allegorical sense of controversial scriptural passages and their heretical opponents for the most part insisting on restricting their meaning. The rigorous, more or less historical exegesis of the school of Antioch had been associated in Newman's mind since *The Arians* with the "literal" sense, while the allegorizing tendencies of the school of Alexandria were those of the champions of orthodoxy. The word, mystical, should be taken therefore as indicating an openness to the mystery of revelation, a capability sorely missed in "the literal and critical interpretation" of scripture that nourished heresies.[11] Putting the case in these terms, the real issue is the continuing ability of the tradition of the church to "know its own mind," even where scriptural demonstrations fall short or a critical interpretation raises difficulties.

In matters of interpreting scriptural prophecies, then, an area where Newman always insisted on the priority of the literal sense, this dialectic tends to take place between two "literal" interpretations, that is, between two incompatible readings of church history (Antichrist or imperial church, in our case). Here, as in the previous case, Newman accepts the interpretation from tradition, but maintains also that the traditional interpretation (the imperial church) is the more literal fulfilment of the prophecies and therefore the more likely. He inadvertently showed the Achilles' heel of his whole construction when he let slip the admission that the Kingdom promises were to be understood literally as eschatological and not as referring to the historical church at all, in the section on "Scripture and its Mystical Interpretation":

---

[10] *Dev*, p. 319; ed. Cameron, p. 336 (VII, iv); ed. Artz, notes 512-518.
[11] *Dev*, p. 282; ed. Cameron, p. 305 (VI, iii, 2).

Christianity developed, as we have incidentally seen, in the form, first, of a Catholic, then of a Papal Church. Now Scripture was made the rule on which this development proceeded in each case, and Scripture moreover interpreted in a mystical sense; and, whereas at first certain texts were inconsistently confined to the letter, and a Millenium was in consequence expected, the very course of events, as time went on, interpreted the prophecies about the Church more truly, and that first in respect of her prerogative as occupying the *orbis terrarum*, next in support of the claims of the See of St. Peter.[12]

Mystical or literal, the church-historical application of messianic prophecies was by now firmly fixed in Newman's mind. Recent biblical scholarship, since the publication of *Jesus' Proclamation of the Kingdom of God* by Johannes Weiss in 1900, has accustomed us to the idea that the connection between the prophetical and Jesuanic proclamation of the Kingdom of God on the one hand, and the church which arose after his resurrection on the other, is problematical. Jesus was intent on an eschatological kingdom of God and spoke of it in a culture shot through with apocalyptic expectations. The church, it is commonly agreed, cannot simply be identified with the promised kingdom.[13] Newman, on the contrary, as we saw in Chapter VII, worked from this identification as early as 1835, as is evident from his sermon, "The Kingdom of the Saints." Even when he contrasted the coming of the church with the coming of the Lord on the last day, it was the church, not the parousia, which he called the kingdom, according to the text, "The kingdom of God cometh not with observation;... the kingdom of God is within you." [14]

For Newman, of course, the church was incomparably greater than the kingdoms of this world: one has only to think of the doctrine of the indwelling Holy Spirit, which makes Christians into the Body of Christ, to realize how different the church is, whether from states or from the Old Testament church.[15] But he stressed just as emphatically the similarities, the earthly reality of the promised kingdom, and did not give way to the temptation to consider the promises "merely"

---

[12] *Dev*, pp. 319-320; ed. Cameron, p. 336 (VII, ɪᴠ).

[13] One can consult recent editions of standard theological lexika and dictionaries. A treatment from a Roman Catholic scholar is Rudolf Schnackenburg, *God's Rule and Kingdom*, 2d ed. (New York: Herder and Herder, 1968), p. 351, and *The Church in the New Testament* (New York: Herder and Herder, 1965), pp. 187-195. Cf. Werner Georg Kümmel, *The New Testament: The History of the Investigation of Its Problems*, tr. S. M. Gilmour and H. C. Kee (Nashville: Abingdon, 1972), pp. 226-230.

[14] *SD*, pp. 308-309 (Lk 17:20-21); cf. *PPS*, III, 266.

figurative or reserved for the future. In his sermon, "Outward and Inward Notes of the Church," of 5 December 1841, he held on to the truth of the outward and public notes set forth in prophecy even while he bewailed their eclipse. While preaching on the "Invisible Presence of Christ" (28 November 1841), he reiterated the visible side of sacramental reality:

> Of course the Kingdom of Christ also, as being in this world, has an outward shape like this world, though it be not of this world; and, as viewed with the eyes of this world, it has an aspect of growth and development like other kingdoms; but after all this is not the true process of its rise and establishment. It came by an inward and secret presence; by outward instruments, indeed, but with effects far higher than those instruments, and really by God's own agency.[16]

A year later the affirmative tone was recovering strength, although he begins his sermon, "Feasting in Captivity" (22 September 1842) with a stark contrast.

> When we reflect upon the present state of the Holy Church throughout the world, so different from that which was promised to her in prophecy, the doubt is apt to suggest itself to us, whether it is right to rejoice when there is so much to mourn over and to fear. Is it right to keep holiday, when the Spouse of Christ is in bondage, and the iron almost enters into her soul? We know what prophecy promises us, a holy Church set upon a hill; an imperial Church, far-spreading among the nations, loving truth and peace, binding together all hearts in charity, and uttering the words of God from inspired lips; a Kingdom of Heaven, upon earth, that is at unity within itself, peace within its walls and plenteousnous within its palaces; "a glorious Church, not having spot or wrinkle or any such thing, but holy and without blemish." And, alas! what do we see? [17]

His imperial ecclesiology then unfolded itself in Sermons XIV-XVII of *Sermons Bearing on Subjects of the Day* in November of 1842, culminating in "The Christian Church an Imperial Power," which we have already analyzed.

It was necessary to recall these sermons in order to establish the context in which Newman so briefly touches upon the role of prophecy in his treatment of the papacy in the *Essay on Development*. The modern reader is liable to overlook or misunderstand the pointers he left to

---

[15] *PPS*, II, 222-225, 244; III, 255 f, 273, 279 f; IV, 169-171; VI, 124-127; VII, 231-233; *SD*, p. 238.

[16] These sermons are from *SD*, citation p. 310.

[17] *SD*, pp. 381-382.

this massive and outdated appeal to prophecy in ecclesiology.[18] Newman held the Christian church to be a continuation of the Jewish [19] in an extraordinarily uncomplicated sense. In his view,

> it is no mere figurative sense in which such words as "power," "kingdom," "rule," "conquest," "princes," "judges," "officers," and the like are used (as if the promised dominion were to be but moral, the promised Church invisible, the promised reign of Christ but spiritual), for this simple reason, that there *has* been, in matter of fact, in Christian times a visible Church, a temporal kingdom, a succession of rulers, such as the prophecies do describe.

---

[18] Nicholas Lash, "Faith and History: Some Reflections on Newman's 'Essay on the Development of Christian Doctrine,' " *Irish Theological Quarterly*, 38 (1971), 234, has endorsed these findings. Alfred Loisy, *Mémoires* (Paris: E. Nourry, 1930), I, 451-452, appropriated the idea of development, but said of Newman's treatment, "Ses idées sur ... la nature des prophéties, sont plutôt d'un théologien que d'un historien bien informé" (c. 1898).

[19] This is the title of Sermon XIV (13 November 1842), from which the following citation comes, *SD*, p. 184.

CHAPTER ELEVEN

DEVELOPMENT AND FULFILMENT, I:
THE FIRST THREE CENTURIES

It is clear from the foregoing that Newman did not try to mobilize the forces of erudition for the exegesis of scriptural texts, but rather for the history of their fulfilment in the successive centuries of church life, especially the fourth and fifth centuries. This happened also to be the area in which he was best qualified. His specialized knowledge did not, however, lead him to insist on particular (individual) points of history. Throughout the *Essay* multitudinous facts confront the reader, but Newman was careful not to run the risk of having his presentation impugned on matters of fact.He did not take advantage of his familiarity with the field to put anything past the less expert reader, as far as I can tell. Instead he deliberately followed the presentation of facts which had found acceptance among opponents of the papacy and Catholicism: Gibbon, the skeptic *par excellence*, Fleury, whose *Histoire ecclésiastique* (1691-1720) was on the Index because of its Gallican leanings, and, in the present case, Isaac Barrow, whose posthumous *Treatise on the Pope's Supremacy* (1680) was a thorough refutation of papal claims as unhistorical.[1] When it came to quoting texts out of the patristic period, Newman used the best editions available; and it could hardly be said that the Catholicism of Jean Hardouin (1646-1729) or Pierre Coustant (1654-1721) affected their painstaking scholarship in editing the texts of councils or the letters of popes.

The critical analysis of Newman's historical arguments which Maurice Nédoncelle has called for repeatedly,[2] will not therefore turn on the facts and utterances which he cited for the most part reliably, but rather on the interpretatory framework and argumentative structure in which he makes use of the facts. At the lower level of historical investigation there is one obvious criticism which calls for discussion; that is Newman's selectivity as to the facts he brings for-

---

[1] The *ODC* can be usefully consulted on all these authors.
[2] Maurice Nédoncelle, "Newman et le développement dogmatique," *Revue des sciences religieuses*, 32 (1958), 204; "The Revival of Newman Studies—Some Reflections," *The Downside Review*, 86 (1968), 392.

ward. Perhaps the best that can be said for him in this regard (limiting the remarks to his treatment of the papacy) is that he lined up his case like a fair and honest defense lawyer who knew that his brief was going to be examined by hostile advocates before an ill-disposed jury. He could afford neither to be caught out in a manifest misstatement of fact nor to forego any rhetorical resources at his command. In fact he was able to turn the tables brilliantly by calling Barrow as a witness for the development of the papacy.

For Newman's purposes there was, after all, more "actual exemplification" of the papal development than he needed, in any reliable source.[3] He therefore chose the one that displayed most clearly an alternative reading of the same evidence, Barrow's *Treatise*. Newman's citations from Barrow are gathered in two series of paragraphs in the *Essay's* chief passage concerning papal supremacy (1845: Chapter III, Section iv, no. 4; 1878: Chapter IV, Section iii). They illustrate his two main points there, that the papal development could hardly be expected to show itself in the conditions of the first three centuries of church life, and secondly, that, as more favorable conditions developed in the fourth and fifth centuries, no one could fail to discern clearly the growth and existence of the papal polity. But before we examine these elements in his argument, we must first turn to that passage in his Introduction where he ran through the pre-Nicene evidence of a seminal Roman primacy in the church.

The context in which he first brought up the historical evidence bearing on papal authority was his discussion of the inadequacy of the Vincentian canon, *Quod semper, quod ubique, quod ab omnibus*.[4] In a single paragraph he mentioned fifteen instances from the letter of Clement (c. A.D. 96) to the time of Cyprian and Pope Stephen in the middle of the third century.[5] No more is claimed for these testimonies than that they show a certain preeminence or special esteem in which the Church of Rome was held by various elements in the early church. Roman church leaders such as Clement, Soter, Victor, Dionysius, and Stephen show a growing consciousness of their authority. Suppliants come to Rome to give their causes added prestige (cited are the heretics Marcion, some Montanists, Praxeas, as well as the orthodox Polycarp

---

[3] See above, Ch. IX, towards the end.

[4] See above, Ch. VIII, notes 8-19.

[5] *Dev*, pp. 22-23; ed. Cameron, pp. 86-87 (in the 3rd ed. shifted from Introduction, no. 18, to IV, iii, 10).

of Smyrna and the bishop of Alexandria, Dionysius). Irenaeus and Tertullian extol the foundation of the Roman Church by Peter and Paul. The Emperor Aurelian refers an ecclesiastical controversy "to the Bishops of Italy and of Rome." Cyprian himself exhorts Stephen in the name of the apostolic foundation of the Roman See not to give any credence to renegade clerics from Africa. Not only African churchmen, but the deposed Spanish bishop Basilides, has recourse to Stephen in Rome. In the whole passage Newman artfully avoided a maximalist interpretation of any of the cases cited, leaving open the question whether there was in fact any theory or practice in the church of the first three centuries which would deserve the name of papal supremacy. He merely observed that a stronger cumulative argument could be drawn from these facts "in favor of the active and doctrinal authority of Rome" than for the doctrine of the Real Presence in the period before Constantine.[6]

Examples of this sort could have been multiplied. But what about all the testimonies in the opposite sense? Cyprian and Firmilian did not recognize the authority of Rome in the question of the baptism of heretics. Polycrates of Ephesus refused to accept the Roman date for Easter, even when Victor insisted vehemently.[7] (It didn't occur to Victor to appeal to Mt 16, apparently.) Newman's reply was that authority in the nature of things calls forth resistance, especially when

---

[6] The "facts" bear up well under examination. Current references can be found in *Dev*, ed. Artz, note 308. The following table supplies references to the convenient *Quellen zur Geschichte des Papsttums und des Römischen Katholizismus* of Carl Mirbt, 6th rev. ed. by Kurt Aland, Tübingen: J. C. B. Mohr (Paul Siebeck), 1967, I:

Clement of Rome	no. 27
Ignatius of Antioch	no. 33
Polycarp of Smyrna	nos. 57-58
Marcion	nos. 55-56
Soter, bishop of Rome	no. 66
Montanists	no. 74
Praxeas	no. 76
Victor, bishop of Rome	no. 92
Irenaeus of Lyons	no. 85
Tertullian	no. 102
Dionysius of Alexandria and Dionysius of Rome	no. 211
Aurelian, Emperor (A.D. 270-275)	no. 214
Cyprian, bishop of Carthage	no. 166
Stephen, bishop of Rome	nos. 197-198

The affair of the Carthaginian clerics Fortunatus and Felicissimus, who come to Rome (Pope Cornelius) to get backing against Cyprian is not mentioned explicitly in the excerpts reprinted in Mirbt/Aland's *Quellen*, but see no. 166.

[7] Cf. *Dev*, ed. Artz, note 302.

it is in the process of establishing itself; moreover, the situation for other Catholic doctrines (Real Presence, apostolic succession) was analogous: before the fourth and fifth centuries the sources simply do not speak that clearly.

There Newman left the matter in the Introduction, to return to it in Chapter III, Section IV, no. 4. The fascinating quality of his historical discussion in the first few pages of this passage stems from his audacious near-acceptance of the thesis that a universal sovereignty in church affairs was unknown in the primitive church. The Petrine primacy of the bishop of Rome was not even consciously adumbrated until Cyprian's time, he seems to say, and not consciously claimed until the fourth and fifth centuries. The word, "consciously," is important, for Newman hedges his historical view of the first three centuries by maintaining that they "may be viewed in the light of the Post-Nicene" centuries, "whereas Protestants resolve the latter into the dimness and indistinctness of the former." [8]

His treatment of the papacy is, I think, the most striking example of Newman's oscillation between the aspect of continuity in development and the aspect of historical novelty. Again, his view of the papacy as a fulfilment of prophecy helps to account for this. If the prophecies apply as he is sure they do, then there is little or no need to establish any continuity between their announcement and their fulfilment —one can treat the three intervening centuries simply as a period of "unfulfilled prophecy." [9] On the other hand he is anxious to assimilate this case also to his idea of development with its strong emphasis on perduring identity. When this motif dominates, then the scarce and ambiguous testimonies from the first three centuries become "a partial fulfilment." [10] The two motifs seem to me to be incompatible and to generate a tension in his picture of the historical development of the papacy that is never resolved. His historical sense tells him that there was a period when nothing of the papacy was discernible, unless you count certain disparate elements which later on will combine to

---

[8] *Dev*, p. 165; ed. Cameron, p. 207; compare *Dev*, p. 179; ed. Cameron, p. 219 (IV, III, 17).

[9] "The *regalia Petri* might sleep, as the power of a chancellor [of the University of Oxford, see ed. Artz, note 300] has slept; not as an obsolete, for it never had been operative, but as a mysterious privilege, which was not understood [!]; as an unfulfilled prophecy." *Dev*, p. 166; ed. Cameron, p. 209 (IV, III, 3).

[10] *Dev*, p. 172; ed. Cameron, p. 214 (IV, III, 9: following this in 1878 is a new sentence, still equivocating: "A partial fulfilment, or at least indications of what was to be, there certainly were in the first age." IV, III, 10).

form papal supremacy. His theory of development, however, leads him to postulate an existing supremacy in some dormant state right back to the beginning of the church.[11]

It is important to illustrate exactly how Newman was of two minds on this question, since Catholic theologians and historians still speak (though less frequently of late) as though Newman's idea of development has provided the key to the problem of the claims that the Pope is no more and no less than the successor of Peter.[12] Along the lines which we may designate as the "unfulfilled prophecy" motif Newman could be very generous in what he later would qualify as unnecessary "concessions to Protestants of historical fact." [13] That is, he could admit that the papal supremacy was simply not present nor dreamed of for generations in the earliest church and that its gradual development was a genuine historical novelty of the fourth and fifth centuries. Thus he not only admitted that Ignatius of Antioch knew nothing of the Pope's authority in the first part of the second century, but that the duty of obedience to bishops (a prior necessity) was not yet generally recognized by Christians. "In the course of time, first the [apostolical] power of the Bishop awoke, and then the power of the Pope.... When the Church, then, was thrown upon her own resources [after the Apostles were gone], first local disturbances gave rise to Bishops, and next ecumenical disturbances gave rise to Popes." [14]

The structures of communion which it was in the Church's nature to set up were neither strictly necessary nor possible as long as a hostile Roman state inhibited the development of Christianity. One could freely concede to Barrow, therefore, that not even Roman bishops in the pre-Constantinian era raised any claims to "universal

---

[11] *Dev*, p. 170; ed. Cameron, pp. 211-212 (IV, III, 7).

[12] See for instance Karl Rahner, "Papst," *LTK*, VIII, 46; Michael Schmaus, "Pope," *Sacramentum Mundi*, V, 42; Georg Schwaiger, *ibid.*, 50. More nuanced is the statement of the Catholic participants in the Lutheran-Catholic Dialogue Group for the United States, "Ministry and the Church Universal: Differing Attitudes toward Papal Primacy," in *Origins*, 3 (14 March 1974), 597-599.

[13] *Dev* (1878), p. viii. Cf. Chadwick, *From Bossuet to Newman*, p. 189, and Newman's letter to Robert Wilberforce of 11 December 1853, *L & D*, XV, 495.

[14] All quotations here and in the following paragraphs are found in *Dev*, pp. 164-169; ed. Cameron, pp. 207-211 (IV, III, 1-6), unless otherwise noted. For Ignatius of Antioch, see also *Dev*, pp. 390-396; ed. Cameron, pp. 394-400 (omitted in rev. ed.).

empire over the consciences and religious practices of men," nor did any party to a doctrinal dispute in this period suppose that "the sentence of the universal pastor and judge" could settle issues in dispute conclusively and efficaciously.

On the other hand, the postulate of continuity in development led Newman to qualify these "concessions" considerably and to plead for the existence "from the first" of "a certain element at work... which, for some reason or other, did not at once show itself upon the surface of ecclesiastical affairs, and of which events in the fourth century are the development." Along this line of thought, the power of the later popes was not simply absent, but rather dormant or provisionally exercised by others (first apostles, later bishops). "This is but natural" in an infant society, the more so in a question of organization, of members' respective rights and duties. The examples of families or colleges, which may go along for generations without serious strife and hence without any clear idea of the precise prerogatives of their various members, seemed an apt illustration to Newman of this point. What he overlooked in this comparison is that family and academic rights are established by convention or decision as the outcome of conflicts that arise, and they may be altered by the same processes. In the central issues of ecclesiastical organization, Newman would admit the fashioning of precedent and structures by this natural process, but not the possibility that what had rightly come into existence could ever be altered henceforth.[15]

The motor and permanent element in the whole development was to be named with a concept of Cyprian's, the *sacramentum unitatis*, the mystery of oneness in the Church with its attendant rights and duties (see above Chapter IX). This is so far removed from providing grounds for the existence of a papal power in the early church that I would hesitate to mention it under the rubric of "continuity," except that Newman so used it. "The *Sacramentum Unitatis* was acknowledged on all hands; the mode of fulfilling and the means of securing it would

---

[15] Here I would again see the influence of the idea that the Church is the Kingdom foretold in prophecy; it would be a falsification of prophecy to admit that the Church had in fact disintegrated into a number of disparate communions. In 1840 Newman had objected to the notion of the development of papal supremacy that, if such a development had been legitimate, another development in reaction to its abuses could certainly not be ruled out, reversing the first one and leading the Church back to a situation resembling that of Cyprian's time, cf. *Essays Historical and Critical*, II, 44.

vary with the occasion; and the determination of its essence, its seat, and its laws would be a gradual consequence of a gradual necessity." [16] St. Paul in his day had had to struggle to gain recognition for his authority as an apostle. It was not surprising that the popes faced the same problem later on. "In either case, a new power had to be defined." It may be noted that even where Newman stressed continuity as best he could, he made no affirmation to the effect that the early Roman bishops were conscious of their elevated position in relation to other churches and bishops, apart from Victor in the second century and Stephen in the third. Nevertheless, the supposition of continuity enabled Newman to interpret the very unflattering picture Barrow gave of the prehistory of the papacy in this way:

> On the whole, supposing the power to be divinely bestowed, yet in the first instance necessarily dormant, a history could not be traced out more probable, more suitable to that hypothesis, than the actual course of controversy which took place age after age upon the Papal Supremacy.

And yet, the first three centuries shed no clear light on the subject. To account for this Newman mixes two mutually exclusive explanations. One of them (the prophecy theory) makes next to no demands on the historical sources anterior to Constantine and Eusebius, since in the nature of an unfulfilled prophecy there would be at the most anticipations of later realities. The other, the dormant power theory, is a hypothesis which, though attractive by reason of the room it opens up for positive historical thinking in the matter of the papacy, is nevertheless quite frail and ready to fall before more solidly-based reconstructions of the incidents which Newman saw (too hastily) as being part of a preordained pattern. As he stated, however, the force of his argument was in the combination of antecedent probabilities with the evidence of the *fourth* and *fifth* centuries. Here again one should distinguish, as Newman did not, between the motifs of prophecy and dormant power (in other words, between historical novelty in the fourth-fifth centuries and continuity from the beginning). The argument from prophetical interpretation in the light of the papal fulfilment would be almost a foregone conclusion. To satisfy himself

---

[16] Newman now understood the *sacramentum unitatis* to involve "an international bond and a common authority," which was "provided" from the first but could not be "consolidated" until persecutions ceased.

and his readers, however, Newman also wished to make a respectable historical case for using the evidence of the imperial church developments to interpret and understand the previous centuries. The most detailed part of his historical treatment of the papal development is therefore in the fourth and fifth centuries, culminating with Pope Leo the Great.

CHAPTER TWELVE

DEVELOPMENT AND FULFILMENT, II:
THE FLOWERING OF ANTIQUITY

A feature of Newman's brief for the papal development which has
so far escaped notice is that it begins as a striking instance of fulfilment
of prophecy but ends on the note of continuity—as though the
Petrine prerogatives were entrusted to popes from the beginning, but
impressed themselves consistently on the record of history starting
only with Pope Julius (A.D. 337-352). There is no reason why the
fulfilment of promises made to Peter could not be partial and frag-
mentary while it was not yet time for the complete antitype to appear.
But if this view were carried through coherently, there would be no
need to read back into the period before Julius what one discovers
from his time onward. But Newman could not confine his argument
to the prophecy theory bare and unaided, however convincing it may
have appeared to him, because he knew or sensed that it would not
measure up to Roman doctrine about the origins of the papacy. As he
was to explain in letters, this doctrine he accepted chiefly on faith from
the communion that he recognized on more general grounds to be
the Church. What his hypothesis about the continuous existence and
development of the papal power availed for was simply to show that
historical objections to this Roman doctrine were not insuperable.[1]

The historical material here is organized according to a pattern in
which a pope is first cited, then one or more contemporaries (if
possible, relative to the same episode). The legendary material about
the Emperor Constantine and Pope Sylvester is of course entirely
omitted and the time between Stephen and Julius is adeptly vaulted
with the remark that the designation *Cathedra Petri*, which Cyprian
seemed to "allow" to the Roman See, became prominent and unfolded
its possibilities in the fourth and fifth centuries. Thus Pope Julius
expostulated with the opponents of Athanasius that they should have

---

[1] Cf. *L & D*, XI, 69, 121, 174-176, 181, 187, 190-192, 238-240, 274-276,
288-291. Extracts from some of these letters of 1846 may also be found in W. Ward,
The Life of Cardinal Newman, I, 129-131 with 621 (to H. Wilberforce), and 160-162
(to J. D. Dalgairns). All quotations in the following paragraphs will be found in
Dev, pp. 172-179; ed. Cameron, pp. 214-219 (IV, III, 11-17).

written to him before mounting any condemnation of the latter, and that this was a custom of long standing, going back to Peter and Paul. The authority of Athanasius himself and Socrates, the church historian, who each report the exchange independently of one another, confirms the claim enunciated by Julius. Skipping over the canons of Sardica (A.D. 343), whose genuineness was not beyond question in Newman's time,[2] and which would not fit Newman's pattern of exposition, he next quotes the famous Pope Damasus (366-384), backed up by Jerome, Basil, and Ambrosiaster. The imperial rescript of 378 and the Edict of Thessalonica (380), signed by all three emperors, are crucially significant steps in the development of papal power, but they do not fit into Newman's scheme either.[3]

Pope Siricius (384-398) expounded a clear awareness of his following Peter in a line of succession, which meant in this case that his jurisdiction extended over Spain. His African contemporary, Optatus of Milevis, for his own anti-Donatist purposes, developing his native tradition, stressed the same Petrine prerogative of the Roman bishop.[4] Then follow the progressively clearer testimonies of Pope Innocent (401-417, supported by Augustine), Pope Celestine (422-432), with Prosper of Aquitaine and, this time a bit pressed, Vincent of Lerins,

---

[2] Cf. Hamilton Hess, *The Canons of the Council of Sardica* (Oxford: Clarendon, 1958), p. 22. Cf. *L & D*, XV, 496 f.

[3] See the recent survey with literature of Rudolf Lorenz, *Das vierte bis sechste Jahrhundert (Westen)*, vol. I, part C1 of *Die Kirche in ihrer Geschichte*, eds. Kurt Dietrich Schmidt and Ernst Wolf (Göttingen: Vandenhoeck & Ruprecht, 1970), here p. 36-37. A more detailed exposition is found in Karl Baus, *From the Apostolic Community to Constantine* and *Die Kirche von Nikaia bis Chalkedon*, respectively vols. I and II/1 of the *Handbook of Church History*, ed. Hubert Jedin (New York: Herder and Herder, 1965 and Freiburg: Herder, 1973). The fullest treatment of all must be Jean Gaudemet, *L'Eglise dans l'Empire Romain (IVe-Ve siècles)* (Paris: Sirey, 1958), the most concise that of Walter Ullmann, *A Short History of the Papacy in the Middle Ages* (London: Methuen, 1972), ch. I. On the relations of Damasus and above all of Ambrose with the East see Francis Dvornik, *Byzantium and the Roman Primacy* (New York: Fordham University Press, 1966), pp. 43-47; Perikles Petros Joannou, *Die Ostkirche und die Cathedra Petri im 4. Jahrhundert* (Stuttgart: A. Hiersemann, 1972); Justin Taylor, "St. Basil the Great and Pope St. Damasus I," *Downside Review*, 91 (1973), 186-203 and 262-274. Antonio Rimoldi, *L'Apostolo San Pietro ... nella Chiesa primitiva dalle origini al Concilio di Calcedonia* (Rome: Gregorian University, 1958), furnishes a detailed discussion of the Petrine traditions.

[4] For this and the attitude of Augustine, who was much more ambiguous about the Roman primacy than Optatus, see Werner Marschall, *Karthago und Rom. Die Stellung der nordafrikanischen Kirche zum Apostolischen Stuhl in Rom* (Stuttgart: A. Hiersemann, 1971).

7

and finally Leo the Great (440-461), confirmed through the words of Peter Chrysologus and the Council of Chalcedon.[5]

Since Leo's significance would detain him in a later chapter, Newman immediately passed over to Barrow's description of the papal developments in the period leading up to Leo. The increasing influence of the Roman See was due in Barrow's view to the power-hungry machinations of Roman clerics, but he could not deny the fact that Rome's prestige reached an impressive level in the church at large. Newman accounted for Barrow's twisted interpretation of these facts by noting that he refused to allow convergence or accumulation of evidences to have any bearing in his investigation. If the individual, isolated testimony did not prove the papal supremacy by itself, then it was totally discarded and not allowed to function in a chain or cable of mutually supporting indications—an impossible procedure for a disciple of Bishop Butler, for whom "probability" was "the guide of life." [6] Barrow's procedures and his polemic intent may well have constituted a hindrance to historical, to say nothing of theological, comprehension, which Newman was able to overcome.[7] Nonetheless Newman's attempt to understand the first three centuries

---

[5] Wilhelm de Vries, "The Primacy of Rome as Seen by the Eastern Church," *Diakonia*, 6 (1971), 221-231, translated from *Stimmen der Zeit*, 186 (1970), 195-202, shows that the expressions of the Council of Chalcedon (A.D. 451) cannot properly be taken as confirmation of Leo's view of papal jurisdiction.

For documentation consult *Dev*, ed. Artz, notes 309-314; supply for Chrysologus Migne, *PL*, 52, 25. Most of the citations in the original can be found in Mirbt/Aland, *Quellen zur Geschichte des Papsttums*, I, under the following numbers:

Pope Julius	no. 271
Athanasius	no. 271
Pope Damasus	not given; *PG*, 82, 1219
Jerome	no. 359
Basil	no. 296
Pope Siricius	no. 343
Optatus	no. 287
Pope Innocent	no. 404
Pope Celestine	not given; *PL*, 50, 427
Pope Leo	not given, but see nos. 441-442
Council of Chalcedon	no. 457

[6] I quote here from Newman's *Grammar of Assent*, p. 237. For Newman's opinion of Barrow's way of dealing with the evidence as contrary to Butler's hermeneutics, cf. *Dev*, pp. 151-157; ed. Cameron, pp. 195-201 (III, 1). Many remarks of this passage are concerned with the way to interpret prophecies; Newman even quotes a Warburtonian lecturer whom he knew at Oriel in support of his criticism of Barrow (John Davison, cf. *Dev*, ed. Artz, note 246).

[7] Newman had still quoted Barrow as an authority in "Catholicity of the Anglican Church" (1840), *Essays Critical and Historical*, II, 21-22.

of the church's life in categories proper to the fourth and fifth centuries was taking the accumulation of probabilities and the patterning of history around a few texts to impermissible lengths. Time has not been kind to this particular example of Newman's method.

Though he made what seemed like a complete outline of a case for the papal supremacy at this point in his *Essay*, Newman was not finished with the theme. It returns in a powerful evocation at the rhetorical heart of the book.[8] The protagonist is Leo I; the drama is that of Chalcedon; and the literary setting is Newman's third and final parallel between the Church of the Fathers and the modern Roman Catholic Church, under the subheading, "The Monophysites."

Newman later told the world in *Difficulties of Anglicans* (1850) and *Apologia pro Vita Sua* how his convictions about the infallible teaching authority of the Church, as exercised by the pope, arose from his study of the early history of dogma, above all from the history of the Council of Chalcedon.[9] He had let Keble know in 1843 that the Monophysite controversy had given rise in him to a "deep impression" that the pope had "a certain gift of infallibility." [10] But at that time he still could not justify these impressions from the summer of 1839 satisfactorily. A good part of the *Essay on Development* is his more or less definite accounting for the disturbing parallels that had loomed up in his reading, especially the key position that Pope Leo had occupied at a critical juncture.[11]

This is the topic, at any rate, of the section on the Monophysites.[12] Leo's position after the important synod at Ephesus in 449 was not unlike that of nineteenth-century popes faced with a vigorous Liberalism, even within the Church: his teaching on the point in question [13] had been rejected and he was excommunicated, with "the Emperor

---

[8] Cf. above, Ch. VIII, note 28.

[9] Heinrich Fries, "Die Dogmengeschichte des fünften Jahrhunderts im theologischen Werdegang von John Henry Newman," in *Das Konzil von Chalkedon*, III, 421-454, esp. 437-443. See also above, Ch. IV, note 1.

[10] Letter of 4 May 1843 in *Correspondence with Keble*, p. 219.

[11] *Ibid.*, p. 24; letter of 5 April 1844 in *Cardinal Newman*, ed. G. H. Harper, p. 43; Maisie Ward, *Young Mr. Newman*, p. 462.

[12] *Dev*, pp. 293-317; ed. Cameron, pp. 315-334 (VI, III, § 3); quotations following are from there, unless otherwise noted.

[13] For which see Aloys Grillmeier, *Christ in Christian Tradition* (New York: Sheed and Ward, 1965), pp. 463-477, and Jaroslav Pelikan, *The Christian Tradition*, I, 256-266.

issuing an edict in approval of the decision of the Council." [14] Leo
had no choice but to take a stand against this decision, with the
felicitous battle cry, *non concilium sed latrocinium Ephesinum* (a "gang
of robbers," as Newman translates). There follows a vivid description
of the odds against Leo and of the plausible arguments of his adversa-
ies.

> Such was the state of Eastern Christendom in the year 449; a
> heresy, appealing to the Fathers, to the Creed, and, above all, to
> Scripture, was by a general Council, professing to be Ecumenical,
> received as true in the person of its promulgator. If the East could
> determine a matter of faith independently of the West, certainly the
> Monophysite heresy was established as Apostolic truth in all its
> provinces from Macedonia to Egypt.
>
> There had been a time in the history of Christianity, when it had
> been Athanasius against the world, and the world against Athanasius.
> The need and straitness of the Church had been great, and one man
> was raised up for her deliverance. In this second necessity, who was
> the destined champion of her who cannot fail? Whence did he come,
> and what was his name? He came with an augury of victory upon
> him, which even Athanasius could not show; it was Leo, Bishop of
> Rome.
>
> Leo's augury of success, which even Athanasius had not, was this,
> that he was seated in the chair of St. Peter and the heir of his preroga-
> tives.[15]

Here Newman added four more testimonies to the Petrine powers
of the pope, which were written at this juncture by Peter Chrysologus,
Theodoret, the Western Emperor Valentinian III, and Leo himself.[16]
He went to cite the acts of the Council of Chalcedon, selecting the
elements which most clearly reflected Pope Leo's primacy as vicar
and heir of Peter. The famous acclamation, "Peter has spoken through

---

[14] Specific parallels were not drawn, except for one allusion to the Council of
Trent, the principle bone of contention between Anglicans and Roman Catholics:
"the Chalcedonian Fathers had ... virtually added to" the Creed; "they had
added what might be called, 'The Creed of Pope Leo.'" This brings to mind
the Tridentine "Creed of Pope Pius," as the Anglican called it, e.g., Froude's
Remains, I, 434. One can't help thinking, however, of the story of French Catholicism's relations with the pope from the opening of the Revolution through the
Civil Constitution of the Clergy to the Napoleonic Concordat—Louis XVI,
like Theodosius II, issued an assembly's decision which the pope refused to
recognize ...

[15] The chair of Peter even then had the significant characteristic of being
called fearful apocalyptic names by heretics, *Dev*, pp. 247-253, 269; ed. Cameron,
pp. 276, 281, 294 (VI, ii, 5, 8, and 17).

[16] The quotation from Chrysologus is the same used previously, with a bit
of context added; the others are new, cf. *Dev*, ed. Artz, note 474.

Leo," is related in context, thus showing the reluctance of the Oriental bishops to treat the papal magisterium as in itself definitive.[17]

The drama of the Council consists according to Newman of the tension between the pope's delegates, who were insisting on the solemn acceptance of Pope Leo's doctrine of the two natures of Christ (in his *Tomus ad Flavianum*), and the greater part of the council fathers, Orientals who didn't see the need of it. Here the civil authority stepped in in the person of the new emperor himself and forced the bishops to choose clearly between Leo and Dioscurus. "And thus ended the controversy once for all." [18]

The Council, after its termination, addressed "a letter to St. Leo; in it the Fathers acknowledge him as 'constituted interpreter of the voice of Blessed Peter,' with an allusion to St. Peter's Confession in Matthew xvi, and speak of him as 'the very one commissioned with the guardianship of the Vine by the Saviour.' " [19]

The one reservation, which Newman's account of the proceedings calls for, is that he overrates the degree of initiative which he attributes to Pope Leo and to his legates at the Council. It was not Leo's idea to mount a full ecumenical council against the Ephesian brigands, but the new emperor in the East, Marcian (under the influence of Pulcheria) insisted upon it. The change of fortune due to the accession of Marcian goes relatively unnoticed in this part of the *Essay*.[20] So does the issue of Constantinopolitan versus Roman hegemony in the Church, which emerged clearly at this Council and which aids comprehension of the Petrine claims considerably.[21]

---

[17] *Acta Conciliorum Oecumenicorum*, ed. Edward Schwartz (Strasbourg, 1914-1938), II, 1, 2, 81. Compare P.-Th. Camelot, *Ephèse et Chalcédoine* (Paris: de l'Orante, 1962), p. 179.

[18] These words must be understood as pertaining to the question of dogmatic orthodoxy alone, as understood by Anglicans to whom the ecumenical councils of antiquity, and Chalcedon in their number, were regarded as infallible. Newman knew that historically the controversy went on and got even worse after Chalcedon.

[19] Cf. Mirbt/Aland, *Quellen zur Geschichte des Papsttums*, I, no. 457.

[20] The replacement is mentioned without emphasis, *Dev*, p. 306; ed. Cameron, p. 325 (VI, III, § 3, 14); see however in another connection, *Dev*, p. 46; ed. Cameron, p. 107 (I, II, 5). On the respective aims of Pope Leo and Emperor Marcian see Monald Goemans, "Chalkedon als 'Allgemeines Konzil'," in *Das Konzil von Chalkedon*, I, 270-272.

[21] Cf. Thomas Owen Martin, "The Twenty-eighth Canon of Chalcedon," *Das Konzil von Chalkedon*, II, 443-458; Anton Michel, "Der Kampf um das politische oder petrinische Prinzip der Kirchenführung," *ibid.*, II, 491-562, and Dvornik, *Byzantium and the Roman Primacy*, pp. 47-54.

Be that as it may, one inescapable fact had impressed itself upon Newman, that Pope Leo exercised a sovereign and infallible act of authority and that he did it in the name of Peter's primacy. Moreover, it was of incalculable benefit to the whole subsequent Church. An authority like that which Leo exercised was far from unwelcome to Newman, once he could legitimate its claim on the hypothesis of developments with the support of prophecy. Nor need one stretch the theory to extravagant lengths to encompass the papacy: by Leo's time the essential development had reached its completion; Tridentine popes did not claim more than Leo did, nor exercise, in principle, a more monocratic power. That is the import of the following passage:

> Such is the external aspect of those proceedings by which the Catholic faith has been established in Christendom against the Monophysites.... the historical account of the Council is this, that a formula which the Creed did not declare, which the Fathers did not unanimously witness, and which some eminent Saints had almost in set terms opposed, which the whole East refused as a symbol, not once, but twice, patriarch by patriarch, metropolitan by metropolitan, first by the mouth of above a hundred, then by the mouth of above six hundred of its Bishops, and refused upon the grounds of its being an addition to the Creed, was forced upon the Council, not indeed as a Creed, yet, on the other hand, not for subscription merely, but for acceptance as a definition of faith under the sanction of an anathema, forced on the Council by the resolution of the Pope of the day, acting through his Legates and supported by the civil power.

In the following pages on the aftermath of Chalcedon, Newman sketches a picture of utmost desolation for a champion of the dogmatic principle: heresies were not diminished after Chalcedon, but grew rank in all quarters. As later he was to make a case for consulting the *laity* in matters of doctrine [22] out of the doctrinal confusions of the episcopacy during the time of the Arian hegemony of the fourth century, so here he made a case for the *papacy* out of the turbulent history of the fifth century.[23] In the year 493, when Gelasius was pope, there was scarcely one province in the inhabited world which he could call Catholic, because of heresies, schisms, and barbarian invasions.

---

[22] In his article "On Consulting the Faithful in Matters of Doctrine" in *The Rambler* (July 1859), 198-230; re-edited under the same name by John Coulson (London: Chapman, 1961).

[23] Fries, in *Das Konzil von Chalkedon*, III, 451. Similarly in his old age, cf. letter of 27 February 1877 in Ward, *Life of Cardinal Newman*, II, 576.

Summing up the case for Catholicism for the third time, he concluded as follows.

> If then there is now a form of Christianity such, that it extends throughout the world, though with varying measures of prominence or prosperity in separate places;—that it lies under the power of sovereigns and magistrates, in various ways alien to its faith;—that flourishing nations and great empires, professing or tolerating the Christian name, lie over against it as antagonist;—that schools of philosophy and learning are supporting theories, and following out conclusions, hostile to it, and establishing an exegetical system subversive of its Scriptures;—that it has lost whole Churches by schism, and is now opposed by powerful communions once part of itself;— that it has been altogether or almost driven from some countries;— that in others its line of teachers is overlaid, its flocks oppressed, its Churches occupied, its property held by what may be called a duplicate succession;—that in orders its members are degenerate and corrupt, and are surpassed in conscientiousness and in virtue, as in gifts of intellect, by the very heretics whom it condemns;—that heresies are rife and bishops negligent within its own pale;—and that amid its disorders and fears there is but one Voice for whose decisions its people wait with trust, one Name and one See to which they look with hope, and that name Peter, and that see Rome;—such a religion is not unlike the Christianity of the fifth and sixth Centuries.

At other places in the *Essay* there were opportunities to insert qualifications. Pope Leo the Great is, of course, the most eminent example of the papal monarchy and infallibility. His was an extraordinary case, and Newman did not want to leave the impression that popes in general acted with his decision and peremptoriness, nor that one should necessarily expect this of Peter's successors. In illustrating how the process of dogmatic development takes the thought of many and various minds as grist for its mill, he was moved to remark:

> The deep meditation which seems to have been exercised by the Fathers on points of doctrine, the debate and turbulence yet lucid determination of Councils, the indecision of Popes, are all in different ways, at least when viewed together, portions and indications of the same process. The theology of the Church is no random combination of various opinions, but a diligent, patient working out of one doctrine from many materials. The conduct of Popes, Councils, Fathers, betokens the slow, painful, anxious taking up of new elements into an existing body of belief.[24]

---

[24] *Dev*, p. 353; ed. Cameron, pp. 363 f (VIII, 1, 10): similarly "The Newman-Perrone Paper on Development," *Gregorianum*, 16 (1935), 416-17.

On almost the last page of his *Essay* he admitted obliquely that an uncritical acceptance of everything a pope proclaims could also be harmful:

> Nor was the development of dogmatic theology, which was then taking place, a silent and spontaneous process. It was wrought out and carried through under the fiercest controversies, and amid the most fearful risks. The Catholic faith was placed in a succession of perils, and rocked to and fro like a vessel at sea. Large portions of Christendom were, one after another, in heresy or in schism; the leading Churches and the most authoritative schools fell from time to time into serious error; three Popes, Liberius, Vigilius, Honorius, have left to posterity the burden of their defence: but these disorders were no interruption to the sustained and steady march of the sacred science from implicit belief to formal statement.[25]

[25] *Dev*, pp. 447 f; ed. Cameron, pp. 443 f (XII, 4). See also his *Select Treatises of St. Athanasius* (1842; London: Longmans, Green, 1881), I, 121-22, note 1; *Arians*, p. 352, note 8.

CHAPTER THIRTEEN

DEVELOPMENT AND FULFILMENT, III:
A CRITIQUE

Newman did not set as much store by his handling of the particular case of the papacy's development as his contemporaries thought he was bound to. His critics battened on the issue and pronounced a verdict of "Not proven."[1] For Henry Wilberforce, as we have seen, it was a sticking-point.[2] Thomas William Allies thought it so important that he wrote two books about it, one on each side of the question.[3] The alternative, papal supremacy or royal supremacy, was equally decisive for other and still more serious minds. Two of them worked out their own way into the Roman Catholic Communion, Henry Edward Manning and Robert Isaac Wilberforce. Two of them remained in the communion of their baptism, William Ewart Gladstone and Richard William Church.[4] The finest theology of papal primacy to come out of Tractarianism—I do not exclude Newman's *Essay on Development* from this judgement—was the work of Robert Isaac Wilberforce.

Robert Wilberforce was the first, or one of the first, to whom Newman had confided (1841-42) the possibility that he could see something in the papacy as accepted among Roman Catholics.[5] The vicissitudes of the next twelve years combined with his talent to make of his *Inquiry into the Principles of Church-Authority* a solid vindication of papal primacy as such. In a way it was the transformation of Newman's hypothesis into more manageable and defensible affirmations, together with a more rigorous argumentation in support of them.

---

[1] See the list of Anglican replies to *Dev* in Chadwick, *From Bossuet to Newman*, p. 164 (note); cf. above, Ch. VIII, note 15, and Ch. IX, note 13.

[2] See above, Introduction.

[3] Thomas William Allies, *The Church of England cleared from the Charge of Schism* (1846); *idem*, *The See of St. Peter* (1850, announcing his switch to Rome).

[4] For the period until 1854, see David Newsome, *The Wilberforces and Henry Manning*. On Manning in particular, see George Huntston Williams, "*Omnium christianorum pastor et doctor*: Vatican I et l'Angleterre victorienne," *Nouvelle revue théologique*, 96 (1974), 113-146 and 337-365. See *ODC* on all these figures.

[5] See above, Ch. V, note 27. Robert Wilberforce replied that Newman surely did not contemplate "joining a communion which is stained by image-worship, saint-worship, the denial of the cup, the Pope's supremacy *de jure divino*," but had to bear correction, cf. Newsome, *The Wilberforces*, p. 291.

Wilberforce also introduced one crucial qualification into the picture of the Church *qua* prophetical Kingdom. The essence of church order does not consist in juridical power (though this follows in due course). The law of its organization is rather "that the same persons, who were individually the dispensers of grace, should collectively be the witnesses to doctrine." [6] From this Wilberforce derived the corollary that church order and the civil order of the state are not necessarily rivals and need not be in perpetual conflict. The root of the conflicts is failure to respect the boundaries of the two organizations' competence. The usefulness of such a distinction was only to impress itself upon Newman much later.

Parallel to this distinction between the Church's proper structures (episcopacy-hierarchy-primacy) and any parallel patterns of organization in civil society, there is the distinction Wilberforce makes between the ecumenical "primacy" (the principle announced in the New Testament of catholic church authority) and "supremacy" (the form this principle assumed in the setting of the Empire). Since royal supremacy can only be interpreted as an unwarranted appropriation by the state of something properly belonging to the Church, it must be repudiated and the primacy must be embraced where it in fact exists. This conclusion does not arise, as in Newman's *Essay*, from an overwhelming deluge of convergent evidence tending to show the identity of Tridentine Catholicism with the Catholic Church of Antiquity, but from an examination of one particular issue, the shape of authority in the church at large, carried out thoroughly and systematically.

Robert Wilberforce had taken the time to investigate the views of leading Catholic theologians on the nature and origins of the papacy, as Newman had not: Möhler, Döllinger, Passaglia, as well as Newman and Allies were cited. A comparison of his work with Newman's is worthwhile in order to make clear the strengths and weaknesses of each in confronting the same question in practically the same situation. Wilberforce was certainly not a patristic scholar on the level with Newman, and so his information is more likely to be garnered at second hand (from Newman, Allies, Möhler, etc.). On the other hand, he was dealing with a more restricted field than that covered by Newman's *Essay*, which meant that he could enter into more detail on the interpretation of particular texts, where Newman sought to put a construction on large patterns discernible in "the disposition, or *lie*,

---

[6] Robert Isaac Wilberforce, *An Inquiry into the Principles of Church-Authority* (London: Longman, Brown, Green and Longmans, 1854), p. 55.

of the evidence," irrespective of the exact interpretation of any given point.[7] When Wilberforce let Newman know that he was laboring over the, to him, key point of Ultramontane Catholicism, the papal supremacy, Newman urged him not to get bogged down in details (as Samuel Wilberforce was also urging from the opposed viewpoint).[8] As for his *Development*, Robert must bear in mind that he had made "a very bold and needless application of" the theory—"with reference to the *facts* of the case." One should not take his factual presentation as being the strongest that could be made.

When Robert Wilberforce came to write up his *Inquiry*, therefore, he left no equivocation regarding the existence of the "primacy" from the beginning of the church, along with the other two forces of church order, the episcopacy and the hierarchy (i.e., the tendency to band together in regional and patriarchal structures of communion). He worked out much more consistently and carefully than Newman had the way in which each emerged as permitted by conditions. Where Newman's treatment may still be thought to be superior is not in his presentation of this specific issue, but rather in the fact that he refused to allow the question of the papal primacy to be crucial at all: he dislodged it from the central position it had occupied and continued to occupy in the minds of most writers involved in the Roman-Anglican controversy by making it a side-issue, subordinate to the truly central question as he saw it, "Which communion is the Church?"[9]

Newman can therefore be given credit for keeping the question of the papal claims in proportion and for reducing their role in the controversy to the rank of difficulties to be dealt with rather than the basic point to be settled. But then he was obliged to *deal* with them, and on this score Robert Wilberforce was much more satisfactory and relied much less on the fragile hypothesis that "the clear light of the fourth and fifth centuries may be fairly taken to illuminate the dim notices of the preceding."[10] In the light of the present status of New Testament and patristic research, this hypothesis seems indistinguishable from a plea to practice systematic anachronism. The early history

---

[7] *Dev*, p. 165; ed. Cameron, p. 207 (IV, III, 1: omitted).

[8] Letter of 11 December 1853, in *L & D*, XV, 495-498; Newsome, *The Wilberforces*, pp. 383-396 ("The Battle of Burton Agnes").

[9] *L & D*, XV, 497; *ibid.*, XI, 190, letter to Henry Wilberforce of 4 July 1846.

[10] *Dev*, p. 179; ed. Cameron, p. 219 (IV, III, 17: "the dim, though definite, outlines traced in the preceding").

of the papacy presents a picture of its developments today which is irreconcilable with Newman's treatment at several important points. Insofar as this picture takes a critical approach to the Bible as a presupposition, both Newman's and Wilberforce's starting point will be found wanting.

To illustrate: unless one starts with the postulate, now widely rejected, that church organization must always have been on one pattern and should remain the same perpetually, one meets clear evidence in the New Testament of a variety of church orders.[11] What this initial lack of uniformity in church structures means for subsequent generations of the church has been worked out with particular éclat by Hans Küng. Put briefly, if the church at Corinth could be a full-fledged Christian church without priests, without even presbyters or bishops with "right of succession" to the Apostle, then the Ignatian arrangement of a monarchical bishop, with a college of presbyters and a third order of deacons, cannot be of the essence of the church, that is, *de iure divino*.

In the course of time, this initial and basic variety of church structures underwent profound modifications, which have been the object of much fruitful research, so that we are in a much better position to describe their intricate evolution than heretofore was the case. Here I can only indicate some milestones in this evolution which determine in outline the context in which the prehistory of the papacy must be seen. One major development was that the original plethora of charismatic ministries which characterized the early Pauline communities gave way in a generation or two to a growing concentration of tasks in the hands of administrative officials. The need which

---

[11] The book to consult for the whole period named in its title is by Hans von Campenhausen, *Ecclesiastical Authority and Spiritual Power in the Church of the First Three Centuries* (Stanford University Press, 1969; originally published in 1953). A large measure of agreement with it is evidenced in, e.g., John Knox, "The Ministry in the Primitive Church," in *The Ministry in Historical Perspectives*, eds. H. Richard Niebuhr and Daniel D. Williams (New York: Harper, 1956), pp. 1-26; Eduard Schweizer, *Church Order in the New Testament* (Naperville, Ill.: Allenson, 1961). After considerable struggling, cf. e.g. Rudolf Schnackenburg, *The Church in the New Testament* (New York: Herder and Herder, 1965), pp. 22-35, this point of view has also found a place in Roman Catholic ecclesiology since Hans Küng's *The Church* (New York: Sheed and Ward, 1967); see *Concilium*, vol. 80 (1972), "Ministries in the Church." I have also found most helpful Adolf M. Ritter, "Amt und Gemeinde im Neuen Testament und in der Kirchengeschichte," in A. M. Ritter and G. Leich, *Wer ist die Kirche?* (Göttingen: Vandenhoeck & Ruprecht, 1968), pp. 16-115.

Christians of the second and third generations increasingly perceived for a stable order and organization, with a view to preserving the Christian heritage handed down from the apostolic age, led to a strengthening of the organizational offices of the church, those of supervision (*episkope*) and service (*diakonia*). The same needs enhanced the usefulness of a patriarchal arrangement such as a board of elders.

A second factor, which the Pastoral Epistles will also reflect, though less distinctly, shows up in Rome before the first century is out: there we see the presbyter-bishop Clement indulging the conception that the Apostles themselves had instituted "bishops and deacons" to head the churches after their departure and, that they had left instructions that "other approved men should succeed to their ministry" after their appointees had died.[12] In the same general situation, the Acts of the Apostles speaks of Paul installing elders (Acts 14:23, cf. 20:28). Neither Clement nor Luke is here preserving historical reminiscence, but instead reflecting conditions of his own later stage of development.

It is with the awareness of these second-generation developments —the trend towards concentration of the many ministries into a few administrative offices, and the trend towards an idea of the apostolic succession of ministers—that we must approach the letters of Ignatius of Antioch. While in the Acts of the Apostles and the Epistle of Clement bishops and presbyters are the same individuals or class of leaders within the community, Ignatius presents us with the "monarchical bishop," the head of the presbyterium and the focus of unity for the whole local church. In the Ignatian usage, which took decades to become standard in other parts of the Christian world, the title of bishop was reserved for the one individual who stood at the head of the community which was clearly structured in ranks: the bishop first, then the presbyterium, the deacons and finally the faithful laity. Prophets, still very much in evidence in other documents from the first part of the second century, find no mention in Ignatius' writings.

Ignatius does not go on to combine his ideal of church order around the bishop with the notion of a juridical link between the episcopate and the Apostles: he does not claim, as does Clement, that the Apost-

---

[12] First Epistle of Clement to the Corinthians, 44.2. Cf. also ch. 42 in any edition of the Apostolic Fathers, as that of Robert M. Grant, *The Apostolic Fathers*, II (New York: Nelson, 1965); or in Mirbt/Aland, *Quellen zur Geschichte des Papsttums*, I, no. 29.

les installed presbyters, much less monarchical bishops.[13] The idea of apostolic succession of bishops is thus not yet present, but another rationale for the authority of the monarchical bishop more than suffices for Ignatius, namely the need for harmony and unity under one bishop in each place: as God is one and Christ is one, so also must the church close ranks about its one bishop.

We have noticed as especially relevant to our present question the circumstance that the Epistle of Clement spoke of a plurality of bishops, also called presbyters, who governed the church of Rome collegially: that is, there is no sign of a monarchical episcopate in Rome at the end of the first century. It would seem now that no significant change had taken place in the constitution of the Roman church by the time, ten or fifteen years later, when Ignatius wrote to it. For though he is anxious to extol the singular place of the bishop in his other letters,[14] there is no mention of the bishop's function and the respect due him in the whole Letter to the Romans. Some cautious scholars do not admit that one can make any inferences from this about the presence or absence of a monarchical bishop in Rome in the Ignatian era; after all, the other letters were directed to communities in Asia Minor with whose problems Ignatius was more or less familiar and had the end in view of edifying and strengthening them, whereas the main purpose of the Letter to the Romans was to make the unusual request that no steps be taken to prevent his martyrdom, which would perhaps be more the concern of Roman laymen than of the clergy.

Others, however, find the most plausible explanation in the *de facto* collegial, not yet monarchical, ruling set-up of the Roman community.[15] Ignatius seems to be conscious that his theory of church government can count on only a very few adherents, in all the world perhaps only certain churches in Asia Minor and in his own community, a minority among the Christians even of Antiochian Syria. As far as Rome is concerned, "The Shepherd" of Hermas still speaks of

---

[13] Newman exploited this circumstance for a *reductio ad absurdum* of the Anglican opposition to development, because Ignatius' silence on the point nullifies the appeal to the Vincentian Canon for the sacred doctrine of apostolic succession of bishops: see above, Ch. VIII, note 19.

[14] Joseph A. Fischer has gathered references in each of the Ignatian letters to the bishop's pre-eminence, cf. *Die Apostolischen Väter* (Munich: Kösel, 1956), p. 128; also Robert M. Grant, *The Apostolic Fathers*, I, 168-69.

[15] Including Raymond E. Brown, *Priest and Bishop: Biblical Reflections* (New York: Paulist Press, 1970), p. 54.

presbyters and bishops *circa* A.D. 140 in such a way as to exclude the monarchical episcopate from the frame of reference.[16] Hegesippus (*circa* 160) is the first witness to a monarchical episcopacy in Rome. Then follows Irenaeus (after 180).

One more document is especially helpful in filling in the picture of the development of church order in the early church, or should we say, in parts of the early church, since the developments evidently varied from locality to locality. The *Didache* or "Teaching of the Twelve Apostles" gives us an intriguing glance into the conditions of one group of Christians in Syria during the time when the allotment of ministries on the charismatic principle as in Paul's writings was becoming a thing of the past and the hierarchical structure with monarchical bishops was apparently still unknown. We see in it vivid indications of some of the factors behind the adoption of the Ignatian type of church order, which arose, as it appears, in the same Antiochene vicinity. (Newman and his contemporaries cannot be faulted for undervaluing the *Didache*, it must be noted, for this writing of sixteen short chapters was not discovered until 1875 nor published until 1883.)

The servants of the church who are prominent in the *Didache* are called "teachers," also "apostles and prophets." [17] What these men have in common is that they are not local people, bound to one community, but itinerant preachers who hold the Eucharist in the community where they happen to be staying. Some prophets may want to settle down, and this is provided for (*Didache* 13). The problem of false prophets is a real one, and several guidelines are given to help discern the true ones from the false, a difficult task (*Didache* 11:3-12).

But that is not all: sometimes no prophet was to be had (*Didache* 13:4)—a shortage seemed to be developing of these traveling charismatics on whom the communities had relied. The *Didache*, however, is not at a loss for advice even in this situation, and proposes letting local residents take over the functions of the disappearing apostles, prophets and teachers. It may not be like the good old days (the

---

[16] Cf. Patrick Burke, "The Monarchical Episcopate at the End of the First Century," *Journal of Ecumenical Studies*, 7 (1970), 508.

[17] Robert A. Kraft, *The Apostolic Fathers*, ed. Robert M. Grant, III, 67; *Didache*, 11:1-6.

implication is), but people out of your neighborhood, who don't necessarily manifest the spontaneous conviction that they have a charismatic vocation to fulfill, can do the essential task too.

> Appoint therefore for yourselves bishops and deacons worthy of the Lord, meek men, and not lovers of money, and truthful and approved, for *they also* minister to you the ministry of the prophets and teachers. Therefore do not despise them, for they are your honorable men together with the prophets and teachers.[18]

What the *Didache* furnishes us is a portrait, missing in Newman's time, of the transition stage between something like the Pauline and something like the Ignatian/Clementine forms of church order. In Paul the apostles, prophets, and teachers exercised the most prominent ministries, surrounded by a variety of others, among whom "moderators" or "supervisors" ("bishops") and "servants" or "waiters" ("deacons") found their modest place. In Ignatius, on the other hand, the prophets are nowhere to be seen, the bishop is in full charge of the teaching, and the presbyters are compared to the apostles (the apostles of the past). The Syrian homeland of the *Didache* for its part does not yet know of the Jewish institution of the presbyterium (elders), it would seem; but as the prophets fade away, the administrative and service ministries must be called upon or created to take up the gap. These bishops and deacons are sought out and appointed, not launched upon their churchly service by an immediate call of God.

This illustrates one relatively unstrained instance of the process that necessarily went on after the first generation in Christian communities everywhere, each with its own peculiarities and at its own pace, the process which provided Max Weber with the vocabulary for his sociological generalizations about the "routinization of charisma."

By juxtaposing Newman's reading and this reading of the historical developments of church office in the first generations of Christianity, I am suggesting that his daring hypotheses are disconfirmed at more than one point. Certain constructions that he wished to maintain regarding the history of the early church are no longer tenable. In the concrete, this means first of all the fiction that there were monarchical bishops in Rome in the first and early in the second century: it is merely an unnecessary theological postulate to hold that Linus, Anacletus, Clement, Evaristus and so forth were sufficiently distinguished from their fellow presbyters as to be considered personal

---

[18] *Didache*, 15:1-2.

successors to Peter. Secondly, one must take seriously the famous passage in Mt 16 and interpret it, not as a prophecy without relevance to the times of the evangelist, but as a commentary on some matter of interest to the Matthaean church.[19] Thirdly, one may not write off the century before Hegesippus, as if all we knew about it were conjecture based on later developments.

A theory which leaves no room for the immense variety of church orders and the very definitely contingent developments which made possible the rise of papal primacy will no longer suffice. We have described only the most striking of these developments in the earliest period before anyone thought of appealing to Mt 16 to support any hierarchical claims: the rise of a distinct form of church order in Pauline communities (exemplified by Corinth) alongside the Judeo-Christian type of church order in which elders played a chief part; the merging of the manifold charismatic ministries found in at least some of the early churches into a more firmly structured order of which administrative officials were the linchpins; concurrently the combination of the presbyteral system of supervision with that of bishops (and deacons); the origin (outside the New Testament canon)[20] of the idea of apostolic succession of office-holders; finally the idea of the sole or monarchical bishop, originating with or at least first attested by Ignatius of Antioch; this at a period some half-century after Paul and Peter had been at Antioch and by a bishop who made no claim to be the Apostles' successor.

These are only the preconditions to a theory of papal supremacy by divine right—the actual formulation of such a doctrine and the appeal to Mt 16 in this sense was the work of still later times and figures of the patristic era. This is not to say that these later patristic [21] and even

---

[19] For exemplification, see *Peter in the New Testament*, eds. Raymond E. Brown, Karl P. Donfried, and John Reumann (Minneapolis/New York: Augsburg/Paulist, 1973); Josef Blank, "The Person and Office of Peter in the New Testament," *Concilium*, 83 (1973), 42-55.

[20] Ritter, *Wer ist die Kirche?* pp. 232-33 discusses the way the notion is only hinted at in Acts and in the Pastoral Epistles. Clement is our first witness, and then in the context of a collegial ruling body of office-holders, not of a single individual as successor to the Apostles. George H. Williams points out that the concept of successors was originally connected with "teachers" in the philosophical and Gnostic traditions, before bishops took it over in relation to church teaching: "The Ministry in the Ante-Nicene Church (c. 125-315)," in *The Ministry in Historical Perspectives*, p. 35.

[21] Cf. Jaroslav Pelikan, *Development of Christian Doctrine* (New Haven: Yale University Press, 1969), pp. 55-62, for further orientation, as well as Wilhelm de Vries, "The Development after Constantine," *Concilium*, 64 (1971), 45-53.

medieval [22] developments are not also of fundamental significance, but the question of origins remains crucial to the Newmanian idea of development.

As we have seen above, Newman relied basically on two approaches to bridge the gap between the position of Peter in the New Testament and the developed doctrine of papal primacy. The idea that the Petrine passages were prophecies and promises, necessarily wrapped in obscurity until they were fulfilled, has not been received in Catholic theology, much less elsewhere. His other approach, that there was at work from the first an element which in due course manifested itself as the supremacy of the pope, was a hypothesis which subsequent research has failed to sustain.[23] Moreover, the two approaches, when combined, tend to cancel one another out,[24] though Newman seems to have thought that they were mutually confirmatory. If this analysis has merit, the conclusion can only be that Newman's application of "development" to the particular case of the papal supremacy does not serve the purpose.

[22] Cf. Yves Congar, *L'Église de saint Augustin à l'époque moderne* (Paris: Cerf, 1970), pp. 89-122 and 227-230, for an admirable survey of the effects of the eleventh-century Gregorian Reform on the concept of papal primacy. A popular treatment of its significance is found in Robert Markus and Eric John, *Pastors or Princes* (Washington: Corpus, 1969). A helpful bibliographical discussion is Anton Weiler, "Church Authority and Government in the Middle Ages," *Concilium*, 7 (1965), 123-36. See also *Le Chiese nei regni dell' Europa occidentale e i loro rapporti con Roma sino all' 800*, Settimana di Studi del Centro Italiano di Studi sull'alto Medioevo, 7 (Spoleto, 1960).

[23] This applies equally to Robert Wilberforce's *Inquiry*, and indeed to all biblical and historical defenses of the papacy which were insufficiently grounded in critical method.

[24] See above, Ch. XI, notes 10 and 11, with the discussion that follows, to the beginning of Ch. XII.

CHAPTER FOURTEEN

THE DEVELOPMENT HYPOTHESIS IN THE SUBSEQUENT DECADES

Newman observed signs of acceptance or rejection of his theory of developments with considerable apprehension in the first years, but after some bad moments his confidence grew and he stopped stressing the tentative nature of his *Essay*. It is true that he did not defend it publicly, except in the most general way, but Owen Chadwick has shown that any serious doubts that Newman may have entertained were passing and inconsequential.[1] It is also apparent, however, that he could retreat to rather anodyne versions of his theory without any awareness that he might be inconsistent. There is an unmistakable fuzziness or elasticity in Newman's mind about how far development may be taken. One does not have to be as inflexible as Döllinger to suspect this.[2] In part this was due to a laudable tentativeness. Having proposed a startling new mode of countering historical difficulties, he was properly non-assertive as to the range of its application.

The papal supremacy, as we have just seen, was to Newman one of those fine determinations of teaching which he was content to accept from the Church, once he had identified which communion was the Church. During the thirty years that elapsed between the first and the second composition of his *Essay on Development*, he left open the ques-

---

[1] Chadwick, *From Bossuet to Newman*, pp. 185-191. For the reception accorded to Newman's *Development* in Catholic theology, see Stephen C. Dessain, "The Reception among Catholics of Newman's Doctrine of Development," *Newman-Studien* (henceforth *NS*), VI (Nuremberg: Glock und Lutz, 1964), pp. 179-191; Bernard-Dominique Dupuy, "L'influence de Newman sur la théologie catholique du développement dogmatique," *ibid.*, pp. 143-165; *idem*, "Newman's Influence in France," *OS*, pp. 147-173; Herbert Hammans, *Die neueren katholischen Erklärungen der Dogmenentwicklung* (Essen: Ludgerus-Verlag, 1965); Paul Misner, "Newman and Theological Pluralism," in *New Dimensions in Religious Experience*, ed. George Devine (Staten Island, N.Y.: Alba House, 1971), pp. 233-244; *Dev*, ed. Artz, pp. xxxii-xl (comprehensive); T. Mark Schoof, *A Survey of Catholic Theology 1800-1970* (New York: Paulist Newman Press, 1970); Georg Söll, *Dogma und Dogmenentwicklung*, Handbuch der Dogmengeschichte, I/5 (Freiburg: Herder, 1971); and Jan Walgrave, *Unfolding Revelation: The Nature of Doctrinal Development*.

[2] Heinrich Fries, "Newman und Döllinger," *NS*, 1 (1948), 35, cites a letter of 1875 from Döllinger to Gladstone, which is disdainful of *Development*, but note the year and circumstances.

tion whether his approach was indeed the proper one to take in regard to the papal claims. In the revised edition of 1878, he clearly treated primacy as one of the chief instances which illustrate his theory, with even greater emphasis than in the first edition. The question just posed was therefore answered in a ringing affirmative, but it was still not altogether clear whether the papal development was a matter of tardy recognition and homogeneous growth, or whether there was not a substantial element of novelty and change in the succeeding stages of the papacy. A discussion of some of his utterances about development and the papacy after 1845 will reveal a tendency towards the first, more traditional, alternative.

It is understandable that Newman wished to assimilate his theology as much as possible to that which he heard in Rome during his stay there from October, 1846 until December, 1847. The so-called "Newman-Perrone Paper" is testimony to this,[3] and it is very evident also in his letters to John D. Dalgairns in Langres, who was charged with overseeing the French translation of *Development*. Thus he wondered "whether perhaps the tradition of the *Roman* Church may not have been developed from the first." [4] It might be enough to believe that the Petrine primacy was known, though largely unexercised, in the early church at Rome, while remaining unknown for a long time elsewhere.[5] If this were the case, then "development" would not have to be pleaded to account for the papal claims. At the most, it would have been a development by sheer expansion and external recognition, but not in the strong sense of substantive evolution. The latter leaves room for newness in the history of dogma and Newman's stronger statements in his *Essay*, especially those framed in terms of prophecy to be fulfilled, seem to endorse it. At the very least his theory envisaged cases that go beyond the merely logical explication of what was implicit.[6]

---

[3] "The Newman-Perrone Paper on Development," ed. T. Lynch, *Gregorianum*, 16 (1935), 402-447. Cf. *Dev*, ed. Artz, notes 692 and 720; Chadwick, *From Bossuet to Newman*, pp. 167, 181-184; Walter Kasper, *Die Lehre von der Tradition in der Römischen Schule* (Freiburg: Herder, 1962), pp. 119-130. Perrone was already much influenced by Möhler.

[4] *L & D*, XI, 290 (of 8 Dec. 1846); cf. *ibid.*, p. 274 (concern about his handling of the pope's supremacy) and p. 280 (Roman tradition suffices for Perrone, no need for Catholic testimonies); "Newman-Perrone Paper," p. 406 (unwillingness to embrace sufficiency of merely local Roman tradition).

[5] Letter to Lord Adare of 31 Aug. 1846, *ibid.*, XI, 240.

[6] These remained for Newman inadequate explanations, cf. Chadwick, *From Bossuet to Newman*, p. 189; Hammans, *Die neueren katholischen Erklärungen*,

Subsequent statements seem to confirm the impression that Newman was willing to defend only that strain in his *Essay* which made minimal concessions to historical difficulties. When it became known that Pope Pius IX wished to define the Immaculate Conception as a dogma, Newman was struck by the confirmation this lent to his theory as opposed to the traditional fixist position of unvarying immutability in doctrine. His manner of writing on this occasion, however, showed that he did not consider the "new" dogma to have been discovered for the first time at that moment when documents began to attest to the belief. Rather, he spoke of the analogy of memory and forgetfulness, of the growth of a globally imparted revelation "in its parts," thus leaving his reader to understand what he would bring out in later letters, that the apostles had had the doctrine, though it was lost sight of for centuries after them.[7] This of course would have startled Perrone, but it concurred with the latter's emphasis on the authority of the living magisterium, which could practically be taken as vouching for tradition without further ado.[8]

In 1853 Newman wrote to an Anglican correspondent that he felt that there had only been an *appearance* of change in church teaching. "As to my book, I could have written its subject on its title page, viz 'The differences and additions in doctrinal teaching observable in the history of the Church are but apparent, being the necessary phenomena incident to deep intellectual ideas.' "[9] He referred to the passages in his Essay where he spoke of the opposition voiced to the ecumenical authority of the early popes, implying that he understood it as due merely to the relative novelty of the phenomenon among the ill-informed. Likewise in writing to Robert Wilberforce in the same year he denied that the difficulties he had raised against Bull regarding the Ante-Nicene writers were more than apparent.[10] Newman did

---

p. 179; Walgrave, *Unfolding Revelation*, p. 304. Anthony A. Stephenson, "Cardinal Newman and the Development of Doctrine," *Journal of Ecumenical Studies*, 3 (1966), 463-485, deplores the confusion perpetrated by Newman's strong doctrine of development and his vacillation between it and an acceptable "weak" notion of the same.

[7] *L & D*, XIII, 81-83 (11 March 1849, to W. G. Ward).

[8] Cf. Walter Kasper, *Die Lehre von der Tradition*, p. 179, also pp. 94-97 and 231-237 about the dogmatization of the Immaculate Conception. On this cf. *L & D*, XVI, 366 (26 January 1855).

[9] *Ibid.*, XV, 371-374 (letter to Edmund Ffoulkes of 1 June 1853).

[10] *Ibid.*, XV, 496 on the discussion of papal supremacy in the Introduction to the *Essay*.

not look back at his book for reference as he wrote these comments; [11] it is surely remarkable how much more consistent they are than the *Essay* itself, excerpting and integrating as they do only the line of argument that is theologically less troublesome and historically less probable.

At length there came a statement which Lord Acton considered a retractation of Newman's hypothesis about developments.[12] Development is "a more intimate apprehension, and a more lucid enunciation of the original dogma... and nothing more." Newman admitted that he may have written confusingly on the subject, but that it was now clear to him that the words "development in dogma" meant "nothing but the process by which, under the magisterium of the Church, implicit faith becomes explicit." Where he differed from Perrone was that the latter admitted even this modest kind of advance in insight only for individual Christians and not for the magisterium. Capping the series of restatements of his development thesis is the so-called "Flanagan Paper" of 15 February 1868.[13] By this time the great issue between W. G. Ward and less zealous Ultramontanes who looked to Newman for guidance was whether papal infallibility should be defined at the Vatican Council. In this context Newman drew out his thinking on the possible extent of dogmatic developments for John Stanislas Flanagan, a former Oratorian colleague whose orientation on dogmatic questions was thoroughly fixist (*semper eadem*).

In this deliberate statement Newman once again concentrated on the psychology of knowing or being-possessed-by deep truths. The analogy of the church's tradition with an individual's memory seems to be the leading idea, so that his forthcoming *Grammar of Assent*, building on the foundation laid in the Oxford University Sermons, must be seen as the later Newman's key to understanding the development of doctrines.[14] In this perspective, questions of historical

---

[11] *Ibid.*, XV, 495; XX, 306.

[12] Cf. Chadwick, *From Bossuet to Newman*, p. 186, text reprinted pp. 243-244 and in *L & D*, XX, 223-224 (to Acton, dated 8 July 1862).

[13] "An unpublished Paper by Cardinal Newman on the Development of Doctrine," ed. C. S. Dessain, in *Journal of Theological Studies*, 9 (1958), 324-335; same, with introductory remarks by Hugo M. de Achával, in *Gregorianum*, 39 (1958), 585-596.

[14] I have not been able to consult William C. Hunt, "Intuition: The Key to J. H. Newman's Theory of Doctrinal Development," a Catholic University dissertation, except in *Dissertation Abstracts*, 27 (1967), 4331A. The point emerges clearly enough already in Jan H. Walgrave, *Newman The Theologian* (London: G. Chapman, 1960).

character recede into the background and the analogy between a human mind and the mind of the church takes over. It is but a small step to the historical implausibilities about the apostles, who must have known, in a way suitable to their circumstances, everything that the church would in the course of the centuries "remember" and proclaim as dogma.

It is not a question, then, of Newman "retracting" his theory with such statements. Rather he was reducing his thought on the subject to a more systematic and coherent view. The lines he emphasized were present in his *Essay*, but there the pressure of facts had prevented him from carrying one theory through consistently, as Nicholas Lash has shown.[15] As he turned back to the themes of his University Sermons and prepared to write the *Grammar of Assent* (1870), the element of theory became stronger and the stubborn facts relaxed their hold on him. One could also say that the interior and psychological element waxed as the historical-sociological interest waned. The papal claims put forth by the First Vatican Council, he was relieved to find, were not identical with those proposed beforehand by Neo-Ultramontanes, and he could accept their substance without difficulty.[16] But what would be his procedure when he once again took up his historical work by re-editing the *Essay on Development*?

One point is abundantly clear: Newman did not set out to bowdlerize his post-Vatican *Development* by eliminating all the themes that did not accord with the more systematic approach he had worked out over the years since the first edition saw the light. He did not seem to think that any major purge was necessary.[17] Respecting the papal

---

[15] As cited above, Ch. VIII, note 6. In a different perspective, John Coulson, *Newman and the Common Tradition*, p. 80, speaks of the rise of the idea of development from the level of hypothesis to that of affirmation during this period.

[16] Ward, *Life of Cardinal Newman*, II, 307 f.

[17] Documentation in Chadwick, *From Bossuet to Newman*, p. 188. Cf. *Dev*, pp. 64 f; ed. Cameron, p. 122: "An empire or a religion may have many changes: but when we speak of its developing, we consider it to be fulfilling, not to be belying its destiny; so much so that we even take its actual fortunes as a comment on its early history, and call its policy a mission. The Popes present a very different appearance to the historian of the world, when in apostolical poverty or in more than imperial power; but, while they protect the poor, reconcile rival sovereigns, convert barbarians, and promote civilization, he recognizes their function in spite of the change, and is contented to praise them." Did Newman delete this in 1878 because he considered it too double-edged and compromising? Or was it due more to the exigencies of his new outline? The passage from which it stems was Ch. I, Sec. III in 1845, but was postponed to Ch. V, Sec. I in 1878; this in itself involved a good deal of *remaniement*. On the other hand, the frank talk of

supremacy, there is not only no sign of strain or retrenchment, but the new order of material gives the case of the papacy a greater prominence than it had enjoyed in the original edition. Among the innumerable minor emendations which he made in 1877-78, however, there were many which reduced the "concessions" of historical fact which he had so liberally indulged in in 1845.[18] Instead of writing that "local disturbances gave rise to Bishops, and... ecumenical disturbances gave rise to Popes" (1845), he modified it to local disturbances giving *exercise* to bishops, ecumenical disturbances giving *exercise* to popes (1878); in the sentence: "While Apostles were on earth, there was need neither of Bishop nor Pope" (1845), it was now a matter of *display* rather than *need*; their power was not simply "dormant" (1845), but it "had no prominence" (1878). Elsewhere, however, the language of dormancy was retained.[19] Despite his intention not to change the substance of the *Essay*, his revision tended to bring it into line as much as possible with the thesis he had developed in the 1850s and 60s that historical change in the dogmatic realm was more apparent than real.

The *Essay*, unread for so many years, had reconquered its author.[20] Two phrases (italicized below) which Newman added in 1878, one at the beginning and the other at the end of what was now Chapter IV, Section III, "The Papal Supremacy," stand in stark contrast to the tentative tone in which he had been accustomed to speak of his treatment of the development of the papacy.

> The *Sacramentum Unitatis* was acknowledged on all hands; the mode of fulfilling and the means of securing it would vary with the occasion; and the determination of its essence, its seat, and its laws would be a gradual supply for a gradual necessity.
> This is but natural, and is parallel to instances which happen daily, *and may be so considered without prejudice to the divine right whether of the Episcopate or of the Papacy.*

> More ample testimony for the Papal Supremacy, *as now professed by Roman Catholics*, is scarcely necessary than what is contained in these passages [from Barrow on the Supremacy]: the simple question

---

"changes" was not so welcome in the revised edition, and may have led to its suppression.

[18] Chadwick, pp. 189 ff; above, Ch. XI, note 13.

[19] *Dev*, pp. 165-167; ed. Cameron, pp. 208 f (IV, III, 2-4).

[20] Maurice Nédoncelle, "Newman et Blondel," *NS*, 6 (1964), 110. But in contrast to Nédoncelle, I do not think that the reconquest was total. The epistemological insights gathered in the *Grammar of Assent* remained dominant over the historian's approach which had been so urgent c. 1845.

is, whether the clear light of the fourth and fifth centuries may be fairly taken to illuminate the dim notices of the preceding.

What he was defending now, it is clear, were the dogmatic claims of Vatican I. The Council had left no ambivalence about the claims that Christ had made Peter the visible head of the church; that the Roman Pontiffs were sucessors of Peter in this office by divine right; and that the primacy consisted in the highest power of jurisdiction over the whole church, bishops as well as lay people. A point that touches historical material very closely is the claim that this succession of popes after Peter was "perpetual," had "always" been the case and had suffered no gap.[21] In thus associating his argument for the papal development with the beliefs expressed in Vatican I, Newman was unwittingly casting a decisive vote in favor of one of the two approaches which had been mixed in the first edition, and remained so in the third. The "unfulfilled prophecy" motif with its corresponding view of history to the effect that many years elapsed before any church leader in Rome considered himself a successor of Peter was allowed to remain, though now more or less as a vestigial remnant. The theme of dormant, or rather, unexercised power was strengthened and made to bear the weight of the argument.

Newman's theory of developments in Christian doctrine and church structures was therefore more consistent in the third edition of 1878 than in his original *Essay*. It treated evidence of true substantive evolution in the papal institution as a matter of outward appearance. Where the evidence did not let itself be so construed, Newman resorted to his old idea of unfulfilled prophecy, and so left the door open a crack for a realistic assessment of the historical situation, though on a level which no longer mattered. In fact he felt entitled to uphold the historical thesis that the papacy was from the first an accoutrement possessed by the church, though the realization of it only sank in gradually and less than universally. The breakthrough to a kind of historical thinking consonant with critical method was presaged in the first edition of *Development*, but the revision represented a step backwards, historiographically speaking. By pushing his insights on the nature of faith and its relationship to reason and science to the utmost (such as he had developed them in his *Grammar of Assent*), Newman had elaborated an approach which relieved him of the task of settling historico-theological problems critically. All this does not

---

[21] DS, nos. 3056-3058.

mean in the least that he slipped into or encouraged any kind of theological obscurantism. It simply means that of the various imaginative lines he embarked upon to render Christianity credible to its cultured despisers, he pursued the line of his University Sermons and rather neglected that of historical criticism.[22]

On the periphery of this increasingly consistent view of developments in church structure as merely accidental and apparent we find a few statements of Newman's which signal a more radical assimilation of historical consciousness, but which he did not follow through. The principle instance consists of the remarks he made on one of his last Anglican attempts to come to grips with the papacy and its claims, "The Catholicity of the Anglican Church" (1840). When he came to reissue it in *Essays Critical and Historical*, II (1871), he replied at some length to his own earlier arguments.[23] If the papacy is a development, he had argued earlier, whence did it derive its legitimation? It is in the nature of developments to continue. Granting that papal power was an apt means of cementing communion in the Middle Ages, why could not the peaceful coexistence of national churches be its counterpart later on? "Why should it not be the intention of Divine Providence, as on the one hand, still to recognize His Church when contracted into a monarchy, so also not to forsake her when relaxed and dissolved again into a number of aristocratic fragments?" To which the Newman of 1871 replied in a footnote:

> "Why not?" because, in fact, it is *not* so dissolved; doubtless, *were* it so dissolved, were the Pope as indistinct a power as he was in the first centuries, and the Bishops as practically independent, the Church would still be the Church.[24]

Lest one feel that this unabashed appeal to fact apart from dogmatic considerations is merely a brief rhetorical thrust without further signi-

---

[22] Compare J. Derek Holmes, "Newman on Faith and History," *Philosophical Studies*, 21 (1973), 202-216, the latest of a series of articles by Holmes on Newman as historian. The controversy between him and Josef Altholz on the question has been analyzed by Martin J. Svaglic in *Victorian Prose*, ed. D. J. Delaura, pp. 156-160. See also Maurice Nédoncelle, "Newman et Blondel," *NS*, 6 (1964), 111-115; Thomas S. Bokenkotter, *Cardinal Newman as an Historian* (Louvain: Pub. Universitaires, 1959), and of course Chadwick, *From Bossuet to Newman*, *passim*, e.g. p. 248: the revised edition of *Dev*, in comparison with the original, "weakened the 'freedom' of the appeal to history."

[23] See above, Ch. IV.

[24] *Essays Critical and Historical*, II, 44, cf. p. 94. Joseph Ratzinger, *Das neue Volk Gottes* (Düsseldorf: Patmos, 1969), pp. 142 f., is too striking a parallel to pass over.

ficance, one must examine the thirty-five page "Note" Newman attached to the same essay in 1871.

The doctrine which he had made the cardinal point of his Anglican ecclesiology was the apostolic succession of (Anglican) bishops. Now Newman was prepared to accept the historical criticism of such as Chillingworth and Macaulay against the naive acceptation of this doctrine, which would postulate an unbroken chain of valid consecrations back to the apostles. Though it would devastate his position of 1840, he insisted that it was a matter of indifference to Roman Catholic apologetics. His reasons are interesting. For the Catholic, he maintained, the apostolic succession of bishops is only a "theological inference" from the "standing fact of the Church, the Visible and One Church, the reproduction and succession of herself age after age." [25] With the church as a whole seen to be apostolic on the evidence of her unity, her continuity, her life, the mere factualness of the apostolic descent of bishops is of lesser moment. The basic apostolicity of the church as a whole even heals whatever rifts may develop in the episcopal lineage, so that "to Catholics the certainty of Apostolic Orders is not a point of prime necessity, yet they possess it; and for Anglicans it is absolutely indispensable, yet they have it not."

What emerges here is a far-reaching relativization of the doctrine of apostolic succession, which is equally a component of the Vatican doctrine of papal primacy. There seems to be no inherent reason why such a relativization could not be analogously applied to all church structures. This would concentrate and locate their theological import in their relationship to the purposes they were created to serve. In this way a reconciliation between theology and history could come about on a far more satisfactory basis than the postulate of merely apparent change which his theory of development had become. But Newman would hold such an approach in reserve for cases in which it seemed unavoidable, necessary. The papacy was, for him, no such case as yet.

This relativizing trait, though a peripheral one in relation to the main course of his thought, brings us back to what was in fact the constant and irreducible core of Newman's Roman Catholic stance regarding doctrines of papal power: that is, that the well-considered judgment of the church could be trusted to define what are the respective powers of its various officers. If the church at length de-

---

[25] *Essays Critical and Historical*, II, 89, see passage starting on p. 84.

clared that the pope was supreme in ecclesiastical jurisdiction and infallible when speaking *ex cathedra*, that declaration bore all the signs of credibility and all contrary historical evidence only amounted to a series of difficulties which could eventually be explained. These difficulties were to himself far from insuperable. This basic attitude persisted from the time he was writing the *Essay on Development* to the end of his life.[26] There is no vacillation whatsoever on this position. Given the state of the evidence as he saw it, the antecedent probabilities properly took charge. Papal supremacy was from first to last a case in which one could fit the facts to a dogmatically given pattern, without loss in intellectual integrity.

One more theme of Vatican ecclesiology which Newman endorsed implicitly may enable us at long last to sum up and conclude this discussion of Newman's thinking on the dogma of papal primacy as a possible development. That is the theme of "divine right." Vatican I anathematized anyone so presumptuous as to declare that the primacy claimed for Peter and for his successors as Roman Pontiffs was not founded by Christ the Lord himself and thus of divine right.[27] Newman was chary of divine-right talk; it ill suited his more grandiose visions of church history as a succession of fulfilments of prophecy up to the medieval apogee, for one thing. His objection would be that it said too little rather than too much. Moreover, he was aware that all developments in history have their human component too.[28] He did not try to sift out what was human from what was divine, as most of those who distinguish divine and human right do.[29] Nevertheless he avowed that the comparatively cautious definition-anathema of Vatican I expressed what he had always held.[30]

But how was this divine-right character of the papal supremacy of jurisdiction covered or anchored in the framework of Newman's development thought? In other words, how did he see it to be a matter of revelation? This is the crucial theological question; Newman

---

[26] Cf. the letter to Henry Wilberforce of 1846, presented in my Introduction and the interpolations (above, Ch. IX, notes 33, 39 and 41) that Newman made while transcribing it in 1876, *L & D*, XI, 190; compare *ibid.*, XX, 304-309, and his letter of 1885 to an unidentified author, "Livius," in Holmes, "Newman on Faith and History," p. 213.

[27] DS, 3058.

[28] Cf. Harper, *Cardinal Newman*, p. 55 (letter to Mrs. William Froude of 29 May 1844).

[29] On the futility of such attempts, see Paul Misner, "Papal Primacy in a Pluriform Polity," *Journal of Ecumenical Studies*, 11 (1974), 248-251.

[30] We shall see that this is no exaggeration in Ch. XV below.

seems again to provide an option to his reader in considering it. One may suppose that Christ let Peter know his awesome responsibilities, the potentialities of which required the developments of centuries to be called forth. This would be the middle way between the postulate of absolute immutability and authentic historical change which seems to characterize Newman's settled views, as in the letter to Flanagan. It cannot be falsified and certainly not proved. However, the immense apparatus of the *Essay*, even in its revised form, contains within itself a more complex account of the revealed character of the papacy, one which can embrace the relativizing trait we have noticed in connection with the apostolic succession of bishops.

Here we face three levels of discourse or three concentric treatments of church unity, of which only the deepest and widest is set forth absolutely—the first two deriving their force from the third. First there are the peremptory-sounding statements in *Development*, chapter IV, section III, number 8 (in the revised edition), about the necessity of a monarchical power in the Church as in a kingdom. This argument purported to establish the papal supremacy as a part of Christianity, not merely by organizational necessity, but by divine institution, for

> it is impossible, if we may so speak reverently, that an Infinite Wisdom, which sees the end from the beginning, in decreeing the rise of an universal Empire, should not have decreed the development of a sovereign ruler.

However, if this stage were to be taken in isolation, the argument would be neither reverent nor convincing. After all, Newman himself had recognized that, though God makes use of human institutions, he may do so for a time, like the monarchy in Israel, and then discard them. In this regard, too, God respects the historical nature of his instruments. "The Jewish polity was an element of earth, made divine by His presence, and while His presence lasted; when He withdrew it, it was again earthly, as it had been at first." [31] If God is to be represented as giving the papacy perpetual duration, this must be made clear in the scriptures—it cannot be deduced from Blackstonian or other political analysis. And Newman recognized this, too; thus, in 1844, he linked the divine right of the papacy with "the prophetic promise to St. Peter as recorded in xvi of St. Matthew." [32]

---

[31] *SD*, p. 97.
[32] Note 28 above; see my Ch. X.

But in the revised edition at least Newman laid too little stress on Matthew 16 to allow the thought that he rested his case for the divine right of papal supremacy principally on this promise, which is nevertheless the clearest that scripture has to offer. The first stage, therefore, is, on Newman's own grounds, not apodictic.

The second stage is broader, deeper, and to Newman much more solid. It brings in Newman's view of the church as a whole, and regards in the first place not so much its organizational set-up as the international unity that should characterize it as an Empire: what I have called in this work his "kingdom-ecclesiology." On this level he had long dealt with the question of whether the church is of human or divine make, a result of revelation and divine grace or a purely human creation, a response, perhaps, to revelation and divine grace but no more. In a sermon called "The Church and the World," he noted that God made use of worldly instruments to further his designs in the world, which explains the assimilation by Jewry and Christendom of so many elements from their pagan surroundings or past. As a history could be written of the Israelite nation on purely natural principles, and as this history would seem to be the parallel of so many other nations' histories, with its rise, limited duration, and fall, so one could take a similar external view of Christianity. I may be pardoned for quoting the following passage at length:

> Its history [Christianity's] is that of a certain principle of universal empire, repressed and thwarted by circumstances; its conquests, indeed, were achieved by moral instruments, "weapons not carnal," as St. Paul speaks, but still they were conquests; and it may be compared to empires of this world, to the conquests of Nebuchadnezzar, or of the Romans, made with the sword; or, again, it may be spoken of as a philosophy, and compared to the philosophies of men. But if it be an empire, if it be a philosophy, as it had its rise, it will have its fall. This is what unbelievers prophesy. They look out calmly and confidently for the fall of Christianity at length, because it rose. Since they read of its beginning, they look for its end; since the world preceded it, they think the world will outlive it. Well, *and were not Scripture pledged that it should continue to the end*, when Christ shall come, I see nothing to startle us, though it were to fall, and other religions to succeed it. God works by human means. As He employs individual men, and inspires them, and yet they die; so, doubtless, He might employ a body or society of men, which at length, after its course of two thousand years, might come to an end. It might be withdrawn, as other gifts of God are withdrawn, when abused. Doubtless Christianity might be such; it might be destined to expire, just as an individual man expires. Nay, it *may* actually be destined so to expire; it may be

destined to age, to decay, and at length to die;—but we know that when it dies, at least the world will die with it. The world's duration is measured by it. If the Church dies, the world's time is run. The world shall never exult over the Church. If the Church falls sick, the world shall utter a wail for its own sake; for like Samson, the Church will bury all with it.[33]

Scriptural promises, therefore, are needed to make any claim of divine right and perpetuity believable, and scriptural promises are at hand. For the papacy as such? No, but for the imperial church, one kingdom over great parts, if not actually over the whole, of the world. Newman found his kingdom-ecclesiology confirmed in the age of the Fathers, besides being the obvious sense of scripture as taught by the church down through the ages. Now, the same basic objection can be made to the doctrine of the imperial church as to that of the papacy: it was not unambiguously revealed in the scripture (one needed the event to make plain what the prophecy was about), and it was not so in the beginning of the church, but was a later human development. For Newman, it was a truism that the *appearance* of the papacy must await the development of the world-wide kingdom that is the church. If, however, the latter is clearly but the unfolding of the divine plan, then what would be more probable than that the papal office, which fits so neatly into the imperial scheme, should be the fulfilment of the promise made to Peter, and hence *iuris divini*?

However, it must be admitted that this second stage does not entirely clinch the matter. The one church with imperial features is certain, but that it is headed by the pope cannot be proved out of scripture. Newman had first to find out which was the one Church, and this process fell within what he was later, in the *Grammar of Assent*, to call concrete reasonings. In concrete matter, coming to a certain conclusion must be based on experience and must make use of a cumulation of probabilities that are too manifold to be marshalled and too fleeting to be formulated. But having found that one Church of Christ with certainty, then if the pope is at the head of it and solemnly claims for his office Petrine authority, this also is certainly so. Thus the third stage, the only stage enjoying certainty, is reached.

For Newman the decisive step was to advance from his "classicist"

---

[33] *SD*, pp. 100 f.

view of the unity of the church in his Anglican time [34]to the view, for him actually more congenial, that the church was still and would remain to the end of time, "a body, visible, one, Catholic, and organized." [35]

---

[34] H. Fries, "J. H. Newman's Beitrag zum Verständnis der Tradition" in *Die mündliche Überlieferung*, p. 81.

[35] *Essays Critical and Historical*, II, 92, compare *Apo*, p. 55. Cf. N. Schiffers, *Die Einheit der Kirche nach John Henry Newman*, pp. 78-90, 235 f.

PART FOUR

COUNTERWEIGHTS TO ABSOLUTISM

CHAPTER FIFTEEN

BETWEEN THE LINES

If Newman had had no greater anxieties in his new religious communion than whether his hypothesis of developments would be allowed, he might have been a happy man. As it was, he gradually fell out with the dominant figures of the church in England and Rome and with some of the aims of the Neo-Ultramontane movement, a story well told by Wilfrid Ward, whose treatment of the subject remains unsurpassed by any other single author who deals in detail with Newman.[1] The new situation in which Newman found himself as a Roman Catholic in the second half of the nineteenth century gave rise to a fundamentally different problem for him—in connection with the papacy—than had been the case in his Anglican years. The application of the idea of developments to papal supremacy was basically a resolution of his Anglican (one can also say, his historical) problem. In his Catholic years he was faced with a problem of church governance and the *abuse* of that church authority which he had so largely endorsed from afar. His response to this issue was as slow in coming, as agonized, and as original and fruitful as his *Essay on Development*.

It must be acknowledged that, apart from Wilfrid Ward, few Newmanists have recognized until recently how large this problem of ecclesiastical abuses loomed in Newman's theological *oeuvre*. Nédoncelle's and Coulson's contributions to this recognition will be mentioned in their place. For now, it suffices to say that Newman did not produce a clear and unveiled statement on the matter until 1877, when he republished his *Prophetical Office* of 1837 in a third edition and provided it with a Preface of ninety-four pages. This Preface, and the *Letter to the Duke of Norfolk* which preceded it by two years, were not the focus of theologians' attention during the first two periods of Newman's influence, which centered respectively on the theory of development and the psychology of faith.[2] Until theologians

---

[1] See his *Life* of Newman (1912) and also his *William George Ward and the Catholic Revival* (1893) with its background material on nineteenth-century Ultramontanism and the new turn it took during the pontificate of Pius IX (1846-1878).

[2] Dupuy, "Newman's Influence in France," *OS*, p. 148.

were ready themselves to face the problems of abuse of authority in the church, Newman's views on authority and freedom were left mostly to the appreciation of social scientists.[3] With Vatican II this state of affairs has changed.

If one were to plot a graph of Newman's attitude toward the primatial powers of the pope throughout his life in the Catholic fold, one would have a very difficult job correlating the psychological and the theological factors. I have no competence in psychology, but at least superficial notice must be taken of the frustrations that Newman felt in the church of Pius IX and that redoubtable Ultramontane, Manning (converted 1851, Archbishop of Westminster 1865-1892). I am sympathetic to the view that these frustrations led to a progressively worse depression and disability to cope, even intellectually, with hierarchical authority. The turning point was the occasion Charles Kingsley gave him to defend both himself and Roman Catholicism by writing the *Apologia pro Vita Sua* in 1864. At this point he still had no better advice to offer those troubled by the oppressive course that Roman ecclesiastical authority was following than to be silent and submit, until Providence should induce a change of heart and policy in the leaders of the church or otherwise overrule their faulty aims. Very slowly he came to a theological basis for resisting church authority in limited but significant ways, while Pius IX and his uncritical supporters were digging in their heels even more firmly than before: the Syllabus of Errors (1864) and the activity surrounding the First Vatican Council (1869-70) indicate what I mean. When occasions presented themselves (Gladstone's pamphlet on the Vatican Decrees in 1874 and the republication of his anti-Roman *Prophetical Office*, now retitled *The Via Media*, in 1877), he elaborated themes new to his readers, explaining why absolutism was out of place in even the most authoritarian church and vindicating the rights of conscience and of a certain theological autonomy even vis-à-vis papal power.

Maurice Nédoncelle points out that in his one purely political essay, on the Crimean War,[4] Newman wrote: "A State or polity implies two things, Power on the one hand, Liberty on the other; a Rule and a Constitution." One could describe the course of Newman's

---

[3] Harold J. Laski, *Studies in the Problem of Sovereignty* (New Haven: Yale Univ. Press, 1917), ch. IV, pp. 121-210; Terence Kenny, *The Political Thought of John Henry Newman* (London: Longmans, Green, 1957).

[4] Nédoncelle, "Newman, théologien des abus de l'Eglise," *Oecumenica*, 2 (1967), 127, citing Newman, "Who's to Blame?" (1855), in *DA*, p. 325. Cf. *L & D*, XVI, 328 and 400.

thought on papal power after *Development* as a struggle for theological balance between these same two elements in *church* polity. For the first several years, he saw no very great reason to depart from the line of his kingdom ecclesiology, which stressed "Rule" one-sidedly. Only reluctantly, impeded by the anti-Liberal arguments which he had been honing for a lifetime, did he come to introduce a measure of "Constitution" into his theological considerations on the church.[5]

One can find statements based on extreme Roman views of papal absolutism. An early one is put in the mouth of the protagonist of Newman's conversion novel, *Loss and Gain* (1848). Speaking of the authority of apostles, Charles Reding declares:

> What that authority was, we see in St. Paul's conduct towards St. Timothy. He placed him in the See of Ephesus, he sent him a charge, and, in fact, he was his overseer or Bishop. He had the care of all the Churches. Now, this is precisely the power which the Pope claims, and has ever claimed; and, moreover, he has claimed it, as being the *successor*, and the sole proper successor of the Apostles, though Bishops may be improperly such also. And hence Catholics call him Vicar of Christ, Bishop of Bishops, and the like; and, I believe, consider that he, in a pre-eminent sense, is the one pastor or ruler of the Church, the source of jurisdiction, the judge of controversies, and the centre of unity, as having the powers of the Apostles, and especially of St. Peter.[6]

Pusey elicited from Newman, at a much later date (1867), a still more intransigent statement, characterizing the pope's jurisdiction as "unlimited and despotic." [7] This declaration cannot be pressed, however, because Newman was exasperated at Pusey and his unrealistic hopes for corporate reunion at the time.

If we return to the years before Newman's disillusionment over the leadership of the hierarchy, we find a more balanced view in the sixth of his *Twelve Lectures addressed in 1850 to the Party of the Religious Movement of 1833*.[8] Here his fine touch for the phenomenological

---

[5] Cf. John Coulson, "Newman on the Church—His Final View, Its Origins and Influence," *OS*, p. 132; compare Ward, *Life*, I, 134.

[6] *Loss and Gain*, p. 394. Newman, perhaps aware that this statement unduly derogates episcopal standing, provided a footnote reference to *Anti-Febronio* (1767) of Francesco Antonio Zaccaria, S.J. Compare Newman's *Lectures on the Present Position of Catholics in England* (1851), p. 112.

[7] Ward, *Life of Cardinal Newman*, II, 217; similarly in *Sermons Preached on Various Occasions*, uniform ed., p. 286.

[8] In *Certain Difficulties Felt by Anglicans in Catholic Teaching* (hereinafter cited as *Diff*), I, 176-186.

description of the church was allowed free rein, for the burden of his argument is how the Church Catholic, as opposed to any branch church like the Church of England, is equipped to deal with the constant pretensions and importunities of the State, which would like to have a servant-church in the sense of a completely subordinate jurisdiction. With a rarely-equalled command of the language and its oratorical possibilities, he draws out the contrast between the aggressive State, striking only to find that it cannot hit a vital spot, and the resilient church, always too supple to suffer a mortal blow. Even a blow at the head, at the pope does not have the desired effect.

> The Church triumphs over the world's jurisdiction everywhere, because, though she is everywhere, for that very reason she is in the fulness of her jurisdiction nowhere. Ten thousand subordinate authorities have been planted round, or have issued from, that venerable Chair where sits the plenitude of Apostolical Power. Hence, when she would act, the blow is broken, and concussion avoided, by the innumerable springs, if I may use the word, on which the celestial machinery is hung.[9]

In the context Newman is not concerned with the questions of origins and early developments, but with recent history and with the shape of church-state relations in his new communion. Nevertheless, it is interesting to note that he does not really regard the church as being set up along consistently centralistic lines, even if he often seems to say so. Authority in the church does not reside in one man alone; rather, the "celestial machinery" (*ius divinum!*) includes auxiliary generators and protective devices as well as a central power.

A hint of the same complexity occurs in the sermon, "Order, the Witness and Instrument of Unity" (1853). After expounding a classic picture of church order according to Ignatius of Antioch (on the supposition that the ecumenical power of the popes had coexisted with the local authority of bishops from the first by divine right) and after evoking once more the *sacramentum unitatis*, Newman apostrophized Bishop Ullathorne as "no longer the mere representative of him who has the plenitude of jurisdiction [the pope], but as the shepherd of a flock..., knit into the body of the faithful whom you rule and whom you serve" and in a fashion responsible to them.[10] That a bishop should take counsel with his clergy in a synod (the occasion for which he was preaching) was as traditional and indispens-

---

[9] *Ibid.*, I, 180.
[10] *Sermons Preached on Various Occasions* (1867, hereafter *Occ Serm*), p. 196.

able a part of well-ordered church life for Newman as it was that the
hierarchy should "consult" the faithful in matters of doctrine.[11]

The lectures delivered in connection with the founding of the
Catholic University in Ireland furnish us with a piquant example of
Newman's changing attitude toward the practical wisdom of papal
policies.[12] While pondering what he should include in the discourses,
he received a letter from Frederick Lucas which encouraged him to
make the most of the pope's authority in backing the costly project.[13]
At any rate, in his introductory lecture,[14] he threw caution to the wind,
presenting it as a lesson of history that the popes' policies had been as
wise as their solemn declarations had been infallible.[15] Later on a
chastened Newman would rue his imprudence.

> I had been accustomed to believe that, over and above that attribute
> of infallibility which attached to the doctrinal decisions of the Holy
> See, a gift of sagacity had in every age characterized its occupants,
> so that we might be sure, as experience taught us, without its being
> a dogma of faith, that what the Pope determined was the very measure,
> or the very policy, expedient for the Church at the time when he
> determined. . . . I am obliged to say that a sentiment which history

---

[11] See Newman, *On Consulting the Faithful in Matters of Doctrine*, ed. with an
introduction by John Coulson (1961). The allusion, of course, is to the controversy
innocently unleashed by Newman's attempt to keep the *Rambler* circle and the
bishops on speaking terms in 1859. Cf. further Josef Altholz, *The Liberal Catholic
Movement in England* (London: Burns & Oates, 1962); Hugh MacDougall, *The
Acton-Newman Relations*; Damian McElrath, *Richard Simpson 1820-1876* (Louvain:
Pub. Univ. de Louvain, 1972); Vincent Blehl, "Newman's Delation: Some
Hitherto Unpublished Letters," *Dublin Review*, no. 486 (1960-61), 296-305 and
idem, "Newman, the Bishops and *The Rambler*," *Downside Review*, 90 (1972),
20-41; Webster T. Patterson, *Newman: Pioneer for the Layman* (Washington:
Corpus Books, 1968).

[12] On the Catholic University and Newman's part in it see *L & D*, XV-
XVIII, *passim*, his "Memorandum about my Connection with the Catholic
University," in Newman, *Autobiographical Writings*, ed. Henry Tristram, pp.
280-333; Fergal McGrath, *Newman's University: Idea and Reality* (London: Long-
mans, Green, 1951); Dwight Culler, *The Imperial Intellect: A Study of Cardinal
Newman's Educational Ideal* (New Haven: Yale Univ. Press, 1955); and, refreshingly
critical of Newman's class-exclusive approach to higher education, which put him
at odds with Cardinal Cullen and later with Manning in England: Vincent
McClelland, *English Roman Catholics and Higher Education, 1830-1903* (Oxford:
Clarendon Press, 1973).

[13] Letter of 9 October 1851 in McGrath, p. 132.

[14] See the passage in the uniform edition of *Idea of a University*, pp. 10-18 and
also some sentences that he edited out of the uniform edition, in Ward's *Life*,
II, 558-559.

[15] Compare *Historical Sketches*, III, 142-167 (from 1854) with *ibid.*, II, xiii
(from 1857).

has impressed upon me, and impresses still, has been very considerably weakened as far as the present Pope is concerned, by the experience of the result of the policy which his chosen Counsellors had led him to pursue. I cannot help thinking in particular, that, if he had known more of the state of things in Ireland, he would not have taken up the quarrel about the higher education which his predecessor left him. . . . I was a poor innocent as regards the actual state of things in Ireland when I went there, and did not care to think about it, for I relied on the word of the Pope, but from the event I am led to think it not rash to say that I knew as much about Ireland as he did.[16]

There can be no question here of recounting all the misfortunes which affected Newman: the Achilles trial, the frustrations of being asked to make bricks without straw, the misunderstandings. The effect of it all, however, was to place in his way, however he might try to avoid it, the question of what measures are advisable in the face of a supernatural authority acting wrongheadedly. Only when he finally saw that there was no justification for certain persistent policies of his church superiors could he envisage working out an appropriate answer to the problem. When he did see it, he found two or three expressive metaphors to describe the situation and its effect on him. In an outpouring to Emily Bowles he wrote that the oppressive attention with which Ultramontanes and curial offices watched his utterances made impossible the kind of intellectual exchange on which a writer was dependent in the formation of his thought. "In former times, primitive and medieval, there was not the extreme centralization which now is in use." Controversies were carried on without calling for an immediate decision by Rome. "*Now*, if I, as a private priest, put anything into print, *Propaganda* answers me at once. How can I fight with such a chain on my arm? It is like the Persians driven on to fight *under the lash*." [17]

This was written the year that a feeling of being wasted had overwhelmed Newman, as recorded in his journal.[18] But even after the worst of that was over and the *Apologia* had shown that he was not going totally to waste, one finds another journal entry which describes, I think, the frame of mind, hardened, but healthier, with which he could approach the tasks which still awaited him: the *Grammar of*

---

[16] *Autobiographical Writings*, ed. Tristram, p. 320, dated 9 Jan. 1873.

[17] *L & D*, XX, 447, dated 19 May 1863. The image reoccurs in *Apo.* p. 239; cf. G. Egner, *Apologia pro Charles Kingsley* (London: Sheed and Ward, 1969), pp. 188-197.

[18] *Autobiographical Writings*, pp. 253-260, dated 21 January 1863.

Assent in which he pulled together the elements of his religious epistemology, and even more, a constructive theology of church structures and their abuse. On 30 October 1867 he opened his journal again—it was not a frequent habit of his—and recalled that he had said to Cardinal Barnabò of Propaganda, "Deus viderit!"

> And now, alas, I fear that in one sense the iron has entered into my soul. I mean that confidence in any superiors whatever never can blossom again within me. I never shall feel easy with them. I shall (I feel) always think they will be taking some advantage of me—that at length their way will lie across mine, and that my efforts will be displeasing to them. I shall ever be suspicious that they or theirs have secret unkind thoughts of me, and that they deal with me with some arrière pensée. And, as it is my happiness so to be placed as not to have much intercourse with them, therefore, while I hope ever loyally to fulfill their orders, it is my highest gain and most earnest request to them, that they would let me alone—and, since I do not want to initiate any new plan of any kind, that, if they can, they would keep their hands off me.[19]

The chain, the lash, the iron in one's soul—such expressions are a measure of the disillusionment which Newman felt. It must be remembered that, as an old Tory, he saw nothing wrong in personal and societal relations of the feudal type, the essence of which is loyalty.[20] It was experience of the contemporary Roman Catholic exploitation of this tradition that enabled him to question and probe it. Given Newman's temperament and background, it was probably necessary that the malfunction of the ecclesiastical machinery be keenly felt, before he would deal critically with it. It was not enough for him to have recognized that hangers-on and careerists would always affect the papacy negatively.[21] He had to be convinced that the papacy itself was entangled, by the set policy of recent popes, in a course of action opposed to the essential interests of the church, and that the effects of this were such as encouraged "toadyism" and discouraged any independent thought.[22]

This brings us to the Temporal Power of the popes, as the question

---

[19] Ward, *Life*, II, 201-202. The Journal entry, under date of 30 Oct. 1867, is given in full in *Autobiographical Writings*, pp. 262-63.

[20] See *Diff*, II, 268.

[21] As he let on as late as 1875, cf. *Diff*, II, 297: "the Rock of St. Peter on its summit enjoys a pure and serene atmosphere, but there is a great deal of Roman *malaria* at the foot of it."

[22] *Autobiographical Writings*, p. 273, dated 10 Sept. 1876.

of the papal states is often referred to. It was on this question that
Newman's very silence seemed disloyalty. During his brief connection
with *The Rambler*, Newman, writing anonymously, had become virtually the only Catholic of Europe to question the necessity for a last-
ditch defense of the papal states, threatened as they were by the
nationalism of the *Risorgimento*, the statecraft of Cavour, the vacilla-
tions of Louis Napoleon, and the hostility of British liberalism.[23]
Otherwise he held his silence until 1866, despite pressures on him to
conform to the obligatory Catholic line that the papal domains were
being annexed illegitimately (which was true, but beside the point).[24]
Manning, for example, at this time provost of Westminster, declared
that "he who lends a hand or a tongue to the dissolution" of the pope's
Temporal Power in Italy contributes "to the dissolution of Christian
Europe," and "will purchase judgment to himself." [25] Of course,
W. G. Ward's *Dublin Review* and, later, the London *Tablet*, chimed in
with disingenuous questions about Newman's failure to take a stand.[26]

   The prospects for dissent on this question among Catholics became
less favorable with the publication, a few months after Newman's
Apologia in 1864, of the papal encyclical *Quanta Cura* and a curious
list of condemned opinions called the Syllabus of Errors. Most of
the positions condemned were those of the liberal opponents of the
papal states; the document had the effect of causing Catholics who
were working for one or another kind of *modus vivendi* with the contemporary European world to take down their shingles and put up
their shutters, for fear of being personally disavowed by Rome.[27] In

---

[23] Letters signed "O. H." and "J. O." in *The Rambler* (May, 1859) 102-105
and 109-113, reprinted in *L & D*, XIX, 527-529 and 534-538; cf. *Wellesley Index
to Victorian Periodicals*, ed. Walter E. Houghton, E. R. Houghton, J. Altholz,
and D. McElrath (Toronto: Univ. of Toronto Press, 1966—), II, 777, and
Hugh MacDougall, *The Acton-Newman Relations*, pp. 58-65, who was the first to
recognize that practically all the "correspondents" on this issue were Newman
himself (cf. *L & D*, XIX, 179).

[24] Ward, *Life of Cardinal Newman*, I, 521-526, 654; II, 215. The mood of the
papal court was described by Odo Russell, whose reports to the Foreign Office
are printed in Noel Blakiston, ed., *The Roman Question* (London: Chapman and
Hall, 1962).

[25] George Huntston Williams, "*Omnium christianorum pastor et doctor*: Vatican
I et l'Angleterre victorienne," *Nouvelle revue théologique*, 96 (1974), 135, citing
H. E. Manning, *Temporal Sovereignty of the Popes* (London, 1860), republished in
The Temporal Power of the Vicar of Jesus Christ, 3d ed. (London: Burns and Oates,
1880), p. 2. See also Edmund Sheridan Purcell, *Life of Cardinal Manning* (London:
Macmillan, 1896), II, 152 f.

[26] *Ibid.*, II, 387-391.

[27] See Roger Aubert, *Le Pontificat de Pie IX* (Paris: Bloud et Gay, 1963),

this atmosphere Newman put aside a project he had considered of answering Pusey's *Eirenicon* on the matter of the papal power.[28] But when the instruction came from Bishop Ullathorne, that all sermons preached on 7 October 1866 be devoted to the obligations of the faithful toward the Holy See, he spoke at length.

What he did *not* say is significant. He did *not* say that the Temporal Power was *necessary* for the papal primacy or its exercise, as Manning, who had been named Archbishop of Westminster in the preceding year, did. Rather he suggested that, as the temporal domains of the pope had been left to him by men, not God, so it was very possible that men, though unjustly, would take them away.[29] He refrained deliberately from calling for the return of the territories already lost to the pope, something that all other leading Catholic figures, including Döllinger, had done.[30] He even hinted that it might be God's will to let the Temporal Power cease:

> We pray when we are uncertain, not when we are certain. If we were quite sure what God intended to do, whether to continue the temporal power of the Pope or to end it, we should not pray.

And again:

> Temporal power has been the means of the Church's independence for a very long period; but, as her bishops have lost it a long while, and are not the less Bishops still, so would it be as regards her Head, if he also lost his.

---

pp. 224-276 or Karl Otmar von Aretin, *The Papacy and the Modern World* (New York: McGraw-Hill, 1970), p. 88 f; Newman's reaction: Ward, *Life*, II, 81 and *L & D*, XXI, 378. Cf. Damian McElrath, *The Syllabus of Pius IX: Some Reactions in England* (Louvain: Pub. Univ., 1964).

[28] Edward Bouverie Pusey, *An Eirenicon* (London, 1865); Newman answered his strictures on Catholic devotion to Mary in *A Letter addressed to the Rev. E. B. Pusey, D.D., on Occasion of his Eirenicon* (1865), reprinted in *Diff*, II, 1-170. But the second installment, on the papacy, was never attempted, cf. MS note of 26 February 1866 in file A 5 23 at the Birmingham Oratory; *Diff*, II, 17; *Autobiographical Writings*, p. 265, and Ward, *Life*, II, 223-228.

[29] Newman, "The Pope and the Revolution" in *Occ Serm*, p. 292. Indeed he went further and asked, p. 293: "His enemies have succeeded, as it would seem, in persuading at least a large portion of his subjects to side with them. This is a real and very trying difficulty. While his subjects are for him, no one can have a word to say against his temporal rule; but who can force a Sovereign on a people which deliberately rejects him? You may attempt it for a while, but at length the people, if they persist, will get their way."

[30] My analysis of this sermon is substantially that of Hugh A. MacDougall, *The Acton-Newman Relations*, pp. 99-102. For this detail, cf. *Occ Serm*, p. 307, as well as Newman's note appended to a letter of his of 13 Feb. 1860, quoted by MacDougall, p. 63, and printed in *L & D*, XIX, 303.

For:

> To say that the Church cannot live except in a particular way, is
> to make it "subject to elements of the earth." The Church is not the
> creature of times and places, of secular politics or popular caprice.
> Our Lord maintains her by means of this world, but these means are
> necessary to her only while He gives them; when He takes them away,
> they are no longer necessary. He works by means, but He is not
> bound to means. He has a thousand ways of maintaining her; He can
> support her life, not by bread only, but by every word that proceedeth
> out of His mouth. If He takes away one defence, He will give another
> instead. We know nothing of the future: our duty is to direct our
> course according to our day; not to give up of our own act the means
> which God has given us to maintain His Church withal, but not to
> lament over their loss, when He has taken them away.[31]

Newman's "non-conformism" in this question of the Temporal
Power of the popes, and at the same time his faith in the spiritual
primacy of popes with or without Papal States, are strikingly illu-
strated in a letter written shortly after his sermon on "The Pope and
the Revolution." He wrote in part:

> Not till some great convulsions take place, which may go on for
> years & years, and when I can do neither good nor harm, and religion
> is felt to be in the midst of trials red-tapism will go out of Rome,
> and a better spirit come in, and Cardinals & Archbishops will have
> some of the reality they had, amid many abuses, in the middle ages.
> At present things are in appearance as effete, though in a different
> way, (thank God) as they were in the tenth century. We are sinking
> into a sort of Novatianism, the heresy which the early Popes so
> strenuously resisted. Instead of aiming at being a worldwide power,
> we are shrinking into ourselves, narrowing the lines of communion,
> trembling at freedom of thought, and using the language of dismay and
> despair at the prospect before us, instead of, with the high spirit of the
> warrior, going out conquering and to conquer ... I believe the
> Pope's spirit is simply that of martyrdom, and it is utterly different
> from that implied in these gratuitous shriekings which surround his
> throne. But the Power of God is abroad upon the earth, and He will
> settle things in spite of what cliques and parties may decide. I am
> glad you like my sermon—the one thing I wished to oppose is the
> coward despairing spirit of the day.[32]

With this sermon he raised his head, warily, and disclosed his
position in the no man's land between those attacking and those

---

[31] *Occ Serm*, pp. 309-313.
[32] Letter of Newman to Emily Bowles, dated 11 Nov. 1866, in *L & D*,
XXII, 314 f; cf. Ward, *Life*, II, 163.

defending the pope. He too wished to defend what he conceived to be the pope's genuine prerogatives, but in the circumstances Pius IX could have used one of Newman's favorite tags [33] against him: "*Non tali auxilio!*" As it was, Manning and Msgr. George Talbot (a sort of liaison man at the Vatican, unfortunately fairly intimate with Pius IX) reinforced each other's suspicions about where Newman's heart was. Not only did he fail to see how crucial the Temporal Power was; he also was avid for educating sons of gentlemen to the point where worldly concerns would make them disloyal too. This was Talbot's view of Newman in May, 1867: "Dr. Newman is the most dangerous man in England, and you will see that he will make use of the laity against your Grace." [34] Viewed from the other side, he seemed more of a pathetic figure, a broken reed. Only with Bishop Ullathorne did some kind of mutual respect survive, and it was in a letter addressed to him during the Vatican Council that a famous unburdening of the heart became public knowledge. Crying out against the sharp practice of zealous Ultramontanes such as Manning and his allies in their loyalty to Pius IX, he called them "an aggressive and insolent faction." [35]

Through all this Newman never counselled disobedience to duly constituted authority, no matter how outrageous its measures.[36] Papal authority, needless to say, was even more immune to criticism than other hierarchical superiors. In the final chapter of the *Apologia*, we may detect with Coulson the first stirrings of what would become a thesis of interdependent functions in the church, subversive of all absolutism.[37] At the same time, we must note that active resistance to any commands of papal authority is in no wise envisaged, and that the notion of limitations in principle to the supreme authority in the

---

[33] Identified for the curious by Dessain in *L & D*, XXII, 315, footnote.

[34] Letter to Manning, in Purcell, *Life of Cardinal Manning*, II, 318.

[35] Charles Stephen Dessain, *John Henry Newman* (London: Thomas Nelson, 1966), 137-138; compare Ward, *Life*, II, 288; cf. Roger Aubert, *Vatican I*, p. 63.

[36] See, for instance, his advice to Acton, *L & D*, XIX, 503-524, esp. p. 523, with the studies cited by the editor.

[37] See references in notes 4, 5, and 11 above, also John Coulson, "The *Apologia* Revalued," in Coulson, A. M. Allchin and Meriol Trevor, *Newman: A Portrait Restored*, pp. 27-61; Edward Kelly, "The *Apologia* and the Ultramontanes," in *Newman's Apologia: A Classic Reconsidered*, ed. Vincent F. Blehl and F. X. Connolly (New York: Harcourt, Brace & World, 1964), pp. 26-46; and J. Derek Holmes, "How Newman Blunted the Edge of Ultramontanism," *Clergy Review*, 53 (1968), 353-362.

church is as yet totally lacking.[38] However, Newman would not rest content with a mystique of obedience, but would draw on unsuspected resources of mental vitality after the storm of Vatican I had passed.

---

[38] G. Egner, *Apologia pro Charles Kingsley*, as cited above note 17.

CHAPTER SIXTEEN

THE VATICAN DECREES AND THE PRIMACY
OF CONSCIENCE

The burning question on papal powers before and after Vatican I
was infallibility—the claim that the pope is able to proclaim truths of
faith infallibly on given occasions. My intention, however, is to
isolate as far as is practicable the more basic issue of papal *primacy* in
Newman's thought, that is, the pope's authority to command obedience, apart from the question of assent. Newman did distinguish the
two issues. Even when he had his difficulties with the notion of
the pope's infallibility, there was never any doubt in his mind about
his primacy. Once, in private notes written before the Council, he
even cited the pope's ruling authority as making it unlikely that he
would be personally infallible as well, on the principle that the combination of supreme executive and legislative (dogmatic teaching)
powers in one person would be, "as human politics teach us, too
great for man to sustain, and a temptation to abuse." [1] But it was
infallibility that stirred up most of the public clamor and private
anxieties that attended the Council. [2]

It was in this atmosphere, therefore, of high party feeling, of being
rushed, of excessive concentration on the one question of infallibility,
that our question, too, that of the pope's primacy of jurisdiction, was
discussed, formulated, and solemnly defined as a dogma of faith. Not
that one can say that the acceptance of this doctrine was not fully
deliberate or did not follow upon sufficient discussion in the council
aula. The most important change effected by the bishops in council
may be summed up by saying that they supplied the dialectic between

---

[1] Notes of 10 July 1866, in file A 5 23 at the Birmingham Oratory. On infallibility, see Gary Lease, *Witness to the Faith: Cardinal Newman on the Teaching Authority
of the Church;* C. S. Dessain, "What Newman Taught in Manning's Church,"
in *Infallibility in the Church: An Anglican-Catholic Dialogue,* by M. D. Goulder and
others (London: Darton, Longman & Todd, 1968), pp. 59-80; and J. Derek
Holmes, "Cardinal Newman and the First Vatican Council," *Annuarium Historiae
Conciliorum,* 1 (1969), 374-398.

[2] Cf. Roger Aubert, *Vatican I,* pp. 70-92; Ward, *Life of Cardinal Newman,* II,
279-289; Cuthbert Butler, *The Vatican Council* (London: Longmans, Green,
1930), I, 81-129; MacDougall, *The Acton-Newman Relations,* pp. 108-139.

papal and episcopal authority which was missing from the draft of the Roman theologians.[3]

It had been long intended by those who were responsible for planning and preparing for the council that it should discuss a wide-ranging "Constitutio" (or solemn conciliar pronouncement) *De Ecclesia*, including a section defining the primacy of the Roman Pontiff. Events, however, had led Pope Pius to cause a chapter on the infallibility of the pope to be added to the schema (in March 1870), and then (in April) to dispose that the chapters about the papacy be taken by themselves as an independent "Constitutio" and be submitted to the council Fathers before the rest of *De Ecclesia*. As it turned out, the Council was not able to deal with the other chapters of the original schema *De Ecclesia*, since Rome was taken by the Italian armies in September 1870 and the Council was not reconvened. But in the amendments which the Council Fathers made in the schema relative to the Petrine primacy one sees that they insisted that due attention be paid to the episcopacy, so that the church would not appear to be structured solely around the Roman Pontiff.

The first sign of this determination to correct the onesidedness of the proposed schema was the amendment adopted in the proem (DS, nos. 3050-51) of *Pastor aeternus*. The schema set forth Christ's will to found a church: "That all may be one," He established in Peter the everlasting principle and the visible foundation of unity in faith and communion. This simple pattern of pope and faithful was not satisfactory, and the Council added the following intermediary member between "that all may be one" and "he established in Peter":

> He sent the apostles, whom he had chosen out of the world, as he himself had been sent by the Father. Likewise he wished there to be pastors and teachers in his church till the end of the world.
>
> But that the episcopacy itself be one and undivided, and in order to maintain the whole multitude of the faithful in unity of faith and communion by means of the unity of the bishops (*per cohaerentes sibi invicem sacerdotes*), he established in Peter the foundation . . .

As is clear, there was no wish to deny or reduce the scale of the Roman primacy—the Fathers wanted merely to guard against the distortion that comes from speaking as if the pope were not merely the supreme, but the *only* authority in the church. Thus there was no opposition, not even from the "Minority," and very little disagreement, about

---

[3] Yves Congar, *L'Eglise de saint Augustine à l'époque moderne*, p. 443; C. Butler, *Vatican Council*, p. 332.

Chapters I and II of the Constitution, which treated of the primacy given to Peter and its continuation in the Roman Pontiffs.

When it came time to debate the third chapter, however, the problem became acute and was intensely discussed. The jurisdiction attributed to the pope is *universalis*: under it comes quite simply every real and juridical person in the church. It is *ordinaria*: that is, not delegated, but belonging to the office itself; *immediata*, i.e. it is within the power of the pope to exercise his jurisdiction directly, dispensing with the normal subordinate authorities; *vere episcopalis*, not merely supplemental to the basic pastoral jurisdiction with which bishops are invested, not merely an *officium inspectionis vel directionis* (DS, no. 3064); it is *suprema*, not in the exclusive sense, since an ecumenical council under the presidency of the pope has the same authority as the pope, but rather in the sense that there is no appeal from his final decision to another instance, not even to an ecumenical council; moreover it is specifically stated that no other power may licitly prevent any member of the church soever from appealing to the judgment of the pope.[4]

How could the pope's jurisdiction over the faithful in the whole world be ordinary and episcopal, without denying or at least reducing to a legal fiction the ordinary and immediate jurisdiction which the bishops exercise in their dioceses? This objection was repeatedly raised on the floor of the Council between June 9 and 14, 1870.[5] The solution hammered out between the Majority and the Minority was two-pronged: *jurisdictio ordinaria*, it was made clear, did not imply an every-day exercise of papal authority within the individual dioceses; was not therefore "ordinary" in the usual sense of the word, but in the canonical sense, which denoted merely that the jurisdiction in question belonged to the pope and the bishops respectively by virtue of their office and not by delegation. On the other hand, a whole additional paragraph was framed (DS, no. 3061) to make plain that the bishops are successors of the apostles in their own right and rule as true pastors in their dioceses. The inopportune and embarrassing procedure by which Manning and Pius IX managed to insert a phrase tending to obscure this balance in the final paragraph of Chapter III need not concern us here, since the amendment was accepted by the Council on the basis of Bishop Zinelli's explanation to the effect that

---

[4] Cf. Herbert Vorgrimler, "Jurisdiktionsprimat" in *LTK*, V, 1220-21; Hans Küng, *Structures of the Church* (New York: Nelson, 1964), pp. 230-244.

[5] Aubert, *Vatican I*, pp. 216, 224.

it was just another way of saying what had already been said elsewhere in the chapter on the pope's supreme power.[6]

It must be confessed that, when Newman came to interpret the Vatican Council, he overlooked or ignored this whole dialectic of papal and episcopal rule, preferring to take an idiosyncratic line (I refer especially to the *Letter to the Duke of Norfolk* of 1875). Unlike moderates such as his own bishop, Ullathorne, and Ketteler, bishop of Mainz, whose aversion to absolutism in all its manifestations was perhaps more natural and deeply-rooted than Newman's, he did not look upon episcopal authority as an important safeguard against abuse of papal authority. This despite the fact that the question was a natural and familiar one to the Anglican, one which he had discussed on a very few occasions also as a Catholic.[7] His lack of interest in bishops' rights is one of those traits which make him an Ultramontane *sui generis*, though he certainly did not favor the centralization of authority in Roman offices which was going on during this period, as attested by a remarkable letter of 1863 and an eloquent passage in the *Apologia*.[8]

The perspective of Newman's *Letter to the Duke of Norfolk* is that of a third party to a battle royal over the meaning of Vatican I.[9]

---

[6] Gustave Thils, *Primauté pontificale et prérogatives épiscopales* (Louvain: E. Warny, 1961), pp. 48-95; cf. Aubert, *Vatican I*, pp. 217-234, and note DS, no. 3115. Manning's phrase in DS, no. 3064, is *aut eum habere tantum potiores partes, non vero totam plenitudinem huius supremae potestatis*.

[7] Those who wish to pursue the matter can start with Newman's references to the passages in Gregory the Great where the latter seems to eschew universal, supra-episcopal authority: see above, Ch. V, note 10; *VM*, I, 188; *L & D*, XIII, 283 and XIV, 350. On the eve of the Council, he wrote about the episcopal vs. the papal wielding of infallibility to Catherine Froude, cf. Harper, *Cardinal Newman*, pp. 193-194; an earlier non-response is in *L & D*, XIV, 301.

[8] Letter to William Monsell of 13 January 1863 in *L & D*, XX, 390-393 (also Ward, *Life*, I, 559-562), and *Apo*, pp. 238-240.

[9] See Josef C. Altholz, "The Vatican Decrees Controversy, 1874-1876," *Catholic Historical Review*, 57 (1971-1972), 593-605. The full title of the *Letter* is *A Letter addressed to His Grace the Duke of Norfolk on Occasion of Mr. Gladstone's Recent Expostulation*, rpt. in the uniform edition, *Diff*, II, 171-378. Alvan S. Ryan has conveniently issued both Gladstone's *The Vatican Decrees in Their Bearing on Civil Allegiance: A Political Expostulation* and Newman's *Letter* in *Newman and Gladstone: The Vatican Decrees* (Univ. of Notre Dame Press, 1962), with an introduction. Bernard-Dominique Dupuy furnishes a valuable introduction and notes to his edition and translation, Newman, *Lettre au Duc de Norfolk* (Paris: Desclée de Brouwer, 1970). Manning's works on the subject are *The Vatican Council and Its Definitions* (1870, rpt. as the third part of *Petri Privilegium*, London, 1871), *Caesarism and Ultramontanism* (1874, rpt. in Manning's *Miscellanies*, 3d. ed., New York: Catholic Publication Society, 1880, pp. 503-550—this may be regarded as the opening shot in the controversy, though it goes back to the earlier opposition between Manning on the one hand and Acton, Döllinger, and Gladstone on

Especially by reason of Manning's opening statement in *Caesarism and Ultramontanism*, the debate was carried on in terms of world-historical significance, almost as a literary British counterpart to the *Kulturkampf* which had broken out at this time in the new German *Reich* of Bismarck. At issue was nothing less than the sovereignty of the state *versus* that of the Church. In Manning's view, only a strong Ultramontane church could provide a bulwark for liberty in the face of the omnicompetent, let us say totalitarian, modern state. Newman, as we shall see, soon was moved to propose a political theory which would deny sovereignty to any form of rule, civil or ecclesiastical, and which would uphold the rights of conscience against both. In striking contrast, Manning felt that the only means to offset state absolutism was the countervailing independent authority of an infallible church. Vatican I had made the most of the pope's infallibility just in time to defend humanity against epochal assaults on its freedom and dignity.

Gladstone, needless to say, disagreed. What Manning's version of the Vatican decrees amounted to was nothing less than an attack on Her Majesty's claim to civil allegiance. If the pope's writ was to control every aspect of a Catholic citizen's moral behavior, then political questions would be fought out between one group of subjects who acknowledged the Queen's authority and another who were loyal to a foreign ruler. He cited *inter alia* the second paragraph, Chapter III, of *Pastor aeternus* (DS, no. 3060):

> This we teach and proclaim: the Lord has disposed that the Roman Church hold a primacy of ordinary power over all other churches, and that this jurisdictional power of the Roman Pontiff, which is a truly episcopal power, is immediate: [that is,] pastors and people of whatsoever rite or dignity, each and all, are bound by the duty of hierarchical subordination and true obedience to it, not only in matters which pertain to faith and morals, but also in those which pertain to the discipline and the regimen of the Church spread throughout the world; so that, unity with the Roman Pontiff (both of communion and of profession of the same faith) being preserved, the Church of Christ may be one flock under one supreme Shepherd. This is the doctrine of Catholic truth, from which no one can stray without loss of faith and salvation.

Manning's *Caesarism* evidently supplied an authoritative exposition

the other), and *The Vatican Decrees in Their Bearing on Civil Allegiance* (London, 1875, a response to Gladstone's *Expostulation*); cf. G. H. Williams, *"Omnium Christianorum Pastor et Doctor,"* *Nouvelle revue théologique*, 96 (1974), 342-354.

of what this passage and similar ones signified for the future of church-state relations. In its intransigence, his piece seemed calculated to show "that the doctrine of infallibility aimed a deadly blow at the old historic scientific and moderate school" of Catholics; and that "it was a degradation of the episcopal order; it carried to the furthest point the spirit of absolutist centralisation... in the Church." [10] As an interpretation of the Council, Gladstone could plausibly argue that the doctrine of *Caesarism* represented "the true sense of the Papal declarations and Vatican decrees, as they are understood by the most favoured ecclesiastics." [11] Gladstone and Manning largely agreed, therefore, on what the Vatican teaching meant, but opposed each other as to the validity of the claims contained in it. Newman occupied another point of vantage altogether, in which he could put both adversaries to flight while remaining himself invulnerable.[12]

Once Newman decided to undertake the answer to Gladstone himself, he brought it to a rapid conclusion and published it in the form of a *Letter to the Duke of Norfolk*, scion of the foremost old Catholic family in England. We shall recur to it in the next chapter in another connection; in this chapter I wish to deal with the role of the individual conscience vis-à-vis the papal primacy as defined in Vatican I and interpreted by John Henry Newman. In continuity with his earlier writings, Newman spoke very warmly and positively of the supremacy even in temporal matters which some popes had claimed and even exercised to a certain extent in the "Age of Faith," when all Europe was united in "Christendom." The power to depose sovereigns was perhaps the most striking example of the kind of temporal power to which popes laid claim in the middle ages. Newman did not disavow it (yet), but he indicated that it had nothing to do with the pope's primacy of divine right. Rather, he saw in it an outmoded international political system, which in its time did the world a good service. In

---

[10] Ward, *Life*, II, 402, quoting Lord Morley's *Life of Gladstone*.

[11] Gladstone, *Vatican Decrees* (ed. Ryan), p. 54. Fortunately for Newman's response, Bishop Joseph Fessler had published a "minimizing" exposition of the Council's teaching, *Die wahre und falsche Unfehlbarkeit der Päpste* (Vienna, 1871). It had received papal approbation and was therefore at least as authoritative as Manning's interpretation. Newman used the French translation (Paris, 1873) for his *Letter*, cf. *Diff*, II, 325 note.

[12] Cf. letter to Frederick Rogers, Lord Blachford, of October 1874 in Ward, *Life*, II, 402: "Gladstone's excuse is, I suppose, the extravagance of Archbishop Manning in his "Caesarism," and he will do us a service if he gives us an opportunity of speaking. We can speak against Gladstone, while it would not be decent to speak against Manning. The difficulty is *who* ought to speak?"

Newman's time, however, unity of faith was gone and hence the use-fulness of the pope as presiding officer of European nations too. Since however Pope Pius IX and papal publicists everywhere still spoke the language of political Christendom,[13] Newman did not want to dismiss it out of hand. Nevertheless it is clear that for him this language has nothing to do with the theology of the Petrine primacy.[14]

Newman proceeded along a parallel line of thought as regards the difficult problem of freedom of conscience. As a young man at Oxford he had adopted a prevalent type of Toryism which made large allow-ances for the right, or rather duty, of State and Church to proceed against a non-conformist individual or minority group who could only appeal to conscience.[15] However, as times changed, he became less rigid, adopting a position much more favorable to individual freedom and unfavorable to compulsion, whether open or disguised, in matters political and religious.

Indeed, his thoughts on the rights of conscience and the political freedom needed to safeguard them approached those of the much-maligned Montalembert, although he could not bear the appellation "Liberal," even in combination with "Catholic." [16] There was this great difference between the "Liberal Catholics' " thinking on freedom of conscience and that of Newman: Newman did not see that the newly celebrated value of individual freedom was so fundamental as to require *necessarily* the reconstruction of societal forms about it.[17] He thought that the rulers of Church and State must *pragmatically* trim their sails to the new breeze, but was not convinced that the theorists of freedom were not throwing out the baby with the bath water.

---

[13] One should note, however, the clear disavowal by Pius IX in 1871 of the temporal authority invested in medieval popes by Christendom, cf. Butler, *Vatican Council*, I, 21 (citing the *Civiltà Cattolica*, August, 1871, p. 485).

[14] *Diff*, II, 220-22; also in *Newman & Gladstone*, ed. Ryan, pp. 108-109.

[15] *Diff*, II, 263-69; cf. above all his letters of 1, 13, and 16 March 1829 in *LC*, I, 177-81, and Alvan S. Ryan, "The Development of Newman's Political Thought," *Review of Politics*, 7 (1945), 239.

[16] Cf. Newman's Note on "Liberalism" from the 1865 (2nd) edition of *Apo*, ed. Svaglic, pp. 254-262, and MacDougall, *Acton-Newman Relations*, p. 151.

[17] Therefore, for all his differing estimation of the concrete situation in Europe, he agreed in principle with the teaching of Pius IX on religious liberty, cf. R. Aubert, "Religious Liberty from 'Mirari vos' to the 'Syllabus'," in *Concilium*, 7 (1965), 50-56.

He could even say, *Diff* II, 268, "No one can dislike the democratic principle more than I do." But see Terence Kenny, *The Political Thought of Newman*, p. 166: "There is good reason for putting very little weight on" this remark.

This all serves as a background to the actual theme of this section, which concerns the rights in conscience one may have, not in public life in general, but where the pope's primatial, Petrine power comes into play. It would have given a false impression of the general tenor of Newman's mind on freedom and authority, had not this background been briefly sketched.

Gladstone, however, did not charge the Vatican Council merely with being illiberal, but with erecting a new affront to all civil authority in its claims. As Gladstone read it, Chapter III of *Pastor aeternus*, not to mention infallibility, attributed to popes an unlimited power over Catholics' consciences. A pope could demand "absolute" and "plenary obedience" not only in the domain of faith, but in that of morals, government, and discipline of the church as well: vast domains not separated "by any acknowledged or intelligible line from the domains of civil duty and allegiance." [18] Newman addressed himself to this question in "§4. Divided Allegiance" of his *Letter to the Duke of Norfolk*.[19] He suggested that, in fact, the pope's decisions hardly played any role at all in the personal lives of Catholics. In practice, Catholics were guided by their moral sense and by the opinions of moral theologians which enjoyed general acceptance. In the preceeding two centuries the Roman See had intervened in moral theology to the extent of condemning some 50 or 60 propositions, but hardly any of these could ever concern the average Catholic.[20]

Newman then does admit that there may be, at least theoretically, cases in which the two supreme jurisdictions, that of the church vested in the pope and that of the state vested in its officers, may run afoul of each other in the same individual, the one common subject.[21] When the individual is faced by contradictory demands of the two authorities, he will most often find that the one is in the wrong and not to be obeyed. This may become clear through many different channels, but if all else failed, "then I must rule myself by my own

---

[18] Gladstone, *The Vatican Decrees*, ed. Ryan, pp. 41-45.

[19] The main reason Newman put forth as to why the obedience spoken of in *Pastor aeternus* cannot be called "absolute" does not fall under the heading of "rights in conscience," and we shall discuss it in the next chapter; but see in this chapter, below, note 30.

[20] *Diff*, II, 227-231. Subsequent history has shown both Gladstone and Manning to have been better prophets than Newman on this score.

[21] Thus already in "Difficulties Felt by Anglicans" (1850) in *Diff*, I, 173-75; in *Letter to Norfolk*, *Diff*, II, 237-45.

judgment and my own conscience. But all this is hypothetical and unreal." [22]

Not that the role of conscience in the government of the church was not important! On the contrary, Newman was at pains to bring out the unique importance of conscience, rightly understood, and to allow "that there are extreme cases in which Conscience may come into collision with the word of a Pope, and is to be followed in spite of that word." [23] But he thought that he must sharply distinguish his own (traditional) conception of conscience as being the voice of God and commanding with divine authority from the "miserable counterfeit" of conscience to which "Liberals" were always appealing, and which was nothing more than the individual man's self-will raised to a first principle of conduct. This latter sense, he explained, was the sense in which Gregory XVI called liberty of conscience a *"deliramentum,"* and in which Pius IX condemned it again in 1864.[24] However, in the true sense of the word, conscience intimates the right and duty of following Divine Authority itself, and in that sense the church herself is built on the voice of conscience. The pope himself, in the most essential core of his office, has no persuasion to fall back on except the force and authority of individuals' consciences; "did the Pope speak against Conscience in the true sense of the word, he would commit a suicidal act. He would be cutting the ground from under his feet." [25] Where there is no revelation concerning a point of conduct, the natural law written by God in our consciences must be our guide. No pope can set himself against that law, any more than he can order what goes against scripture or the articles of the faith.[26]

There remains therefore the particular possible case, where conscience is to be taken as a sacred and sovereign monitor and its dictate must prevail even against the voice of the pope. But this only after

> serious thought, prayer, and [the use of] all available means of arriving at a right judgment on the matter in question. And further, obedience to the Pope is what is called "in possession"; that is, the *onus probandi* of establishing a case against him lies, as in all cases of exception, on the side of conscience. Unless a man is able to say to himself, as in the Presence of God, that he must not, and dare not, act upon the Papal

---

[22] *Diff*, II, 244.
[23] *Ibid.*, p. 246. Pages 246-61 comprise "§ 5. Conscience."
[24] DS, nos. 2730 and 2979.
[25] *Diff*, II, 252.
[26] *Ibid.*, pp. 254 and 242.

injunction, he is bound to obey it, and would commit a great sin in disobeying it.[27]

Newman brought his section on conscience to a close with citations from different schools of moral theology within the church, all proclaiming the primacy of conscience. Then he added "one remark," one of his best known:

> Certainly, if I am obliged to bring religion into after-dinner toasts, (which indeed does not seem quite the thing) I shall drink—to the Pope, if you please,—still, to Conscience first, and to the Pope afterwards.[28]

In order to make still more precise the character of papal jurisdiction, Newman made much of the fact that no claim of infallibility was involved in its exercise. If, for example, an interdict or any other part of a pope's public policy were endowed with infallibility, then the individual conscience would truly have to accept it inwardly, and Catholics would be "moral and mental slaves," as Gladstone charged.[29] "But a Pope is not infallible in his laws, nor in his commands, nor in his acts of state, nor in his administration, nor in his public policy." That means that, like those of any other duly established authority, the pope's commands are to be obeyed on principle, though there will also be cases where conscience must refuse obedience. For "all general rules have exceptions." [30]

Thus Newman at length clearly stated that the pope is not the despot of souls. A letter to Lord Blachford explains why he had never before, for instance in some subordinate clause of his sermon on "The Pope and the Revolution," hinted that disobedience to the pope was thinkable.

> As to Canon Neville's passage, you must recollect what a strong thing it is to tell the party spirit, and the enthusiasm, and the sentiment

---

[27] *Ibid.*, p. 258. Cf. John Coulson, *OS*, p. 133, for the contrast with Lord Acton's conception of conscience.

[28] *Diff*, II, 261. Cf. Dupuy's notes in *Lettre au Duc de Norfolk*, pp. 254-262.

[29] *Diff*, II, 224; for the whole argument, *ibid.*, pp. 256-57.

[30] *Ibid.*, pp. 337-338; cf. p. 243: "When, then, Mr. Gladstone asks Catholics how they can obey the Queen and yet obey the Pope, since it may happen that the commands of the two authorities may clash, I answer, that it is my *rule*, both to obey the one and to obey the other, but that there is no rule in this world without exceptions, and if either the Pope or the Queen demanded of me an 'Absolute Obedience,' he or she would be transgressing the laws of human society. I give an absolute obedience to neither."

unreasoning and untheological, of Catholics, that the Pope is ever to be disobeyed.[31]

But obedience to conscience creates the basis on which the popes rule; when and if they proceed against the authority of conscience, their rule must be ignored.

---

[31] Letter of 11 April 1875 in Ward, *Life*, II, 408. Cf. *Diff*, II, 357-58: Neville, of Maynooth, also spoke of a case where a soldier could continue in the Queen's service, ignoring a papal excommunication against same, on the ground that force and fear dispense from ecclesiastical censures. Newman had a different reason, but was glad to find Catholic support for the very idea "that the Pope is ever to be disobeyed." Compare the gingerly first approach to the matter in Newman's letter to the *Times*, dated 9 September 1872 (letter 28 in Vatican I Collection, Book 47, Birmingham Oratory).

CHAPTER SEVENTEEN

INTERDEPENDENT FUNCTIONS IN THE CHURCH:
THE *SCHOLA THEOLOGORUM*
AND THE EXTENT OF PAPAL POWER

In his valuable study of Newman's preface to the third edition of
the *Via Media* (1877), John Coulson has pointed out that Newman
there completed a step which forms the bridge between our present
chapter and the preceding one. To maintain the ultimate primacy of
conscience over all human authority, even that of the pope, is necessary and right as far as it goes. But left at that, the practical effect
would be minimal, for it requires that an individual, with his doubts,
fears and weaknesses, assert himself over against an otherwise un-
restricted authority—a counsel of heroism which Newman himself
thought was unreal or at least unusual. And yet a pope is exposed to
the same temptations to ambition and tyranny that beset other
rulers.[1]

Is there no remedy for this in the ecclesiastical set-up? Must members
of the Roman Catholic Church stand to the supreme authority as so
many unstable iron filings in the magnetic field of its massive appeal
to conscience? Or is there another factor at work in this field, which
could offset the one-sided influence of authority? Newman evolved
his answer on the basis of the distinction of three "offices" in the
church, the kingly, the priestly and the prophetical,[2] as we shall see
in a little more detail shortly. He now (1877) came to see in the prophetical function of the church, as expressed in the *Schola Theologorum*,
the semi-institutional buttress of the individual conscience against

---

[1] *VM*, I, xli. Newman did not admit this readily, compare *Diff*, I, 237, dating
from 1850. Cf. John Coulson, "Newman on the Church—His Final View, Its
Origins and Influence," *OS*, pp. 123-143; *idem, Newman and the Common Tradition*, esp. pp. 165-183.

[2] The notion of the "three offices" of Christ and of the church became wide-
spread, first in Protestant theology, and then, in the nineteenth century, in
Catholic theology as well, cf. G. H. Williams, *"Omnium christianorum pastor,"*
Nouvelle révue théologique, 96 (1974), 360, and Josef Fuchs, "Origines d'une triologie
ecclésiologique à l'époque rationaliste de la théologie," *Revue des sciences philo-
sophiques et théologiques*, 53 (1969), 185-211. Eusebius is a patristic source, cf.
Coulson, *Newman and the Common Tradition*, p. 168, and Per Beskow, *Rex Gloriae*
(Stockholm: Almqvist & Wiksell, 1962).

the tendency of the kingly function in the church to make excessive use of its authority. According to Coulson:

> The proper question to ask then is what ensures that the Church functions as a living whole instead of an abstraction of discordant and self-conceived parts? Newman's answer is that it is the prophetical office, *not the unaided power of conscience*, which has to be opposed to the institutional excesses of the Church. "Theology," he says, "is the regulating principle. Its absence has been the cause of our late and present internal troubles," since never is religion in greater danger than when "the Schools of theology have been broken up and ceased to be." [3]

This, however, was the rather unexpected conclusion—a "breakthrough" really—of a long development.

Already as an Anglican Newman had perceived that the whole reality of the church was too great to be summed up in any one manifestation of itself, say that of apostolic succession.[4] He saw for instance that besides the form-giving function of the episcopate, the church needed a more creative force to maintain the vitality of the truths entrusted to it at its founding. The Prophetical Office was not simply a matter for the bishops, the official teachers. "Almighty God placed in His Church first Apostles, or Bishops, secondarily Prophets. Apostles rule and preach, Prophets expound. Prophets or Doctors are the interpreters of the revelation." And so he set up his famous distinction: the Episcopal Tradition is infallible, but limited to the fundamental truths of revelation; the Prophetical Tradition is manifold, vast, without strict boundaries, but providing " 'the mind of the Spirit,' the thought and principle which breathed in the Church." [5]

It was fully congruous to Newman's theology that he also considered worship to be "as fundamental a note of the Church as its prophetical and episcopal traditions;" [6] which then suggested of itself the pattern of the "three offices." In the early 1840s Newman became dismayed to find the Episcopal Tradition (or kingly function) so ineffective in the Church of England, for he felt that "the Church's free exercise of its kingly function was the precondition for the effective exercise of its

---

[3] Coulson, *OS*, p. 135. Cf. Ward, *Life*, II, 374 for the quotations. Emphasis mine.

[4] Cf. Coulson, *OS*, pp. 125-28; also *VM*, I, xciv.

[5] *VM*, I, 250 251 (being the *Prophetical Office* of 1837); cf. Günter Biemer, *Newman on Tradition*, pp. 46-48.

[6] Coulson, *OS*, p. 130.

priestly function." [7] This lent an additional urgency to the authoritarian side of his thoughts for decades, as we have already seen in many examples. After his conversion, however, he recognized the vigor of the kingly and priestly functions in the Roman Catholic Church, but became increasingly convinced that the weakness of the prophetical office, the theological discipline in the church, was the source of many of the ills that were befalling Christianity. Among these ills were those with which he had reproached the Catholic Church in his lectures on the *Prophetical Office* (1837), namely authoritarian and devotional excesses. The remedy he suggested in the Preface to its third edition (1877) was the strengthening of the prophetical function in the church through the recognition that the work of theologians was of eminent importance.

This intimate connection, almost identification, between the prophetical office and the *Schola Theologorum* results in large part from the mental framework Newman erected for his special purposes in the Preface of 1877. Before examining this, however, we must turn to Newman's previous use of the notion of the *Schola Theologorum*.

This concept in Newman's Catholic outlook appears to take over the function which was proper to "Antiquity" according to his Anglican way of thinking. The phrase itself emerges for the first time to my knowledge in correspondence with an Anglican clergyman in 1863, and what is more, apparently in connection with the controversy brewing up as to what a Catholic must believe of the pope's privileges.

> By the Schola theologorum is meant the teaching of theologians. It applies to all times as the Fathers to the early times. We speak of the *consensus Patrum*—and so I spoke of the unanimous decision of the Schola.
>
> Dr. Manning could not have made it a *condition* of your reception that you should believe in the Pope's Temporal Power as inseparable from His Office as Vicar of Christ. He would have put a catechism into your hands, and you would not have found that Doctrine in any authorized catechism. [8]

Where one found agreement among the voices of the Church of the Fathers (Antiquity), there was an infallible utterance. But according to Augustine's *Securus judicat orbis terrarum*, this infallibility was not a

---

[7] *Ibid.*, pp. 131-32.
[8] Letter to Mr. Brownlow of 1 November 1863 in Ward, *Life*, I, 653-54 and *L & D*, XX, 552 f.

thing of the past. The judgment of the whole world could now be found there, where amidst many disputed questions the theologians of the church in communion with Rome nevertheless agreed. Thus one arrives at the idea of a single *Schola Theologorum* in the abstract, elevated above the controversies of the concrete "theological schools."

In his earlier Catholic years Newman did not lay so much emphasis on *theologians* as the mouthpiece of this acceptance on the part of the whole church of the true sense of Catholic doctrine. He did so later in order to preserve due liberty of thought against enthusiastic, but theologically rash, popular publicists and prelates.[9]

This is the motive behind Newman's appeal to the judgment of the *Schola Theologorum* in the *Letter to the Duke of Norfolk*. He made this appeal in the first place to combat exaggerated notions of papal infallibility, and secondarily also to correct Gladstone's view of what the newly defined papal primacy purported. Newman had before this protested against the slighting of the painstaking, time-consuming theological process on the part of the "aggressive party" of Ultramontanes before and during the Vatican Council. Now he distinguished sharply between the utterances of any one person or particular school and the final judgment which only time could make possible. There was after all more than one admissible opinion regarding the interpretation of the Vatican decrees current in the Catholic communion, and in the end a moderate view, hedged around with lawyerlike clauses, would prevail. "None but the *Schola Theologorum* is competent to determine the force of Papal and Synodal utterances, and the exact interpretation of them is a work of time." Part of the work of the *Schola Theologorum* is a "legitimate minimizing" and circumscription of the exact import of conciliar and papal definitions, which require in the nature of the case this expert examination. For "the Church, as guided by her Divine Master, has made provision for weighing as lightly as possible on the faith and conscience of her children."[10]

Although the time had not come when one could confidently assert that this and this was the consensus of the *Schola* in the interpretation of the Vatican decrees, still there were points where obviously a less rigorous interpretation than that of Gladstone on the pope's powers had its supporters. A Manning might enjoy ever so much favor in Rome—still his views on interpretation of the conciliar

---

[9] Cf. letter to Isy Froude of 29 July 1875 in Ward, *Life*, II, 564.
[10] *Diff*, II, 333-34.

documents were worth only as much as the theological reasoning which backed them up. A calm look at the wording of the Constitution *Pastor aeternus* itself, with a view to determining its sense according to the traditions and usages of theologians was what was needed, and Newman assays this very briefly under the heading of the "Sovereignty" of the pope.

Gladstone had made out of the Vatican Council's declaration of the pope's universal jurisdiction a claim to "general authority over us in all things whatsoever." [11] The papal jurisdiction there described is rightly called "universal" in the sense that it holds sway over every person and juridical person in the Roman communion, but Gladstone thought that its *object* was simply uncircumscribed, and extended to all matters of personal and public conduct. Newman's main effort, therefore, was concentrated on the task of showing that *disciplina* and *regimen* were words of a well-defined and fairly narrow meaning in church usage, and could not be used as a catch-all. They were *not*

> words of such lax, vague, indeterminate meaning, that under them any matters can be slipped in which may be required for the Pope's purpose in this or that country, such as, to take Mr. Gladstone's instances, blasphemy, poor-relief, incorporation, and mortmain.[12]

On the contrary, "discipline" pertains to the ordering of the liturgy and the administration of the clerical office-holders in the church and of her temporal possessions—all strictly internal affairs, of no interest to a state which does not want to meddle. Thus is it described in church law and by leading authors like Perrone.

> So too the word "regimen" has a definite meaning, relating to a matter strictly internal to the Church: it means government, or the mode or form of government, or the course of government; and, as, in the intercourse of nation with nation, the nature of a nation's government, whether monarchical or republican, does not come into question, so the constitution of the Church simply belongs to its nature, not to its external action. Certainly there are aspects of the Church which involve relations toward secular powers and to nations, as, for instance, its missionary office; but regimen has relation to one of its internal characteristics, viz., its form of government, whether we call it a pure monarchy or with others a monarchy tempered by

---

[11] Newman's phrase, *Diff*, II, 233; cf. Gladstone, *The Vatican Decrees*, pp. 38-42, citing the decree (DS, no. 3064) which states that the papal jurisdiction applies *non solum in rebus, quae ad fidem et mores, sed etiam in iis, quae ad disciplinam et regimen Ecclesiae per totum orbem diffusae pertinent*.

[12] *Diff*, II, 234.

aristocracy. Thus Tournely says, "Three kinds of regimen or government are set down by philosophers, monarchy, aristocracy, and democracy." [13]

Gladstone's chief mistake, therefore, according to Newman, was to press the meaning of the words "discipline and regimen" too far. But he had also taken other liberties with the text. He had, for instance, spoken of "absolute obedience" so often, that any reader, who had not the passage before him, would think that the word "absolute" was the Council's word, not his.[14] He translated "doctrina" (in the last sentence of DS, no. 3060) by the word "rule," so as to be able to state that according to the Vatican Council no one could *disobey* the pope without endangering his salvation. Actually, as Newman points out, the decree merely states "that no one can *disbelieve* the *duty* of obedience and unity without such risk." [15]

Newman's most pregnant remark on the interpretation of papal primacy as defined in *Pastor aeternus* is perhaps his noticing that the primacy is explicitly defined in relation to its *purpose*, the unity of the church as "one flock under one supreme shepherd." Apart from the familiar themes of Newman's "kingdom-ecclesiology" which reappear in the following excerpt, one may also see in it a reminder that the *raison d'être* of the papal primacy are its spiritual duties on the ecumenical plane, and that it need not intrude itself into local problems, particularly when these are of a predominantly secular character.

> I consider this passage to be especially aimed at Nationalism: "Recollect," the Pope seems to say, "the Church is one, and that, not only in faith and morals, for schismatics may profess as much as this, but one, wherever it is, all over the world; and not only one, but one and the same, bound together by its one regimen and discipline,—the same rites, the same sacraments, the same usages, and the same one Pastor; and in these bad times it is necessary for all Catholics to recollect, that this doctrine of the Church's individuality and, as it were, personality, is not a mere received opinion or understanding, which may be entertained or not, as we please, but is a fundamental, necessary truth."
>
> This being, speaking under correction, the drift of the passage,

---

[13] *Ibid.*, 235. It must be admitted that Newman's effort at elucidating these points is not a very successful one, in that it only partly coincides with the Council's intended meaning and does not meet Gladstone's objection, which has to do with the thorny area of *materia mixta*, to speak canonically, or to use Newman's term, the *pomoerla* (*Apo*, p. 230).

[14] *Diff*, II, 233.

[15] *Ibid.*, cf. also pp. 341-42.

I observe that the words "spread throughout the world" or "universal" are so far from turning "discipline and regimen" into what Mr. Gladstone calls a "net," that they contract the range of both of them, not including, as he would have it, "marriage," here, "blasphemy" there, and "poor-relief" in a third country, but noting and specifying that one and the same structure of laws, rites, rules of government, independency, everywhere, of which the Pope himself is the centre and life. And surely this is what every one of us will say as well as the Pope, who is not an Erastian, and who believes that the Gospel is no mere philosophy thrown upon the world at large, no mere quality of mind and thought, no mere beautiful and deep sentiment or subjective opinion, but a substantive message from above guarded and preserved in a visible polity.[16]

The hope which Newman here intimated that theologians would succeed in hedging papal claims about looks rather misplaced in view of the integralist dominance of the succeeding decades. Nevertheless one can maintain with Harold Laski that Newman did avoid falling into the all-or-nothing trap set by the concept of "sovereignty." [17] If the monistic, absolutistic notion of sovereignty was a mistake as applied to civil jurisdiction, the same could be said of papal power, at least in cases of conflict with conscience. Beyond that, however, was there any factor at the level of structures ("regimen") which could correct absolutist tendencies after Vatican I? Finally, with a deceptive air of uttering no particular novelties, Newman surmounted all the ingrained obstacles that had kept him from saying so in the past.

His last theological essay to be included in his collected works, the Preface of 1877 (in *Via Media*, I), is an analysis of abuses in the church, abuses stemming from an undue monopoly whether of the priestly (worshiping) office, the prophetical (teaching) office, or the kingly (ruling) office.[18] The church has a "many-sided mission." Abuses arise not only from the sinful proclivities of its members and leaders, but also from concentrating on one of its aims (say, solidarity among its members) at the expense of others (holiness, truth). The goal of

---

[16] *Diff*, II, 236.

[17] Harold J. Laski, *Studies in the Problem of Sovereignty*, 201-207, p. 202: the *Letter to the Duke of Norfolk* is "perhaps the profoundest discussion of the nature of obedience and of sovereignty to be found in the English language;" p. 207: Newman lays down "a theory of liberty" based on consent, not power.

[18] Besides Coulson, see also Richard Bergeron, *Les abus de l'Eglise d'après Newman*, with a preface by Maurice Nédoncelle (Montreal: Bellarmin, 1971).

truth is the special province of theologians, not of the pope ("He strangles, while they prate," *L&D*, XX, 391). It is striking how Newman consistently aligns the prophetical or teaching office with "the schools" or "theology," and not with the official *magisterium* of the pope and bishops.

The bishops hardly come in for mention as official teachers in the Preface. The pope stands in Newman's typology as the embodiment of the ruling or kingly function in the church, leaving the *Schola Theologorum* to typify the prophetic function and the "pastor and flock" to stand for the priestly function.

> I will but say in passing, that I must not in this argument be supposed to forget that the Pope, as the Vicar of Christ, inherits these offices and acts for the Church in them. This is another matter; I am speaking here of the body of Christ, and the sovereign Pontiff would not be the visible head of that Body, did he not first belong to it . . .
> Christianity, then, is at once a philosophy, a political power, and a religious rite: as a religion, it is Holy; as a philosophy, it is Apostolic; as a political power, it is imperial, that is, One and Catholic. As a religion, its special centre of action is pastor and flock; as a philosophy, the Schools; as a rule, the Papacy and its Curia.[19]

The distribution of the notes of the church and its various components under the three offices is rather artificial, but it does serve as a usable framework for Newman's reflection on the multiplicity of diverse forces in the church and excludes from the outset the tendency to reduce church life to one of its functions, a besetting sin of Ultramontanes. Infallible definitions, for instance, are undoubtedly the province of the ruling power—but only as taking over and sanctioning the accomplishments of the prophetical office, when necessity induces it to make such a rare move.[20] Here the emphasis is on the work of theologians that precedes and follows authoritative doctrinal decisions of the hierarchy. These theologians may not be the "official

---

[19] *VM*, I, xl. He goes on to say that the religious element was the first to develop, the philosophical more tardily, and the imperial last of all; then p. xli: "Truth is the guiding principle of theology and theological inquiries; devotion and edification, of worship; and of government, expedience. The instrument of theology is reasoning; of worship, our emotional nature; of rule, command and coercion. Further, in man as he is, reasoning tends to rationalism; devotion to superstition and enthusiasm; and power to ambition and tyranny."

[20] *Apo*, p. 224: "Such is the infallibility lodged in the Catholic Church, viewed in the concrete, as clothed and surrounded by the appendages of its high sovereignty: it is, to repeat what I said above, a supereminent prodigious power sent upon earth to encounter and master a giant evil [the bent of the human intellect towards rationalism]."

teachers" in the church, yet they are a constitutional element which cannot be ignored. By reason of their learned appropriation of and reflection upon the tradition, they exercise the prophetical (or, as Newman disconcertingly says, the philosophical) function. They form, in their ensemble, a body of teachers and a body of teaching which is as indispensable to the church as its priests and rulers.

In fact, Newman went even further. To the prophetical office, in the shape of the *Schola Theologorum*,[21] he attributed a certain superiority relative to the other two functions of the church. For the other two functions are more liable to abuse.

> I say, then, Theology is the fundamental and regulating principle of the whole Church system. It is commensurate with Revelation, and Revelation is the initial and essential idea of Christianity. It is the subject-matter, the formal cause, the expression, of the Prophetical Office, and, as being such, has created both the Regal Office and the Sacerdotal. And it has in a certain sense a power of jurisdiction over those offices, as being its own creations, theologians being ever in request and in employment in keeping within bounds both the political and popular elements in the Church's constitution.[22]

This would seem to imply a radical subordination of institutional authority (and popular devotion) to the judgment of theologians, and to deprive acts of authority, even of the highest, papal, authority, of their peremptory character. But if Newman did not want the fate of the church to be left solely in the hands of its rulers, he did not deliver it altogether into the hands of its theologians either. The ruling function, embodied in the hierarchy, must feel the restraint of

---

[21] The idea was already in his head in 1875, as described in a letter to Lord Blachford of 5 Feb. 1876 in Ward, *Life*. II, 374. Some allusions in the letter are to be understood in the light of the recipient's long career in the civil service.
"[T]he Schola Theologorum is (in the Divine Purpose, *I* should say) the regulating principle of the Church, and, as lawyers and public officers (if I may thus speak *coram te*) preserve the tradition of the British *Constitution*, in spite of the King, Lords, and Commons, so there is a permanent and *sui similis* life in the Church, to which all its acts are necessarily assimilated, nay, and under the implied condition of its existence and action such acts are done and are accepted." Newman thought this was what Acton meant when he said, recklessly, "that it is no matter what Councils or Popes decree or do, for the Catholic body goes on pretty much as it did, in spite of all" (compare *Selections from the Correspondence of the First Lord Acton*, ed. J. N. Figgis and R. V. Laurence, London, 1917, I, 119-124). And he went on to speculate: "Where would Ward have been if there had been theological schools in England? Again, the Archbishop [Manning] is not a theologian, and, what is worse, the Pope is not a theologian, and so theology has gone out of fashion."
[22] *VM*, I, xlvii-xlviii.

theology, but likewise theology must temper its logical reasoning, when it threatens to lose contact with concrete reality, by taking into consideration the needs and capabilities of the church in its other two functions, as a worshipping community organized in a polity.[23]

In short, Newman, who did not utilize the dialectic of episcopal and papal powers within the ruling functions of the church, recognized in the Preface to the third edition of *Via Media* a *dialectic of functions* within the church, which could not be reduced to functions of the hierarchy. He went a good piece further here than he had in a letter to Isy Froude, where he described the *Schola Theologorum* as partaking of the passive infallibility of the *Ecclesia discens*.[24] Here it is no longer merely a question of the rare infallible definitions, but of the day-to-day interplay of functions in the church. Deleterious tendencies showed themselves constantly in the seats of authority in the church and especially in the bureaucracy pertaining thereto. The remedy had to be just as constantly active, in the theological schools. Because of theology's intrinsic closeness to the heart of the Christian religion, revelation, Newman allowed himself the paradox that the prophetical office "has in a certain sense a power of jurisdiction over" the regal office and the sacerdotal.

Newman's broad use of the word "theology" can easily cause confusion. On the one hand, he seems to conceive it as the intellectual work pursued by theologians, in the *Schola Theologorum*. But what he really means by theology, when, as above, its primacy over church authority is affirmed, is made clear in the sentence: "[Theology] is commensurate with Revelation, and Revelation is the initial and essential idea of Christianity." Theologians of Newman's persuasion today would speak preferably of the church being under the judgment of the Word of God, and would be careful not to create the impression that professional theologians had a monopoly in the understanding of this Word. They would stress not only the distinction between church authority and divine authority, but also that between the Word of God and its human expression, at which theologians toil. But Newman's concern was simpler, more directly practical in the context in which he wrote: he wanted to show that the best will in the world would not enable the hierarchy to dispense with careful reflection and the return to the sources, in a word, with theology; and that the indiscriminate

---

[23] For examples, see *VM*, I, li-lxix, lxxxi-xciii. Cf. Paul Misner, "Theologians and the Papacy," *The Newman*, 4 (1969), 190-198.

[24] Letter of 28 July 1875 in Ward, *Life*, II, 564.

subordination of this work to the felt needs of the hierarchy as of the people could only be unhealthful in the long run.

In what concerns the relationship of theology and the papal office in detail, Newman mentions that "Popes, such as Liberius, Vigilius, Boniface VIII, and Sixtus V, under secular inducements of the moment, seem from time to time to have been wishing, though unsuccessfully, to venture beyond the line of theology." [25] The names of Liberius and Vigilius (mostly coupled with Honorius) are familiar to the reader of Newman's other works and letters: they were popes who did not always prove equal to the blandishments, threats and tortures of the Byzantine Emperors and who subscribed to heterodox creeds.

The names of Boniface VIII and Sixtus V, however, are much more interesting and to the point. The reader of Newman's other works is unprepared for this. The seventy-six year old Newman now for the first time alluded to certain papal pretensions associated with the names of these popes and suggested that they would have committed the church to the theory of papal power as supreme even over the state in the latter's own area of autonomy, had it not been for theologians who subsequently whittled away at the papal declarations until that which had to be held as of faith was properly limited. [26]

As Père Chenu has pointed out, the Bull *Unam Sanctam* which Boniface VIII published in 1302 is "a classic example for the use of *loci theologici*." [27] For when Boniface defined solemnly that every human creature was subject to the Roman Pontiff, he meant that Philip the Fair had no right to oppose him in administrative and financial matters in the French church, that even as king he had to submit to the pope. These motives, however, are detached by theological commentary from the solemn definition itself. Nor are the theological explanations given for the defined proposition themselves held to be defined. Rather, the theologians have the task of digging down to the lasting basic doctrine, and in this task they must have regard for other truths (in this case especially the rightful autonomy of the secular world). They must also determine which expressions in the defined propositions are less than adequate to the truth being

---

[25] *VM*, I, xlviii.

[26] This stands in startling contrast to § 3 of the *Letter to the Duke of Norfolk*, "The Papal Church." But there is no outright contradiction. In the *Letter*, after all, he had hinted that the full extent of claims to political power, such as Boniface VIII made, were not of divine right, while here he carefully notes that he was unsuccessful in dogmatizing what seems to be the immediate import of his Bull.

[27] Marie-Dominique Chenu, art. "Unam Sanctam" in *LTK*, X, 462.

defined, as being based on faulty presuppositions or limited mental horizons which are, again, *not* defined. Chenu formulates then the truth which can be regarded as defined in *Unam Sanctam* as follows: all human activity, that of rulers included, stands under the moral law and under grace, nothing is excepted from its sway; the political sphere must also submit to moral requirements, it must be of service to man and responsible before God. This reinterpretation by theologians certainly illustrates what Newman meant by the function of the *Schola Theologorum*, though it no doubt goes further than would have been possible for Newman.

Sixtus V (1585-90) has not come down in history as another Boniface VIII, but it was under this aspect of papal pretensions to jurisdiction even in civil affairs that Acton wrote about him.[28] In particular, Acton had related in the *Rambler* how Robert Bellarmine had fallen into disfavor with Sixtus V, because in his principle work, the *Controversiae*, he upheld the view that the pope's power to intervene in the civil sphere was only indirect, *ratione peccati*. The pope put the *Controversiae* on the Index of Forbidden Books, until such a time as Bellarmine would see fit to uphold the *direct control* of the pope over every earthly power.[29] Then, however, the pope predeceased the theologian (just as Pius IX would die in time to permit Newman's full and definitive emergence from under the cloud), and Bellarmine could set forth his theory again, not of course as infallible, no more than Sixtus V had been in this question, but as an admissible interpretation.

It is probably this question of church-state relations, and more particularly this incident between a pope and a theologian, to which Newman was referring when he mentioned Sixtus V in the preface to the third edition of *Via Media*. It illustrates very well what he had written to Isy Froude in 1875:

> [The Schola Theologorum] acts with great force both in correcting popular misapprehensions and narrow views of the teaching of the active *infallibilitas*, and, by the intellectual investigations and disputes which are its very life, it keeps the distinction clear between theological truth and theological opinion, and is the antagonist of dogmatism.[30]

---

[28] Cf. Lord Acton, *Essays on Church and State*, ed. by Douglas Woodruff (New York: Thomas Y. Crowell, 1968), p. 256.

[29] Cf. *ibid.*, pp. 277-78, where Acton quotes Bellarmine's autobiography, p. 22. The essay originally appeared in *The Rambler* of February 1859 under the title, "The Catholic Press."

[30] Letter of Newman to Miss Eliza Margaret Froude of 28 July 1875 in Ward, *Life*, II, 564.

This is, of course, no primrose path for theology. There are times, as he had charged in his *Prophetical Office*, and as he now rephrased it in his new Preface, when "the Regal function of the Church, as represented by the Pope, seems to be trampling on the theological, as represented by Scripture and Antiquity." [31] Newman felt he was living in such times. He was too reserved to draw the applications for his own times of his theology of abuses in the church. He didn't mention in the Preface to the third edition of *Via Media* the controversy over the Temporal Power of the Pope, or the definitions of the primacy and infallibility of the pope at the first Vatican Council, or the bad effects of over-centralization stemming from England's status as a missionary country under the control of Propaganda in Rome, or what he considered the inadequacies of the leading Roman school of theology at the time. But it is clear that these and similar conditions were the real object of his considerations, since Newman never wrote anything out of pure antiquarian interest.

For all that, Newman would not have the prophetical office of the church rule the roost unchallenged;

> theology cannot always have its own way; it is too hard, too intellectual, too exact, to be always equitable, or to be always compassionate; and it sometimes has a conflict or overthrow, or has to consent to a truce or a compromise, in consequence of the rival force of religious sentiment or ecclesiastical interests; and that, sometimes in great matters, sometimes in unimportant.[32]

In fact, he went so far as to enounce a "principle of expediency" which seems almost to nullify the principle insisted upon earlier, that "Theology is the fundamental and regulating principle of the whole Church system."

In the last pages of his Preface he presented several examples of how the hierarchical authorities in the church, and pre-eminently the pope, had pushed through measures which they obviously held to be necessary for the good of the church, even though no one could adequately defend them theologically at the time. The cases of Liberius and Honorius belong of course in another category, for they committed "acts simply unjustifiable... real betrayals of the truth." [33] But in the other dozen examples he retails, Newman held the measures

---

[31] *VM*, I, xliv.
[32] *Ibid.*, I, xlviii-xlix.
[33] *Ibid.*, p. lxxxii.

in question to have been recognized with the passage of time as justified, even theologically. And yet they were decided upon on the basis of expediency, the guiding principle, not of theology, but of government, a sort of *raison d'église*.[34]

One case of this sort was that of Pope Leo IX, who in 1049 attempted to attack the abuse of simony in root and branch by declaring that all simoniacal ordinations were null and void. He was soon forced however to take a milder line, because practically every ordination was tainted by simony, if not directly, then somewhere in the ordaining prelate's background. "Such a mode of resolving a point in theology," argues Newman,

> is intelligible only on the ground laid down above, that a certain quasi-doctrinal conclusion may be in such wise fatal to the constitution, and therefore to the being of the Church, as *ipso facto* to stultify the principles from which it is drawn, it being inconceivable that her Lord and Maker intended that the action of any one of her functions should be the destruction of another. In this case, then, He willed that a point of theology should be determined on its expediency relatively to the Church's Catholicity and the edification of her people, —by the logic of facts, which at times overrides all positive laws and prerogatives, and reaches in its effective force to the very frontiers of immutable truths in religion, ethics, and theology.[35]

Newman admits that this principle of expediency is difficult to apply properly [36] and open to abuses. One feels on careful reading that what he means is not what one normally understands by expediency at all, but rather the insight that is reserved to those who do not let dogma and tradition degenerate into ideology, confronting them instead with facts and actual conditions. In his own vivid and highly individual way he was defending the priority of pastoral interests in theology.

It is worthy of note that most of Newman's illustrations of the proper functioning of this principle of expedience are aimed against rigorism. The Roman See distinguished itself in the ancient church by its mildness of discipline and by its opposition to all varieties of rigorism and Novatianism, as Newman's chief examples, having to do with the requirements for the validity of baptism and orders, and

---

[34] *Ibid.*, p. xli. Of course this was a "high, generous expediency," p. lxxxix, but opposed to the primacy of theological reasoning all the same.

[35] *Ibid.*, I, lxxxvi. One notes that Newman carefully exempts any truly immutable, dogmatic truth from this kind of manipulation.

[36] *Ibid.*, p. lxxxiii.

for the readmission of sinners or *lapsi* into communion with the church, instruct us.[37] These cases lend themselves to Newman's point, because the rigorist side seemed at the time to have irrefragable theological reasons for their position, and the Roman Pontiffs had to fight them down with seemingly inadequate theological weapons, mainly an appeal to pragmatic considerations. In such cases, the practical spirit which seemed to animate the Roman See in the old days was a needful antidote against theological rigorism.[38]

If each of the three functions within the church can maintain itself against the others, and each can vindicate to itself a certain priority, what does this mean except, as Coulson says, that there is "a dialectic of functions" within the church, that none must be exercised in a vacuum, and that each must expect clashes and challenges? [39] Since the emphasis in the second half of the nineteenth century was so exclusively on the ruling function in the Catholic Church, with theological schools weakened or absent in many parts of the Catholic world, and with those that remained under too close surveillance by Roman authorities, Newman stressed the importance of theology having its say too, and on more or less equal terms.

The net effect of all this is to give quite a different picture of the pope's primatial powers than that presented to Pusey in 1867.[40] The pope remains the supreme judge, and there is no appeal from his definitive verdict to any other court, as far as the legal channels are concerned. But the church is a many-sided phenomenon, not merely or even chiefly a juridical structure. It is to Newman's credit that, toward the end of his writing career, he took up two themes in the concrete, conscience and the *Schola Theologorum*, which manifested aspects of the church's being which were more essential than the ruling power itself. If the church were a theocracy, as Newman's earlier "kingdom ecclesiology" would give one to understand, then ruling power would coincide with wisdom and justice, and one would have no standing to oppose its authoritative directives. But in fact all church authority is *derived* from divine authority and divine revelation, and these remain sovereign and independent of their creation, church authority. The conscience and the theology which correspond

---

[37] *VM*, I, lxxxvi-xciii; cf. also p. xlviii; Newman had spoken of the danger of a new Novatianism in the contemporary church in a letter of 11 Nov. 1866, cf. *L & D*, XXII, 314.

[38] See especially *VM*, I, lxxxviii-xci.

[39] Coulson, *OS*, pp. 138, 142.

[40] See above, Ch. XV, note 7.

to that sovereign authority and that sovereign Gospel, enjoy therefore a certain autonomous standing even in the church, whether in peaceful cooperation or in self-assured confrontation with the ruling function.

Newman had put church authority, what he now called the regal office of the church, on a pedestal during his long fight against state supremacy over the church and against undue trust in reason where religion was concerned. In his preface to the third edition of the *Via Media* he pulled it down from its pedestal and bade it take its place in the arena with "theology" and "devotion".' With this he gave the underpinnings of much that he had formerly written about the church a mighty shake. The assumption, for instance, that authority in the church was modelled on that of a secular empire, would be drawn into question as soon as critical biblical studies were recognized as a legitimate part of "theology."

Newman did not realize this, of course. He included in the 1877 preface an impressive page of unadulterated kingdom-talk in the style of his old sermons.[41] And the ecclesiological assumptions of the *Essay on Development* did not seem in the least questionable to him when he revised this for republication in the following year. Nevertheless, by vindicating for theology the role of "fundamental and regulating principle of the whole Church system," [42] he opened the door in principle to the thoroughgoing revision of ecclesiology which is now underway with the aid of the whole modern instrumentarium of historical and theological scholarship. By laboriously and delicately introducing an element of "Constitution" beside that of "Rule" into his ecclesiology, he recovered the balance that had been so seriously threatened in the Ultramontane revival.

---

[41] Cf. *VM*, I, lxxx.
[42] *Ibid.*, I, xlvii.

NEWMAN'S PLACE IN THE HISTORY
OF ECCLESIOLOGY

To attempt to fix Newman's position on the ecclesiological map, or, to use another metaphor, to plot his course on the relevant theological trajectories, is no easy task, and I shall not try to be definitive. Nevertheless, some sketchy comparison and contrast with others' views on the theology of the church and of the papacy is necessary to gauge his significance. The examination of Newman's writings gives rise to very few occasions to refer to the age-old Roman Catholic domestic debate on the powers of the papacy. Newman was not familiar with its course, until he had to concern himself with it in the 1870s, and even then, as we have seen, he could not enter into the problematic with the same mastery that marked his participation in the Roman-Anglican debate from Antiquity. Still, he has an undeniable place in the Roman Catholic controversy; with Yves Congar's aid, we can see where he fits in.

The initial and basic connection to be established is of course that between Newman's ecclesiology and the Catholic consensus of the Fathers. This at once sets him apart from the majority of modern theologians, whose judgment on patristic ecclesiology is itself basically conditioned by the stand which each takes on the Reformation vis-à-vis medieval Latin theology. Newman claimed once that he started out reading the Fathers with a Protestant theological system in his head; [1] but we know that this did not long remain dominant. When his *Essay on Development* overcame his difficulties against seeing the Roman communion as the heir of the patristic church, he endorsed the medieval Latin developments to the extent that Rome had endorsed them, but without really appropriating them into his theological culture. Thus he could say to Pusey in 1867:

> For myself, hopeless as you consider it, I am not ashamed still to take my stand upon the Fathers, and do not mean to budge. The history of their times is not yet an old almanac to me. Of course I maintain the value and authority of the "Schola," as one of the *loci theologici*; nevertheless I sympathize with Petavius in preferring to the "conten-

---

[1] *Diff*, I, 371; compare *Apo*, pp. 35 f.

tions and subtle theology" of the middle age, that "more elegant and fruitful teaching which is moulded after the image of erudite Antiquity." The Fathers made me a Catholic, and I am not going to kick down the ladder by which I ascended into the Church. It is a ladder quite as serviceable for that purpose now, as it was twenty years ago. Though I hold, as you know, a process of development in Apostolic truth as time goes on, such development does not supersede the Fathers, but explains and completes them.[2]

On the special question of papal powers, however, this starting point creates a predisposition towards one of the two main tendencies which Yves Congar has found among Catholic theologians.[3] He notes that before about A.D. 1300, theologians treated of the church and its nature and mission at various places in their work, but never devoted a separate treatise or a special section within a *Summa* to it. Questions regarding the juridical constitution of the Church were left to the canonists. But the canon-law treatment of church structures had long been marked by the typical Western Christian tensions between pope and emperor.

Meanwhile, the *theological* understanding of the church that the Fathers had developed (the church as Body of Christ, sacrament of Christ its Head) gave way in the thirteenth century to a purely metaphorical, corporative understanding: the church was now often called the "mystical body" simply in the sense of societal body as distinguished from an individual, physical body. Hence the pope could easily be called the head of the church in the pedestrian sense, although it was not forgotten that Christ was his Body's "invisible" Head.

Christendom, as constituting one body with one head, was a well elaborated theme of thirteenth-century thinkers. This corporative conception of Christian society could be and was developed in two opposite directions. Those who attached great weight to hierarchical values and those in the Roman tradition of Gregory VII underlined the unity of the body to the aggrandizement of the head, the papacy. The opposite tendency—to stress the corporative value whereby all members of the body had their part to play, the part of the head being in the main a summing up and expression or "representation" of the

---

[2] *Diff*, II, 24.

[3] In the following I rely principally upon Yves Congar, *L'Eglise de saint Augustin à l'époque moderne* (rich documentation); in broader lines, *idem*, "The Historical Development of Authority in the Church. Points for Reflection," in *Problems of Authority*, ed. John M. Todd (Baltimore: Helicon Press, 1962), pp. 119-150.

life of the whole body—was operative in the work of some canonists, even before Jean of Paris took up this viewpoint and elaborated it theologically.[4] Nor did Jean of Paris remain the sole representative of a Catholic school of thought on church powers which was opposed to the hierocratic thinking of the Roman sort: he was followed by whole ranks of writers who prepared the ground for late medieval conciliarism and even for representative democracy. To pursue that development would carry us too far afield. Suffice it to have pointed out what kind of context has conditioned the debate on papal powers from that time until very recently.[5]

Two poles emerged, Boniface VIII [6] typifying the one and Jean of Paris the other, which have dominated Catholic theological treatises *De Ecclesia* ever since. The ecclesiological writer has occupied himself in the main with the categories of power juridically conceived. Our question, therefore, of papal primacy was never far from the center of attention in the history of ecclesiology from 1300 until 1950 and on into the present day. The lines have been drawn by and large between those theologians who choose the papal pole as their point of departure, thus approaching the "lower ranks" in the church through a consideration of the pope as source or summit of all ecclesiastical powers, and those others who prefer to start with the church as *ekklesia*, as that prior totality which is the congregation of all the faithful, and then proceed to locate the pope within the church. For instance, conciliarist theologians naturally gravitated to the *ekklesia*-pole, while Roman theologians have generally worked down from the papal peak.[7]

As for the role of Vatican I in this perspective, it seems to mark the

---

[4] Jean Quidort (of Paris) wrote *De potestate regia et papali* in 1302/03, cf. Congar, *L'Eglise*, p. 283, citing Brian Tierney, *Foundations of Conciliar Theory* (Cambridge, Mass.: Harvard Univ. Press, 2d ed. 1968).

[5] Cf. Yves Congar, "Geschichtliche Betrachtung über Glaubensspaltung und Einheitsproblematik," in *Begegnung der Christen*, (Stuttgart: Evangelisches Verlagswerk, Frankfurt: J. Knecht, 1959), p. 414.

[6] Congar, *L'Eglise*, p. 229.

[7] The doctrine of papal infallibility did not originate in papalist circles, but emerged from the controversy about evangelical (Franciscan) poverty in the early fourteenth century, as Brien Tierney has shown in *Origins of Papal Infallibility 1150-1350* (Leiden: E. J. Brill, 1972). In Guido Terreni (Gui Terré), however, a Carmelite who died as bishop of Elne in 1334, the doctrine found a champion who rendered it serviceable to the papal cause. Congar, while accepting Tierney's central findings, shows how Thomas Aquinas had prepared the way for this development in "Saint Thomas Aquinas and the Infallibility of the Papal Magisterium (Summa Theol., II-II, q.1, a.10)," *Thomist*, 38 (1974), 81-105.

beginning of the end, to show the first symptoms of the eventual breakdown of the papalist approach in Catholic ecclesiology, paradoxical as this may sound. Its decisions in ecclesiology were, it is true, wholly concerned with the question of powers, papal powers as it turned out; and its thought was couched in juridical categories. That much it had in common with its precedents in the history of the debate. But despite the fact that it was clearly a papal Council, meeting in Rome and borne along on a seemingly irresistible tide of Ultramontane feeling, it did not in fact come down on the side of the hierocratic papalist tradition, any more than it favored the conciliarist-representative-episcopalist tradition. Seen from the perspective of one hundred years, Vatican I's decree on papal powers seems to have been the awkward[8] but efficacious attempt to secure the untrammeled leadership position of the pope within the Roman Catholic Church, while rejecting onesided hierocratic views inconsistent with the church's larger and more authentic tradition. In other words, the *ekklesia*-pole in ecclesiological theory could rise again and attain its natural dominance, once the extreme (but not unprecedented) doctrine of the church as seen from the papal pole had been aired and rejected in ecumenical council.[9]

This schematic interpretation of the history of the Catholic debate on the papal powers seems well-founded, as it emerges from Congar's erudite studies and surveys. It provides us with an instrument

---

[8] "Awkward" because the decree was mired in juridical thought-patterns inappropriate to its object and because within these limitations the overriding concern of the Council Majority was to let the pope appear as not subject to any human authority, hence not *bound* by any considerations of a corporative inspiration either. Compare Yves Congar, "L'ecclésiologie de la Révolution Française au Concile du Vatican, sous le signe de l'affirmation de l'autorité," in *L'Ecclésiologie au XIXᵉ siècle*, ed. M. Nédoncelle (Paris: Cerf, 1960), pp. 111-14.

[9] Cf. Heinrich Fries, "Ex sese, non ex consensu ecclesiae," in *Volk Gottes*, ed. R. Bäumer and H. Dolch (Freiburg: Herder, 1967), pp. 480-500, who shows that the approach from the totality of the faithful (*ekklesia*) to the ministerial functions (among which are those of the pope) is in possession of the Catholic theological scene today, including Vatican II; and that Vatican I at least left the way open for this development to take place, although the very questions it decided (papal primacy and infallibility) would seem calculated to impose the other, "papalist" approach.

It was very plausibly argued as recently as 1960 that this way was no longer open, viz. by Walter Ullmann, *The Medieval Papacy, St. Thomas and Beyond* (London, 1960), p. 31. He claimed that Pius XII's encyclical *Mystici Corporis* of 1943 had settled this option in the papal sense. This aspect of Pius XII's teaching, among, others, was not sanctioned by Vatican II, however: cf. Yves Congar, *L'Eglise* p. 473, note 2.

for clarifying Newman's place in the extended history of this debate, the more useful in that it corresponds well to the basic element which separated Newman's characteristic handling of this question from that of most of his Catholic theological contemporaries. Apart from the few surviving theological Gallicans, perhaps only Möhler in the nineteenth century operated consistently from the *ekklesia*-pole. The Catholicizing wing of Anglican theologians had of course stuck to this approach,[10] and even though the Catholic authors Newman read after his conversion were all practitioners of the papal approach, Newman continued, with few and superficial lapses, to recur first and last to the total church, treating the position of the pope as a question of secondary importance.

The most striking evidence of this assertion is no doubt the letter Newman wrote to Henry Wilberforce about the *Essay on Development* together with explanatory notes with which he glossed it when he copied it in 1876.[11] For a few years after 1846 he tried to think in a more Roman fashion, but his characteristic view of the church-as-a-whole as the primary ecclesiological horizon surfaced briefly in 1859 (*On Consulting the Faithful in Matters of Doctrine*) and reappeared with ever-increasing clarity in the 70s. Thus his strongest argument for the authority of the Vatican Council's decrees was not their confirmation by the pope, but their reception by the whole Roman Catholic communion with few exceptions.[12] Commenting on his previous Anglican stand on the catholicity of the church, he wrote in 1871: "were the Pope as indistinct a power as he was in the first centuries, and the Bishops as practically independent, the Church would still be the Church." [13] On Anglican orders: "Our starting-point is... the standing fact of the Church.... She is not based upon her Orders; she is not the subject of her instruments." [14] Even Newman's insistence on authority in religion is best understood against this background; this helps explain why Newman did not become increasingly intransigent in his advanced years, but instead worked out positions to blunt the edge of Ultramontanism.

This last remark, however, calls for another mode of situating Newman ecclesiologically, by comparison with contemporaries who

---

[10] Note in particular Robert Isaac Wilberforce, as above, Ch. XIII, note 6.

[11] *L & D*, XI, 190.

[12] Cf. letter of 24 Nov. 1870, Ward, *Life*, II, 376 as well as *Essays Critical and Historical*, II, 109.

[13] *Ibid.*, p. 44 note.

[14] *Ibid.*, p. 88, "Note on Essay X."

were facing some of the same questions he faced. John Coulson has recently enriched our knowledge of the immediate English background to Newman's view of the church by arguing persuasively the existence of a "common tradition" about church and society of which Samuel Taylor Coleridge, Frederick Denison Maurice, and Newman were the most conspicuous exponents. The tradition which was common to these three and opposed to the utilitarian thought of the period held "that the Church manifests the presence of Christ sacramentally to the world." [15] This aspect of Coleridge's thought—can one say of the romantic movement in Christian theology?—was of course attuned to the patristic idea of the church which Newman assimilated so thoroughly. Both factors bring him into affinity with the Catholic Tübingen School of the same period, the patristic *ressourcement* and the romantic sense for symbol, tradition, life.[16]

But the comparison with F. D. Maurice is perhaps the more enlightening, as it brings out the difference between two thinkers who proceeded in diverging directions on the basis of a common tradition. Starting with Coleridge's plea for a national church that would not evaporate into a phantom or a metaphor, Newman, under the impulse of his prophetic view of the imperial church, as I think, turned more and more away from the national component of Coleridge's vision and towards the international communion which secured the truth of faith with the most adequate safeguards, defiant if it must be of too close an arrangement with the societies in which it lived. With this went a myopia in regard to the responsibility of Christians to the commonwealth. Maurice, on the other hand, developed a theology of the Kingdom of Christ which stressed this social concern as the very test of the church's reality and sacramentality.[17] One may also note Maurice's continuing attachment to the Reformers, whereas Newman broke with the common Protestant estimation that a "fall" had taken place in the Catholic Church from which the Reformation had to rescue true Christians.

The importance of Newman's extreme and all too realistic kingdom ecclesiology, which he took over from his preaching into the *Essay on Development*, has not previously been recognized. Yet it was this ecclesiological imperialism, if I may thus label it, which drove Newman inexorably on, away from any Via Media outside the communion

---

[15] Coulson, *The Common Tradition*, p. v.
[16] Cf. T. M. Schoof, *A Survey of Catholic Theology 1800-1970*, p. 170.
[17] Coulson, *The Common Tradition*, p. 188 and *passim*.

of the world-wide church. It was to him inherently implausible that this vast church should not be the Kingdom whose features he found already in Old Testament prophecy. When we recall in this connection what Newman has told us about the impression made on him in 1839 by Augustine's *Securus judicat orbis terrarum*, the two influences render each other more intelligible. That which made Newman overcome his objections and hesitations, and seek admission into the Roman Catholic Church, was (on the theological level at least) not so much the appeal which authority exercised on him (as is commonly maintained), but primarily the appeal of an actually united and international communion. This it is which separates Newman from William Palmer of Worcester College, the theoretician of the "Branch Theory" of church unity.[18]

When Newman visited the Roman schools, the "common tradition" served him well, for Perrone too appreciated the sacramental nature of the church as the romantic movement had rediscovered it, though, as we have noted, in a papalist orientation which in his case owed much to the spirit of the Restoration after Napoleon.[19] What disconcerted Perrone and the other Roman theologians was Newman's seeming acceptance of historical change in the realm of dogma and his relative frankness about the historical reality of the church's past. They were not used to this; and the succeeding generation of theologians were even less prepared to cope with it, as the Neo-Thomistic revival gained momentum and "speculative" theology was accorded pride of place ahead of the "positive" theology practiced by Perrone.[20] On the matter of authority in the church there was much common ground between Newman and the Roman School during the first years of his Catholic life. As we have seen, the situation became strained during the struggle for the Temporal Power of the pope, but given his views on the authoritarian nature of revealed religion and the imperial character of the church, he saw the growing reliance upon doctrinal authority in the church as a legitimate response to the increased pretensions of rationalism.[21] However, Newman did

---

[18] William Palmer, *Treatise on the Church of Christ* (1838), cf. *ODC*, 1009.

[19] Walter Kasper, *Die Lehre von der Tradition in der Römischen Schule*, pp. 47-54; Congar, *L'Eglise*, pp. 429 f, 435.

[20] Edgar Hocedez, *Histoire de la théologie au XIXᵉ siècle* (Brussels: L'Edition universelle, 1947), III, 45-52 and 162 f; cf. Paul Misner, "Newman and Theological Pluralism," in *New Dimensions in Religious Experience*, ed. George Devine (Staten Island, N.Y.: Alba House, 1971), pp. 234 f.

[21] *Apo*, p. 220.

not want to see authority exercised to the detriment of theological research and general culture within the church. While composing and delivering his lecture on *The Idea of a University*, he could still feel that his convictions on this score were not out of harmony with the ideals dominant in the Catholic Church of that period. But from *Apologia* onwards, he sought consciously to mitigate and reconcile, against the dominant mood, the use of authority with due freedom of scholarship.

Finally, in the Preface to the Third Edition of *Via Media*, he arrived at a theory of the interplay of functions within the church. One could equally well call this a theory of the non-predominance of any one church function over the others, although Newman in fact was at pains to give "Theology" the preference over the ruling and the worshiping functions. What this epochal step meant in Newman's own development was a final answer to his own Anglican difficulties as expressed above all in *Prophetical Office*, and at the same time a corrective to the excesses of his earlier kingdom-ecclesiology.

His overriding concern at the end of his career was that none of the functions of the church should atrophy through the overbearing, perhaps pathological, vitality of the office of supreme direction given in the papacy. Other sources must flow, other projects go forward than those which the ruling power is fitted to command. Newman's idea of a pope's place within the church and his dependence upon other members and other functions is perhaps nowhere better put than in these words:

> When our Lord went up on high, He left His representative be-
> hind Him. This was Holy Church, His mystical Body and Bride,
> a Divine Institution, and the shrine and organ of the Paraclete, who
> speaks through her till the end comes. She, to use an Anglican poet's
> words, is "His very self below," as far as men on earth are equal to the
> discharge and fulfilment of high offices, which primarily and supremely
> are His. . . . The sovereign Pontiff would not be the visible head of
> that Body, did he not first belong to it.[22]

---

[22] *VM*, I, xxxix-xl. The Anglican poet is John Keble, see above, Ch. II, note 5.

BIBLIOGRAPHY

I. SOURCES

A. *Works of John Henry Newman*

The uniform edition of Newman's works (see L&D, XI, p. xxv), published by Longmans, Green and Co., has been used wherever not otherwise specified. The list here presented indicates the chronological sequence of those works of Newman which I consulted, and where they are to be found in the uniform edition.

1. *Sermons*

The World our Enemy. *PPS*, VII, III (8 March 1829).

Abraham and Lot. *PPS*, III, I (19 July 1829).

The Unity of the Church. *PPS*, VII, XVII (8, 15, and 22 November 1829).

Submission to Church Authority. *PPS*, III, XIV (29 November 1829).

Stedfastness in the Old Paths. *PPS*, VII, XVIII (21 March 1830).

Wilfulness of Israel in rejecting Samuel. *PPS*, III, II (9 May 1830, rewritten).

St. Peter's Authority. MS Sermon no. 246 at the Birmingham Oratory (29 June 1830).

The Self-wise Inquirer. *PPS*, I, XVII (24 October 1830).

The World's Benefactors. *PPS*, II, I (30 November 1830).

St. Paul's Conversion viewed in reference to his Office. *PPS*, II, IX (25 January 1831).

Christian Nobleness. *SD*, pp. 137-149 (22 May 1831).

Use of Saints' Days. *PPS*, II, XXXII (30 November 1831)

The Usurpations of Reason. *Fifteen Sermons preached before the University of Oxford*, pp. 54-74 (11 December 1831).

Contest between Faith and Sight. *Ibid.*, pp. 120-135 (27 May 1832).

Human Responsibility, as Independent of Circumstances. *Ibid.*, pp. 136-155 (4 November 1832).

The Immortality of the Soul. *PPS*, I, II (21 July 1833).

Self-Denial the Test of Religious Earnestness. *PPS*, I, V (22 December 1833).

The Christian Ministry. *PPS*, II, XXV (14 December 1834).

The Gospel Witnesses. *PPS*, II, XVII (27 December 1834).

The Indwelling Spirit. *PPS*, II, XIX (end of 1834).

The Gospel, a Trust committed to us. *PPS*, II, XXII (end of 1834).

The Glory of the Christian Church. *PPS*, II, VIII (end of 1834).

The Kingdom of the Saints. *PPS*, II, XX (early 1835).

The Kingdom of the Saints. *PPS*, II, XXI (early 1835).

Acceptance of Religious Principles Compulsory. *PPS*, IV, IV (22 March 1835).

Contest between Truth and Falsehood in the Church. *PPS*, III, XV (17 May 1835).

The Gift of the Spirit. *PPS*, III, XVIII (8 November 1835).

Regenerating Baptism. *PPS*, III, XIX (15 November 1835).

Elisha a Type of Christ and His Followers. *SD*, pp. 164-179 (14 August 1836).

The Church and the World. *SD*, pp. 78-111 (1 January 1837).

The Communion of Saints. *PPS*, IV, XI (14 May 1837).

The Call of David. *PPS*, VIII, IV (25 June 1837).

The Spiritual Presence of Christ in the Church. *PPS*, VI, X (6 May 1838).

The Fellowship of the Apostles. *PPS*, VI, XIV (5 October 1839).

Divine Calls. *PPS*, VIII, II (27 October 1839).

Condition of the Members of the Christian Empire. *SD*, pp. 256-274 (31 May 1840).

Implicit and Explicit Reason. *Oxford University Sermons*, pp. 251-277 (29 June 1840).

The Three Offices of Christ. *SD*, pp. 52-62 (25 December 1840).

Judaism of the Present Day. *PPS*, VI, XIII (28 February 1841).

Wisdom, as contrasted with Faith and with Bigotry. *Oxford University Sermons*, pp. 278-311 (1 June 1841).

Invisible Presence of Christ. *SD*, pp. 308-323 (28 November 1841).

Outward and Inward Notes of the Church. *SD*, pp. 324-342 (5 December 1841).

Elijah the Prophet of the Latter Days. *SD*, pp. 367-380 (12 December 1841).

Grounds for Steadfastness in our Religious Profession. *SD*, pp. 343-366 (19 December 1841).

The Work of the Christian. *SD*, pp. 1-13 (23 January 1842).

Feasting in Captivity. *SD*, pp. 381-394 (22 September 1842).

The Christian Church a Continuation of the Jewish. *SD*, pp. 180-198 (13 November 1842).

The Christian Church an Imperial Power. *SD*, **pp.** 218-236 (27 November 1842).

Sanctity the Token of the Christian Empire. *SD*, pp. 237-255 (4 December 1842).

The Theory of Developments in Religious Doctrine. *Oxford University Sermons*, pp. 312-351 (2 February 1843).

The Apostolical Christian. *SD*, pp. 275-292 (5 or 12 February 1843).

Wisdom and Innocence. *SD*, pp. 293-307 (19 February 1843).

Connexion between Personal and Public Improvement. *SD*, pp. 126-136 (4 June 1843).

The Parting of Friends. *SD*, pp. 395-409 (25 September 1843).

Christ upon the Waters. *Occ Serm*, pp. 121-162 (27 October 1850).

Order, the Witness and Instrument of Unity. *Occ Serm* pp. 183-198 (9 November 1853).

The Pope and the Revolution. *Occ Serm*, pp. 281-316 (7 October 1866).

2. *Other Works*

(1825-26.) "The Miracles of Scripture." *Two Essays on Biblical and on Ecclesiastical Miracles*, pp. 1-94. 11th edition. London, 1897.

(1830.) "Suggestions in behalf of the Church Missionary Society." *VM*, II, 9-17.

(1833.) *The Arians of the Fourth Century*. New edition. London, 1897.

(1833.) "Separation of Friends." *Verses on Various Occasions*, p. 195. New edition. London, 1896.

(1833.) "The Cruel Church." *Lyra Apostolica*, p. 184. Ed. H. C. Beeching. London, 1901.

(1833.) Tract 1: Thoughts on the Ministerial Commission.
Tract 11, 20; The Visible Church.
Tract 15: On the Apostolical Succession in the English Church. *Tracts for the Times*, I. London, 1834.

(1833-36.) "The Church of the Fathers." *Historical Sketches*, I, 338-442. New edition. London, 1891. *Historical Sketches*, II, 1-210. New edition. London, 1898.

(1834.) Tract 33: Primitive Episcopacy. *Tracts for the Times*, I. London, 1834.

(1834.) Tracts 38, 41: *Via Media*, I, II. *VM*, II, 19-48.

(1834-35.) "The Convocation of the Province of Canterbury." *Historical Sketches*, III, 337-421. New edition. London, 1897.

(1835.) "Restoration of Suffragan Bishops." *VM*, II, 49-91.

(1836.) "Home Thoughts Abroad." Rpt. under the title "How to accomplish it" in *DA*, pp. 1-43.

(1836.) Tract 71: On the Mode of conducting the Controversy with Rome. *Tracts for the Times*, III. London, 1836. Rpt. *VM*, II, 93-141.

(1836.) Tract 73: The Introduction of Rationalistic Principles into Revealed Religion. *Essays Critical and Historical*, I, 30-99.

(1836.) "The Brothers' Controversy." Rpt. under the title "Apostolical Tradition" in *Essays Critical and Historical*, I, 102-137.

(1837.) *Lectures on the Prophetical Office of the Church viewed relatively to Romanism and Popular Protestantism*. London, 1837. Rpt. in *VM*, I, 1-355.

(1837.) Tract 79: On Purgatory (Against Romanism—No. 3). *Tracts for the Times*, IV. London, 1837.

(1837.) Tract 82: Letter to a Magazine in behalf of Dr. Pusey's Tracts on Holy Baptism. *Tracts for the Times*, IV. London, 1837. Rpt. in *VM*, II, 143-194.

(1837.) "The Fall of La Mennais." *Essays Critical and Historical*, I, 138-172.

(1838.) Tract 83: Advent Sermons on Antichrist. *Tracts for the Times*, V. London, 1840. Rpt. as "The Patristical Idea of Antichrist" in *DA*, pp. 44-108.

(1838.) *Lectures on the Doctrine of Justification*. 7th edition. London, 1897.

(1838.) *Letter to the Margaret Professor of Divinity on Mr. R.H. Froude's Statements on the Holy Eucharist*. *VM*, II, 195-257.

(1838.) "Medieval Oxford." *Historical Sketches*, III, 313-335.

(1838.) Tract 85: Lectures on the Scripture Proof of the Doctrines of the Church. Part I. *Tracts for the Times*, V. London, 1840. Rpt. as "Holy Scripture in its Relation to the Catholic Creed" in *DA*, pp. 109-253.

(1838.) "Palmer's Treatise on the Church." Rpt. as "Palmer's View of Faith and Unity" in *Essays Critical and Historical*, I, 179-215.

(1839.) "Jacobson's Apostolical Father." Rpt. as "The Theology of St. Ignatius" in *Essays Critical and Historical*, I, 222-261.

(1839.) "State of Religious Parties." Rpt. as "Prospects of the Anglican Church" in *Essays Critical and Historical*, I, 263-307.

(1840.) "The Catholicity of the Anglican Church." *Essays Critical and Historical*, II, 1-73.

(1840.) "Todd's Discourses on Antichrist." Rpt. as "The Protestant Idea of Antichrist" in *Essays Critical and Historical*, II, 112-185.

(1841.) *Tract 90: Remarks on Certain Passages in the Thirty-nine Articles*. London 1841. Rpt. in *VM*, II, 259-348.

(1841.) "Milman's View of Christianity." *Essays Critical and Historical*, II, 186-248.

(1841.) *Letter to Dr. Jelf in Explanation of the Remarks*. *VM*, II, 365-391.

(1841.) *Letter to the Bishop of Oxford in the Same Subject*. *VM*, II, 395-424.

(1841.) "The Reformation of the Eleventh Century." *Essays Critical and Historical*, II, 249-317.

(1841.) "Private Judgment." *Essays Critical and Historical*, II, 336-374.

(1841.) *Select Treatises of St. Athanasius*. 2 vols. 7th edition. London, 1897.

(1843.) "The Miracles of Early Ecclesiastical History." *Two Essays on Biblical and Ecclesiastical Miracles*, pp. 95-390. 11th edition. London, 1897.

(1845.) *An Essay on the Development of Christian Doctrine*. London, 1845. 2nd edition. London, 1846.

(1847.) "The Newman-Perrone Paper on Development." Ed. T. Lynch. *Gregorianum*, 16 (1935), 404-444.

(1848.) *Loss and Gain.* 12th edition. London, 1896.

(1850.) *Twelve Lectures addressed to the Anglican Party of 1833. Diff,* I.

(1851.) *Lectures on the Present Position of Catholics in England.* New edition. London, 1896.

(1852.) *Discourses on the Scope and Nature of University Education. The Idea of a University.* London, 1873, pp. 1-239.

(1854.) "Office and Work of Universities." Rpt. as "Rise and Progress of Universities" in *Historical Sketches,* III, 1-251.

(1855.) *Callista, a Tale of the Third Century.* New edition. London, 1895.

(1855.) "Who's to Blame?" *DA,* pp. 306-362.

(1858.) "St. Cyril's Formula, μία φύσις σεσαρκωμένη. *Tracts Theological and Ecclesiastical,* pp. 329-382. New edition. London, 1895.

(1859.) *On Consulting the Faithful in Matters of Doctrine.* Ed. John Coulson. London, 1961.

(1864.) *Apologia pro Vita sua. Apo.*

(1865.) *Letter addressed to the Rev. E. B. Pusey, D.D., on Occasion of his Eirenicon. Diff,* II, 1-118.

(1865-68.) Notes in preparation of my proposed Second Pamphlet to Pusey on the Pope's Powers . . . MS A 5 23 at the Birmingham Oratory.

(1866.) "An Internal Argument for Christianity." *DA,* pp. 363-398.

(1870.) *An Essay in Aid of a Grammar of Assent.*

(1875.) *A Letter addressed to His Grace the Duke of Norfolk on Occasion of Mr. Gladstone's Recent Expostulation.* In *Newman and Gladstone: The Vatican Decrees,* pp. 73-228. Ed. Alvan S. Ryan. Notre Dame, 1962. Also in *Diff,* II, 171-378.

(1877.) *The Via Media of the Anglican Church.* Vol I: *Lectures on the Prophetical Office of the Church,* 3rd edition. Vol II: *Occasional Letters and Tracts.* New edition. London, 1895-96.

(1878.) *An Essay on the Development of Christian Doctrine.* 3rd rev. edition.

(1884.) *On the Inspiration of Scripture.* Ed. J. Derek Holmes and Robert Murray. London, 1967.

3. Letters and Diaries

Newman, John Henry. *Autobiographical Writings.* Ed. H. Tristram. New York, 1957.

Cardinal Newman and William Froude, F. R. S.: A Correspondence. Ed. Gordon H. Harper. Baltimore, 1933.

Letters and Correspondence of John Henry Newman during his Life in the English Church. Ed. Anne Mozley. 2 vols. London, 1897.

The Letters and Diaries of John Henry Newman. Ed. Charles Stephen Dessain and others. Vols. XI—XXVI. London, 1962-74.

B. *Other Primary Sources*

Acton, John Emerich Edward Dalberg. *The Correspondence of Lord Acton and Richard Simpson.* Ed. Josef Altholz and Damien McElrath. 2 vols. Cambridge, England, 1971-73.

——. *Essays on Church and State.* Ed. Douglas Woodruff. New York, 1953.

——. *Essays on Freedom and Power.* Ed. Gertrude Himmelfarb. Boston, Mass. and Glencoe, Ill., 1949.

——. *The History of Freedom and Other Essays.* Ed. J. N. Figgis and R. V. Laurence, London, 1907.

Allies, Thomas W. *The Church of England Cleared From the Charge of Schism.* London, 1846.

——. *The See of St. Peter.* London, 1850. 3rd ed. with Preface, London, 1866.

Bagot, Richard, D.D. *A Charge Delivered to the Clergy of the Diocese of Oxford.* Oxford, 1838.

Barrow, Isaac. *Treatise on the Pope's Supremacy. Enchiridion Theologicum Anti-Romanum,* II. Ed. "E.C." of St. Alban's Hall. Oxford, 1836.

Bowden, John William, with R. H. Froude, John Keble, J. H. Newman, R. I. Wilberforce and Isaac Williams. *Lyra Apostolica.* Ed. H. C. Beeching. London, 1901.

Bull, George. *Defensio Fidei Nicaenae,* I, II. Vols. 4 and 5 of *The Works of George Bull,* collected and rev. by the Rev. Edward Burton, M. A. Oxford, 1827.

Cyprian. *De lapsis and De ecclesiae catholicae unitate.* Ed. Maurice Bévenot. Oxford, 1971.

Döllinger, Ignaz von. *Briefwechsel* (with Lord Acton). Ed. Victor Conzemius. 3 vols. Munich, 1963-1971.

English Historical Documents, 1833-1874. Ed. G. M. Young and W. D. Handcock. London, 1956.

Faussett, Godfrey. *The Revival of Popery.* 3rd ed. Oxford, 1841.

——. *The Thirty-Nine Articles.* Oxford, 1841.

Feßler, Joseph. *Die wahre und die falsche Unfehlbarkeit der Päpste.* 3rd ed. Vienna, 1871.

Froude, Richard Hurrell. *Remains.* 4 vols. London, 1838-1839.

Gladstone, W. E. *The Vatican Decrees in their Bearing on Civil Allegiance: A Political Expostulation.* London, 1874.

Homilies. Certain Sermons or Homilies appointed to be read in Churches in the time of the late Queen Elizabeth . . . A new edition. Oxford, 1822.

Janus. *Der Papst und das Concil.* Leipzig, 1869.

Keble, John. *The Christian Year* (1827). Oxford, 1876.

Manning, Henry Edward. "Caesarism and Ultramontanism." *Miscellanies.* 3rd ed. New York, 1880. Pp. 503-550.

——. *The Oecumenical Council and the Infallibility of the Roman Pontiff.* London, 1869.

——. *Petri Privilegium.* London, 1871.

——. *Temporal Sovereignty of the Popes.* London, 1860.

——. *The Vatican Council and Its Definitions.* London, 1870.

Maurice, Frederick Denison. *The Epistle to the Hebrews.* London, 1846.

Milman, Henry Hart. "Newman on the Development of Christian Doctrine." *Savanarola, Erasmus, and Other Essays.* London, 1870.

Milner, Joseph. *The History of the Church of Christ.* 4 vols. Ed. Thomas Grantham. London, 1847.

Möhler, Johann Adam. *Die Einheit in der Kirche oder das Prinzip des Katholizismus.* Ed. Josef Rupert Geiselmann. Cologne, 1957.

Mozley, James B. *The Theory of Development.* London, 1878.

Nelson, Robert. *The Life of George Bull, D.D. The Works of George Bull.* Ed. Edward Burton. Vol. I. Oxford, 1827.

Newton, Thomas. *Dissertations on the Prophecies.* New ed. 2 vols. London, 1820.

Palmer, William. *A Narrative of Events connected with the Publication of the Tracts for the Times.* New ed. London, 1883.

——, and John Henry Newman. "On the Apostolical Succession in the English Church." Tract No. 15. *Tracts for the Times,* I. New ed. London, 1838.

Perrone, Giovanni. *Praelectiones Theologicae.* Vol. II. Regensburg, 1854.

Pusey, Edward Bouverie. *The Articles Treated on in Tract 90 reconsidered and their interpretation vindicated in a Letter to the Rev. R. W. Jelf, D. D., Canon of Christ Church.* 2nd ed. Oxford, 1841.

——. *An Eirenicon, . . .* Oxford, 1865.

———. *Is Healthful Reunion Impossible?* *A Second Letter to . . . Newman.* Oxford and London, 1870.

Whately, Richard. *The Errors of Romanism traced to their Origin in Human Nature.* London, 1830.

Whitby, Daniel. *A Paraphrase and Commentary on the New Testament.* 2 vols. 4th ed. London, 1718.

Wilberforce, Robert Isaac. *An Inquiry into the Principles of Church-Authority.* London, 1854.

II. SECONDARY WORKS

Acta Conciliorum Oecumenicorum. Ed. Edward Schwartz. Strasbourg, 1914-1938.

Allchin, A. Macdonald. "The Theological Vision of the Oxford Movement." *OS*, pp. 50-75.

Allen, Derick W., and A. Macdonald Allchin. "Primacy and Collegiality: an Anglican View." *Journal of Ecumenical Studies*, 2 (1965), 68-80.

Altaner, Berthold. "Zur Geschichte des päpstlichen Primats." *Theologische Revue*, 37 (1938), 329-39.

———. *Patrologie.* 5th ed. Freiburg, 1958.

Altholz, Joseph L. *The Liberal Catholic Movement in England: the "Rambler" and its Contributors 1848-1864.* London, 1962.

———. "The Vatican Decrees Controversy, 1874-1875." *Catholic Historical Review*, 57 (1971-72), 593-605.

American Essays for the Newman Centennial. Ed. John K. Ryan and Edmond D. Benard. Washington, 1947.

The Apostolic Fathers. Ed. Robert M. Grant. 6 vols. New York, 1965-1968.

Die Apostolischen Väter. Ed. Joseph A. Fischer. Munich, 1956.

Aretin, Karl Otmar von. *The Papacy and the Modern World.* New York, 1970.

Artz, Johannes, "Entstehung und Auswirkung von Newmans Theorie der Dogmenentwicklung." *Theologische Quartalschrift*, 148 (1968), 63-104 and 167-198.

———. Introduction to Newman, *über die Entwicklung der Glaubenslehre.* Mainz, 1969.

Aubert, Roger. *Le pontificat de Pie IX (1846-1878).* Vol. XXI of *Histoire de l'Église depuis les origines jusqu'à nos jours.* Fondée par A. Fliche et V. Martin. Paris, 1963.

———. "Religious Liberty from 'Mirari vos' to the 'Syllabus'." *Concilium*, 7 (1965), 50-56.

———. *Vatican I.* Vol. 12 of *Histoire des conciles oecuméniques*, ed. Gervais Dumeige. Paris, 1964.

Bacht, Heinrich. "Primat und Episkopat im Spannungsfeld der beiden Vatikanischen Konzile." *Wahrheit und Verkündigung.* Ed. Leo Scheffczyk, Werner Dettloff and Richard Heinzmann. Paderborn 1967. II, 1447-1466.

Baker, William J. "Hurrell Froude and the Reformers." *Journal of Ecclesiastical History*, 21 (1970), 243-259.

Bardy, Gustave, ed. and tr. Eusèbe de Césarée, *Histoire ecclésiastique.* Paris, 1952-1960.

Batiffol, Pierre. *Saint Grégoire le Grand.* 2nd ed. Paris, 1928.

———. *Le Siège apostolique (359-451).* Paris, 1924.

Benn, Alfred William. *The History of English Rationalism in the Nineteenth Century* (1906). 2 vols. Rpt. New York, 1962.

Bennett, Gareth Vaughan, "Patristic Tradition in Anglican Thought, 1660-1900." *Oecumenica 1971-1972: Tradition in Lutheranism and Anglicanism.* Ed. G. Gassmann and V. Vajta. Minneapolis, 1972. Pp. 63-85.

Bergeron, Richard. *Les abus de l'église d'après Newman*: *Étude de la Préface à la troisième édition de La Via Media*. Montréal, 1971.
Beskow, Per. *Rex Gloriae*: *The Kingship of Christ in the Early Church*. Stockholm, 1962.
Best, G. F. A. "The Protestant Constitution and Its Supporters." *Transactions of the Royal Historical Society* (series 5), 8 (1958), 105-127.
Betz, Otto. "Felsenmann und Felsengemeinde." *Zeitschrift für die neutestamentliche Wissenschaft und die Kunde der älteren Kirche*, 48 (1957), 49-77.
Biemer, Günter. *Newman on Tradition*. Rev. ed. New York, 1967.
——. *Überlieferung und Offenbarung*: *die Lehre von der Tradition nach John Henry Newman*. Freiburg, 1961.
Blank, Josef. "The Person and Office of Peter in the New Testament." *Concilium*, 83 (1973), 42-55.
Blehl, Vincent F. "Newman, the Bishops and *The Rambler*." *Downside Review*, 90 (1972), 20-40.
——. "Newman's Delation: Some Hitherto Unpublished Letters." *Dublin Review*, 486 (1960-61), 296-305.
Bokenkotter, Thomas S. *Cardinal Newman as an Historian*. Louvain, 1959.
Bouyer, Louis. *Newman*: *His Life and Spirituality*. Cleveland/New York, 1960.
——. Introduction and notes to Newman, *Essai sur le développement de la doctrine chrétienne*. Paris, 1964.
Brilioth, Yngve. *The Anglican Revival*: *Studies in the Oxford Movement*. London, 1925.
——. *Three Lectures on Evangelicalism and the Oxford Movement*. London, 1934.
Brown, Raymond E. *Priest and Bishop*: *Biblical Reflections*. New York, 1970.
Burke, Patrick. "The Monarchical Episcopate at the End of the First Century." *Journal of Ecumenical Studies*, 7 (1970), 499-518.
Butler, Cuthbert. *The Life and Times of Bishop Ullathorne*. 2 vols. London, 1926.
——. *The Vatican Council*. 2 vols. London, 1930.
Byrne, James J. "The Notion of Doctrinal Development in the Anglican Writings of J. H. Newman." *Ephemerides Theologicae Lovanienses*, 14 (1937), 230-286.
Camelot, Pierre-Thomas. *Ephèse et Chalcédoine*. Vol. 2 of *Histoire des conciles oecuméniques*. Ed. Gervais Dumeige. Paris, 1962.
Cameron, James M. Introduction to Newman, *An Essay on the Development of Christian Doctrine*, the ed. of 1845. Baltimore, 1974.
——. "Newman and the Empiricist Tradition." *OS*, pp. 76-96.
Campenhausen, Hans von. *Ecclesiastical Authority and Spiritual Power in the Church of the First Three Centuries*. Stanford, 1969.
Caspar, Erich. *Die älteste römische Bischofsliste*. Schriften der Königsberger Gelehrten Gesellschaft, Geisteswissenschaftliche Klasse, 2. Jahrg., Heft 4. Berlin, 1926.
——. *Geschichte des Papsttums von den Anfängen bis zur Höhe der Weltherrschaft*. 2 vols. Tübingen, 1930-1933.
——. "Primatus Petri." *Zeitschrift der Savigny-Stiftung für Rechtsgeschichte*, 47, Kanonistische Abteilung, 16 (1927), 253-331.
Cauwelaert, R. van. "L'intervention de l'église de Rome à Corinthe vers l'an 96." *Revue d'histoire ecclésiastique*, 31 (1935), 267-306.
Chadwick, William Owen. *From Bossuet to Newman*: *the Idea of Doctrinal Development*. Cambridge, 1957.
——. *The Victorian Church*. 2 vols. London, 1966-1970.
Le Chiese nei regni dell'Europa occidentale e i loro rapporti con Roma sino all' 800, Settimana di Studi del Centro Italiano di Studi sull'alto Medioevo, 7 (Spoleto, 1960).

Church, Richard William. *The Oxford Movement: Twelve Years, 1833-1845.* Ed. Geoffrey Best. Chicago, 1970.

Colson, Jean. *L'Épiscopat catholique. Collégialité et Primauté dans les trois premiers siècles de l'Église.* Paris, 1963.

——. *Klemens von Rom.* Stuttgart 1962.

Conciliorum Oecumenicorum Decreta. Ed. G. Alberigo. 3rd rev. ed. Freiburg, 1973.

Congar, Yves. *L'Église de saint Augustin à l'époque moderne.* Paris, 1970.

——. "Geschichtliche Betrachtungen über Glaubensspaltung und Einheitsproblematik." *Begegnung der Christen.* Ed. Maximilian Roesle and Oscar Cullmann. Stuttgart/Frankfurt, 1959. Pp. 405-429.

——. "Saint Thomas Aquinas and the Infallibility of the Papal Magisterium (Summa Theol., II-II, q. 1, a. 10)." *The Thomist,* 38 (1974), 81-105.

Conzemius, Victor. "Die 'Römischen Briefe vom Konzil'." *Römische Quartalschrift,* 59 (1964), 186-229 and 60 (1965), 76-119.

Coulson, John, ed. John Henry Newman, *On Consulting the Faithful in Matters of Doctrine.* London, 1961.

——. *Newman and the Common Tradition. A Study in the Language of Church and Society.* Oxford, 1970.

——. "Newman on the Church—his final view, its origins and influence." *OS,* pp. 123-143.

—— with A. M. Allchin and Meriol Trevor. *Newman: a Portrait Restored: an Ecumenical Revaluation.* London, 1965.

Cross, Frank Leslie. *John Henry Newman.* London, 1933.

Culler, Dwight. *The Imperial Intellect: A Study of Cardinal Newman's Educational Ideal.* New Haven, 1955.

Cullmann, Oscar. *Petrus: Jünger — Apostel — Märtyrer.* Munich, 1967.

——. "Petrus, Werkzeug des Satans und Werkzeug Gottes." *Vorträge und Aufsätze.* Ed. Karlfried Fröhlich. Tübingen 1966.

Davis, H. Francis. "Doctrine, Development of." *A Catholic Dictionary of Theology.* London, 1967. II, 177-189.

——. "Le rôle et l'apostolat de la hiérarchie et du laicat dans la théologie de l'Église chez Newman." *L'Ecclésiologie au XIXᵉ siècle.* Ed. M. Nédoncelle. Paris, 1960. Pp. 329-349.

Dawson, Christopher. "Newman and the Modern World." *The Tablet,* 226 (5 August 1972), 733-734.

——. *The Spirit of the Oxford Movement.* London, 1933.

DeLaura, David J., et al. *Victorian Prose. A Guide to Research.* New York, 1973.

Dessain, Charles Stephen. *John Henry Newman.* London, 1966.

——. "The Newman Archives at Birmingham." *NS,* 3 (1957), 269-279.

——. "The Reception among Catholics of Newman's Doctrine of Development." *NS,* IV (1964), 179-191.

The Documents of Vatican II. Ed. Walter M. Abbott. New York, 1966.

Dupuy, Bernard-Dominique. "L'influence de Newman sur la théologie catholique du développement dogmatique." *NS,* IV (1964), 143-165.

——. "Newman's Influence in France." *OS,* pp. 11, 147-173.

——. Introduction and notes to Newman, *Lettre au Duc de Norfolk.* Paris, 1970.

Dvornik, Francis. *Byzantium and the Roman Primacy.* New York, 1966.

Egner, G. *Apologia pro Charles Kingsley.* London, 1969.

Faber, Geoffrey. *Oxford Apostles: a Character Study of the Oxford Movement.* London, 1936.

Fries, Heinrich. "Die Dogmengeschichte des fünften Jahrhunderts im theologischen Werdegang von John Henry Newman." *Das Konzil von Chalkedon.* Ed. Alois Grillmeier. Würzburg, 1954. III, 421-454.
——. "Ex sese, non ex consensu ecclesiae." *Volk Gottes.* Ed. R. Bäumer and H. Dolch. Freiburg, 1967. Pp. 480-500.
——. "J. H. Newmans Beitrag zum Verständnis der Tradition." *Die mündliche Überlieferung.* Ed. Michael Schmaus. Munich, 1957. Pp. 33-122.
——. "Newmans Bedeutung für die Theologie." *NS,* I (1948), 181-198.
——. "Newman und Döllinger." *NS,* I (1948), 29-66.
——. *Die Religionsphilosophie Newmans.* Stuttgart, 1948.
Fuchs, Josef. "Origines d'une trilogie ecclésiologique à l'époque rationaliste de la théologie." *Revue des sciences philosophiques et théologiques,* 53 (1969), 185-211.

Gaudemet, Jean. *L'Église dans l'Empire Romain (IV-V siècles).* Paris, 1958.
Goemans, Monald. "Chalkedon als 'Allgemeines Konzil'." *Das Konzil von Chalkedon.* Ed. Aloys Grillmeier. Würzburg, 1951. I, 251-289.
Gooch, George P. *History and Historians in the Nineteenth Century* [1913]. Boston, 1959.
Gorce, Denys. *Newman et les Pères.* Bruges, 1947.
Greenfield, Robert H. "The Attitude of the Tractarians to the Roman Catholic Church 1833-1850." Unpublished diss., Oxford, 1956 (in Bodleian Library, Oxford).
Grillmeier, Aloys. *Christ in Christian Tradition.* New York, 1965.
Guitton, Jean. *The Church and the Laity.* New York, 1965.
——. *La Philosophie de Newman (Essai sur l'idée de développement).* Paris, 1933.

Haller, Johannes. *Das Papsttum. Idee und Wirklichkeit.* Vol. I: *Die Grundlagen.* Stuttgart, 1934.
Hammans, Herbert. *Die neueren katholischen Erklärungen der Dogmenentwicklung.* Essen, 1965.
Handbuch der Dogmengeschichte. Ed. M. Schmaus, A. Grillmeier, and L. Scheffczyk. Freiburg, 1951—.
Handbuch der Kirchengeschichte. Ed. Hubert Jedin. Freiburg, 1962—. E.T. (in part), *Handbook of Church History.* New York, 1965—.
Härdelin, Alf. *The Tractarian Understanding of the Eucharist.* Uppsala, 1965.
Harrold, Charles Frederick. *John Henry Newman: An Expository and Critical Study of His Mind, Thought and Art.* New York, 1945.
Heiler, Friedrich. *Altkirchliche Autonomie und päpstlicher Zentralismus.* Munich, 1941.
Hemmerdinger, Bertrand. "La Prépondérance de l'Église de Rome en 95." *Revue des sciences philosophiques et théologiques,* 47 (1963), 58-60.
Herman, Emil. "Chalkedon und die Ausgestaltung des konstantinopolitanischen Primats." *Das Konzil von Chalkedon,* II, 459-490.
Hernegger, Rudolf. *Macht ohne Auftrag.* Olten, 1963.
Hertling, Ludwig. *Communio: Church and Papacy in Early Christianity.* Tr. and ed. Jared Wicks. Chicago, 1972.
Hess, Hamilton. *The Canons of the Council of Sardica.* Oxford, 1958.
Hocedez, Edgar. *Histoire de la théologie au XIXᵉ siècle.* 3 vols. Brussels, 1947.
Hofmann, Fritz. "Der Kampf der Päpste um Konzil und Dogma von Chalkedon von Leo dem Grossen bis Hormisdas (451-519)." *Das Konzil von Chalkedon,* II, 13-94.
Hofstetter, Karl. "Das Petrusamt in der Kirche des 1.-2. Jahrhunderts: Jerusalem-Rom." *Begegegnung der Christen.* Ed. Maximilian Roesle and Oscar Cullman. Stuttgart/Frankfurt, 1959. Pp. 373-389.

Holmes, J. Derek. "Cardinal Newman and the First Vatican Council." *Annuarium Historiae Conciliorum*, 1 (1969), 374-398.
——. "How Newman Blunted the Edge of Ultramontanism." *Clergy Review*, 53 (1968), 353-362.
——. "Newman on Faith and History." *Philosophical Studies*, 21 (1973), 202-216.
——. "A Note on Newman's Historical Method." *OS*, pp. 97-99.
Horst, Fidelis van der. *Das Schema über die Kirche auf dem I. Vatikanischen Konzil*. Paderborn, 1963.
Hunt, R. W. "Newman's Notes on Dean Church's Oxford 'Movement'." *Bodleian Library Record*, 8 (1969), 135-57.
Hutton, Richard H. *Cardinal Newman*. 2nd ed. London, 1891.

Infallibility in the Church. Ed. M. D. Goulder. London, 1968.
Ingram, Kenneth. *John Keble*. London, 1933.

Jalland, Trevor Gervase. *The Church and the Papacy*. London, 1949.
Joannou, Perikles Petros. *Die Ostkirche und die Cathedra Petri im 4. Jahrhundert*. Stuttgart, 1972.
Jones, Owain W. *Isaac Williams and His Circle*. London, 1971.
Journet, Charles. *Primauté de Pierre*. Paris, 1953.

Karrer, Otto. *Um die Einheit der Christen*. Frankfurt, 1953.
——. "Apostolische Nachfolge und Primat." *Fragen der Theologie heute*. Ed. Johannes Feiner, Josef Trütsch and Franz Böckle. Einsiedeln, 1957. Pp. 175-206.
——. "Das Petrusamt in der Frühkirche." *Festgabe Joseph Lortz*. Ed. Erwin Iserloh and Peter Manns. Baden-Baden, 1957. I, 507-525.
——. "Das Bischofsamt und das Petrusamt in der Kirche." *Volk Gottes*. Ed. R. Bäumer and H. Dolch. Freiburg 1967. Pp. 54-83.
Kasper, Walter. *Die Lehre von der Tradition in der Römischen Schule*. Freiburg, 1962.
——. "Primat und Episkopat nach dem Vatikanum I." *Theologische Quartalschrift*, 142 (1962), 47-83.
Kempf, Friedrich. "Die päpstliche Gewalt in der mittelalterlichen Welt." *Miscellanea Historiae Pontificiae 21: Saggi storici intorno al papato*. Rome, 1959. Pp. 117-169.
Kenny, Terence. *The Political Thought of John Henry Newman*. London, 1957.
Das Konzil von Chalkedon. Geschichte und Gegenwart. Ed. Aloys Grillmeier and Heinrich Bacht. 3 vols. Würzburg, 1951-1954.
Kümmel, Werner Georg. *The New Testament: The History of the Investigation of Its Problems*. Nashville, 1972.
Küng, Hans. *Structures of the Church*. New York, 1964.
——. *The Church*. New York, 1967.

Lash, Nicholas. *Change in Focus*. London, 1973.
——. "Faith and History: Some Reflections on Newman's 'Essay on the Development of Christian Doctrine'." *Irish Theological Quarterly*, 38 (1971), 224-241.
——. "The Notions of 'Implicit' and 'Explicit' Reason in Newman's University Sermons: A Difficulty." *The Heythrop Journal*, 11 (1970), 48-54.
Laski, Harold J. *Studies in the Problem of Sovereignty*. New Haven, 1917.
Lease, Gary. *Witness to the Faith. Cardinal Newman on the Teaching Authority of the Church*. Pittsburgh, 1972.
Léonard, Augustin. "La Foi principe fondamental du développement du dogme." *Revue des sciences philosophiques et théologiques*, 42 (1958), 276-286.

Liddon, Henry Parry. *Life of Edward Bouverie Pusey*. 4 vols. London, 1893-97.
Loisy, Alfred. *Mémoires pour servir à l'histoire religieuse de notre temps*. 3 vols. Paris, 1930-31.
Lorenz, Rudolf. *Das vierte bis sechste Jahrhundert (Westen)*. Vol. I, part C of *Die Kirche in ihrer Geschichte*. Ed. K. D. Schmidt and E. Wolf. Göttingen, 1970.
Ludwig, Joseph. *Die Primatworte Mt 16, 18.19 in der altkirchlichen Exegese*. Münster, 1952.
Lutheran/Roman Catholic Dialogue Group for the United States. "Ministry and the Church Universal: Differing Attitudes toward Papal Primacy." *Origins*, 3 (14 March 1974), 585-600.

McAdoo, Henry Robert. *The Spirit of Anglicanism: A Survey of Anglican Theological Method in the Seventeenth Century*. New York, 1965.
McClelland, Vincent Alan. *English Roman Catholics and Higher Education, 1830-1903*. Oxford, 1973.
McCue, James F. "The Roman Primacy in the Second Century and the Problem of the Development of Dogma." *Theological Studies*, 25 (1964), 161-196.
MacDougall, Hugh A. *The Acton-Newman Relations*. New York, 1962.
McElrath, Damian. *Richard Simpson 1820-1876*. Louvain, 1972.
———. *The Syllabus of Pius IX: Some Reactions in England*. Louvain, 1964.
McGrath, Fergal. *Newman's University: Idea and Reality*. Dublin, 1951.
Markus, Robert, and Eric John. *Pastors or Princes. A New Look at the Papacy and Hierarchy*. Washington, 1969.
Marot, Hilaire. "The Primacy and the Decentralization of the Early Church." *Concilium*, 7 (1965), 9-16.
Marschall, Werner. *Karthago und Rom. Die Stellung der nordafrikanischen Kirche zum Apostolischen Stuhl in Rom*. Stuttgart, 1971.
Martin, Thomas Owen. "The Twenty-eighth Canon of Chalcedon." *Das Konzil von Chalkedon*, II, 443-458.
Meyendorff, John, Alexander Schmemann, Nicolas Afanassieff, and Nicolas Koulomzine. *The Primacy of Peter*. London, 1963.
Michel, Anton. "Der Kampf um das politische oder petrinische Prinzip der Kirchenführung." *Das Konzil von Chalkedon*, II, 491-562.
The Mind of the Oxford Movement. Ed. Owen Chadwick. Stanford, Cal., 1960.
The Ministry in Historical Perspectives. Ed. H. R. Niebuhr and D. D. Williams. New York, 1956.
Misner, Paul. "Newman and the Tradition Concerning the Papal Antichrist." *Church History*, 42 (1973), 377-395.
———. "Newman and Theological Pluralism." *New Dimensions in Religious Experience*. Ed. George Devine. Staten Island, New York, 1971. Pp. 233-244.
———. "Newman's Concept of Revelation and the Development of Doctrine." *The Heythrop Journal*, 11 (1970), 32-47.
———. "Papal Primacy in a Pluriform Polity." *Journal of Ecumenical Studies*, 11 (1974), 239-260.
———. "Theologians and the Papacy." *The Newman*, 4 (1969), 190-198.
Mörsdorf, Klaus. "Die Entwicklung der Zweigliedrigkeit der kirchlichen Hierarchie." *Münchener Theologische Zeitschrift*, 3 (1952), 1-16.
———. "Die Unmittelbarkeit der päpstlichen Primatialgewalt im Lichte des kanonischen Rechtes." *Einsicht und Glaube*. Ed. Joseph Ratzinger and Heinrich Fries. Freiburg, 1962. Pp. 464-478.
Mysterium Salutis: Grundriss heilsgeschichtlicher Dogmatik. Ed. Johannes Feiner and Magnus Löhrer. Einsiedeln, 1965—.

Nédoncelle, Maurice. "L'Apologia de Newman dans l'histoire de l'autobiographie et de la théologie." *Interpretation der Welt*. Ed. H. Kuhn. Würzburg, 1965. Pp. 571-585.

——. "Le développement de la doctrine chrétienne: J. B. Mozley, critique anglican de Newman." *Oecumenica 1971-1972: Tradition in Lutheranism and Anglicanism*. Ed. G. Gassmann and V. Vajta. Minneapolis, 1972. Pp. 156-172.

——. "Newman et Blondel: la théologie des développements doctrinaux." *NS*, VI (1964), 105-122.

——. "Newman et le développement dogmatique." *Revue des sciences religieuses*, 32 (1958), 197-213.

——. "Newman, théologien des abus de l'Eglise." *Oecumenica*, 2 (1967), 116-132.

——. "The Revival of Newman Studies—Some Reflections." *Downside Review*, 86 (1968), 385-394.

——. "La Suprématie papale d'après l'Essai sur le développement de Newman." *Parole de Dieu et sacerdoce. Études présentées à Mgr. Weber*. Ed. E. Fischer and L. Bouyer. Paris, 1962. Pp. 139-152.

Nédoncelle, Maurice, et. al. *L'Ecclésiologie au XIXe siècle*. Paris, 1960.

Newman's Apologia: A Classic Reconsidered. Ed. Vincent F. Blehl and F. X. Connolly. New York, 1964.

Newsome, David. "The Evangelical Sources of Newman's Power." *OS*, pp. 11-30.

——. *The Wilberforces and Henry Manning: The Parting of Friends*. Cambridge, Mass., 1966.

Nicholls, David. "Newman's Anglican Critics." *Anglican Theological Review*, 47 (1965), 377-395.

Norman, E. R. *Anti-Catholicism in Victorian England*. London, 1968.

Oakley, Francis. *Council Over Pope? Towards a Provisional Ecclesiology*. New York, 1969.

O'Connell, Marvin R. *The Oxford Conspirators: A History of the Oxford Movement 1833-45*. New York, 1969.

Oepke, Albrecht. "Der Herrnspruch über die Kirche Mt 16, 17-19 in der neuesten Forschung." *Studia Theologica*. Lund, 1950. II, 110-165.

The Oxford Movement. Ed. Eugene R. Fairweather. New York, 1964.

Parker, Thomas M. "The Rediscovery of the Fathers in the Seventeenth-century Anglican Tradition." *OS*, pp. 31-49.

Patterson, Webster T. *Newman: Pioneer for the Layman*. Washington, 1968.

Pelikan, Jaroslav. *The Christian Tradition: A History of the Development of Doctrine*. Vol. I: *The Emergence of the Catholic Tradition (100-600)*. Chicago, 1971.

——. *Historical Theology: Continuity and Change in Christian Tradition*. Philadelphia, 1971.

Peter in the New Testament. Ed. R. E. Brown, K. P. Donfried, and J. Reumann. Minneapolis/New York, 1973.

Problems of Authority. Ed. John M. Todd. Baltimore, 1962.

Purcell, Edmund Sheridan. *Life of Cardinal Manning*. 2 vols. New York, 1896.

Quellen zur Geschichte des Papsttums und des römischen Katholizismus. Comp. Carl Mirbt. 6th ed. rev. by Kurt Aland. Vol. I: *Von den Anfängen bis zum Tridentinum*. Tübingen, 1967.

Quinn, J. Richard. *The Recognition of the True Church According to John Henry Newman*. Washington, 1954.

Rahner, Karl. "Zur Frage der Dogmenentwicklung." *Schriften zur Theologie*, VI, 49-90. Einsiedeln, 1954—.
——. "Überlegungen zur Dogmenentwicklung." *Schriften*, IV, 11-50.
——. "Zur Theologie des Symbols." *Schriften*, IV, 275-311.
——. "Was ist eine dogmatische Aussage?" *Schriften*, V, 54-81.
——. , and Joseph Ratzinger. *The Episcopate and the Primacy*. New York, 1962.
Ratzinger, Joseph. "Das geistliche Amt und die Einheit der Kirche." *Die Autorität der Freiheit*. Ed. Johann Christoph Hampe. Munich, 1967. II, 417-433.
——. *Das neue Volk Gottes*. Düsseldorf, 1969.
——. "Primat, Episkopat und Successio apostolica." *Catholica*, 13 (1959), 260-277.
Rimoldi, Antonio. *L'Apostolo San Pietro*. Rome, 1958.
Ritter, Adolf M., and G. Leich. *Wer ist die Kirche?* Göttingen, 1968.
Robbins, William. *The Newman Brothers: An Essay in Comparative Intellectual Biography*. Cambridge, Mass., 1966.
The Roman Question: Extracts from the despatches of Odo Russell from Rome 1858-1870. Ed. Noel Blakiston. London, 1962.
Ryan, Alvan S. "The Development of Newman's Political Thought." *The Review of Politics*, 7 (1945), 210-240.

Sandeen, Ernest R. *The Roots of Fundamentalism: British and American Millenarianism 1800-1930*. Chicago, 1970.
Schiffers, Norbert. *Die Einheit der Kirche nach John Henry Newman*. Düsseldorf, 1956.
Schmid, Josef. "Petrus 'der Fels' und die Petrusgestalt der Urgemeinde." *Begegnung der Christen*. Ed. Maximilian Roesle and Oscar Cullman. Stuttgart/ Frankfurt, 1959. Pp. 347-359.
Schnackenburg, Rudolf. *The Church in the New Testament*. New York, 1965.
——. *God's Rule and Kingdom*. 2nd ed. New York, 1968.
Schoof, T. Mark. *A Survey of Catholic Theology 1800-1970*. New York, 1970.
Schreiber, Ottis Ivan. "Newman's Revisions in the Essay on the Development of Christian Doctrine." In Newman, *An Essay on the Development of Christian Doctrine*. Ed. C. F. Harrold. New York, 1949. Pp. 417-435.
Schulze-Kadelbach, Gerhard. "Die Stellung des Petrus in der Urchristenheit." *Theologische Literaturzeitung*, 81 (1956), 1-14.
Schweizer, Eduard. *Church Order in the New Testament*. Naperville, Ill., 1961.
Seppelt, Franz Xaver. *Geschichte der Päpste von den Anfängen bis zur Mitte des 20. Jahrhunderts*. 4 vols. 2nd ed. Munich, 1954-1957.
Seynaeve, Jaak. *Cardinal Newman's Doctrine on Holy Scripture*. Louvain, 1953.
——. "Newman (doctrine scripturaire du Cardinal)." *Dictionnaire de la Bible*, *Supplement*, 6 (1960), 427-474.
Sheridan, Thomas L. *Newman on Justification: A Theological Biography*. Staten Island, New York, 1967.
Stanley, David Michael. "Kingdom to Church: the Structural Development of Apostolic Christianity in the New Testament." *Theological Studies*, 16 (1955), 1-29.
Stephenson, Anthony A. "Cardinal Newman and the Development of Doctrine." *Journal of Ecumenical Studies*, 3 (1966), 463-485.
——. "The Development and Immutability of Christian Doctrine." *Theological Studies*, 19 (1958), 481-532.
Stern, Jean. *Bible et Tradition chez Newman*. Paris, 1967.
——. "L'Infaillibilité de l'Eglise dans la pensée de Newman." *Recherches de sciences religieuses*, 61 (1973), 161-185.

——. "Traditions apostoliques et Magistère selon J. H. Newman." *Revue des sciences philosophiques et théologiques*, 47 (1963), 55.

Tavard, George H. *The Quest for Catholicity: A Study in Anglicanism*. London, 1963.
Taylor, Justin. "St. Basil the Great and Pope St. Damasus I." *Downside Review*, 91 (1973), 186-203 and 262-274.
Thils, Gustav. *Primauté pontificale et prérogatives épiscopales: "potestas ordinaria" au concile du Vatican*. Louvain, 1961.
——. *La primauté pontificale. La doctrine de Vatican I. Les voies d'une révision*. Gembloux, 1972.
Trevor, Meriol. *Newman*. Vol. I: *The Pillar of the Cloud*. Vol. II: *Light in Winter*. London, 1962.

Ullman, Walter. *The Growth of Papal Government in the Middle Ages*. 2nd ed. London, 1962.
——. *The Medieval Papacy, St. Thomas and Beyond*. London, 1960.
——. *A Short History of the Papacy in the Middle Ages*. London, 1972.

Valeske, Ulrich. *Votum Ecclesiae*. Munich, 1962.
Vargish, Thomas. *Newman: The Contemplation of Mind*. New York, 1970.
Vidler, Alec R. *The Church in an Age of Revolution*. London, 1965.
Vögtle, Anton. "Der Petrus der Verheissung und der Erfüllung." *Münchener Theologische Zeitschrift*, 5 (1954), 1-47.
Vries, Wilhelm de. "The Development after Constantine." *Concilium*, 64 (1971), 45-53.
——. "The Primacy of Rome as Seen by the Eastern Church." *Diakonia*, 6 (1971), 221-231.
Walgrave, Jan H. *Newman the Theologian*. London, 1960.
——. *Unfolding Revelation: The Nature of Doctrinal Development*. Philadelphia, 1972.
——. Introduction to Newman, *Essai sur le développement de la doctrine chrétienne*. Paris, 1964. Pp. 7-48.
Walker, G. S. M. *The Churchmanship of St. Cyprian*. Richmond, Va., 1968.
Ward, Maisie. *Young Mr. Newman*. New York, 1952.
Ward, Wilfrid. *The Life and Times of Cardinal Wiseman*. 2 vols. 2nd ed. London, 1897.
—— *The Life of John Henry Cardinal Newman*. 2 vols. London, 1912.
—— *Last Lectures by Wilfrid Ward*. London, 1918.
—— *William George Ward and the Catholic Revival*. London, 1893.
—— *William George Ward and the Oxford Movement*. London, 1889.
Warre Cornish, Francis. *The English Church in the Nineteenth Century*. 2 vols. London, 1910.
Watkin, Aelred, and H. Butterfield. "Gasquet and the Acton-Simpson Correspondence." *The Cambridge Historical Journal*, 10 (1950), 75-105.
Weatherby, Harold L. *Cardinal Newman in His Age: His Place in English Theology and Literature*. Nashville, 1973.
Weiler, Anton. "Church Authority and Government in the Middle Ages." *Concilium*, 7 (1965), 123-136.
Wellesley Index to Victorian Periodicals. Ed. W. E. Houghton, E. R. Houghton, J. Altholz and D. McElrath. 2 vols. Toronto, 1966-1972.
Willam, Franz. "Kardinal Newman über Primat und Episkopat (1849)." *Orientierung*, 27 (1963), 162-164.

Williams, George Huntston. *"Omnium christianorum pastor et doctor*: Vatican I
　　et l'Angleterre victorienne." *Nouvelle revue théologique*, 96 (1974), 113-146 and
　　337-365.
Winter, Michael M. *Saint Peter and the Popes*. Baltimore/London, 1960.
Wuyts, A. "Le 28ᵉ canon de Chalcédoine et le fondement du primat romain."
　　Orientalia Christiana periodica, 17 (1951), 265-282.

INDEX OF PERSONS

INDEX OF SUBJECTS